Asian NIEs and the Global Economy

Asian NIEs
&
the Global Economy

Industrial Restructuring &

Corporate Strategy in the 1990s

Edited by Gordon L. Clark & Won Bae Kim

The Johns Hopkins University Press

Baltimore and London

© 1995 The Johns Hopkins University Press
All rights reserved. Published 1995
Printed in the United States of America on acid-free paper
04 03 02 01 00 99 98 97 96 95   5 4 3 2 1

The Johns Hopkins University Press, 2715 North Charles Street
Baltimore, Maryland 21218-4319
The Johns Hopkins Press Ltd., London

Library of Congress Cataloging-in-Publication Data will be found at the end of this book.

A catalog record for this book is available from the British Library.

ISBN 0-8018-5105-X

For our children (and their futures)

Peter Clark

Suh-Young Kim

&

Ghee-Young Kim

Although the dynamism continues, Japan and the four little dragons [Hong Kong, Singapore, Korea, and Taiwan] have begun to undergo drastic changes, changes sufficiently fundamental that in the early 1990s we may speak of the end of the era of industrial breakthrough. Signs of basic change began to appear in Japan in the 1970s, after the first oil shock, and in the four little dragons in the late 1980s, after their currencies rose in value against the U. S. dollar. These changes help us see the nature of these societies during their several decades of industrial breakthrough in sharper relief.

—Ezra Vogel, *The Four Little Dragons*

Contents

Preface

In May 1993, the East-West Center in Honolulu hosted a major international conference on industrial restructuring and corporate strategy in the Asian newly industrialized economies (NIEs). The conference reported the results of a large multiyear research project on industrial restructuring and corporate strategy, which began in early 1991. This project was funded in part by the Population Program of the East-West Center and by research institutes and centers in Hong Kong, Korea, Singapore, and Taiwan. The research project drew, in part, upon recent research in the United States and elsewhere on the nature and scope of industrial restructuring since the mid 1980s and emphasized the interrelationships between the restructuring of labor-intensive industries and the strategies used by corporations to cope with, and respond to, radically changing global economic conditions. Over the two years of the project, participants met a number of times to present background papers and to design and coordinate the implementation of a common cross-economy survey for a comparative analysis of the corporate logic of industrial restructuring in the Asian NIEs. The basic survey instrument is shown in the appendix to this book. Reports, papers, and background analyses for the project have been published in two special issues of the journal *Environment and Planning A,* in 1993 and 1994.

The conference had three distinct parts, now reflected in the contents and structure of this book. Part 1, Global Economic Forces, introduces the significance of the project, linking it to contemporary patterns and processes operating at the global level. This part includes an introductory chapter by the editors, a major chapter devoted to global political economy, and a chapter that sets corporate strategy in the context of competing explanations of the growth of the Asian NIEs. Part 2, Dimensions of Corporate Strategy, is the heart of the book. It comprises five separate papers reporting on the results of the common survey of corporate strategy, including two separate reports on Korea. These chapters are stories or arguments about restructuring in their own right, a set of five papers on the empirical results of the survey reflecting the particular issues and circumstances of the different Asian NIEs. As well, comparisons are drawn between the city-state economies of Hong Kong and Singapore and the larger economies of Korea and Taiwan. Part 3, Asian NIEs in Perspective, then pools the empirical data in a set of econometric models designed to make more general arguments about industrial restructuring in the Asian NIEs. It makes reference to issues of political economy (for example, the relative significance of the state and the market) and to the capacity of Asian corporations to frame strategies in response to the accelerating economic imperatives of global competition. The last chapter of the book reflects upon the likely separate futures of the Asian NIEs, noting the increasing significance of China for the long-term growth of these economies. As well, we briefly consider some of the unresolved questions in each economy relating to the processes of industrial restructuring.

The East-West project was designed to expand our knowledge of the contemporary economic experience of the Asian NIEs and to provide an in-depth empirical reference point for understanding the particularities of the responses of each economy's firms to recent economic events. Our interest in articulating the logic and mechanisms of Asian restructuring has also prompted an interest in the experience of other countries, like the United States and those of western Europe, that have gone through a sustained period of industrial restructuring. Thus, in an important way, this book brings together a general interest shared by many researchers and policy makers around the globe about the strategies of restructuring, with a particular interest in the experience of the Asian NIEs. Inevitably, general theoretically driven arguments about the options and strategies of restructuring available to corporations overlap and intersect with particular issues and debates about the recent performance of the NIEs. Here, we focus on corporate restructuring strategies in labor-intensive industries, paying particular attention to the devices used by corporations to control labor costs and encourage labor flexibility through a combination of strategies, including technological change. As is well appreciated in the West, these strategies are also intimately and inevitably geographical; the project was about both industrial restructuring and the expanding geographical reach of corporate strategy.

Research in the United States and Europe has shown that to maintain international competitiveness, firms, localities, and nation-states have to be able to adjust their production, organization, and processes to changing economic circumstances. Given the scramble for market share, a fixed configuration of production would be a long-term competitive liability. Adjustment to these circumstances, whether induced by the market (as in Western economies) or by macroeconomics or industry policy (as in the Asian context), may involve the reorganization of production and labor use in industries, thereby affecting the livelihood of workers and the transformation of localities. Of the various empirical issues addressed in the study, we consider the following: (1) The underlying economic forces causing industrial restructuring; (2) How restructuring operates at the firm level, and what these processes are like in the local context. For example, does restructuring involve plant closure and relocation, product diversification, switching to other lines of production, automation, flexible production systems, subcontracting, corporate reorganization, or other options? (3) How restructuring affects labor and labor-management relations. For example, does part-time employment and subcontracting not only lower workers' wages and benefits but also weaken the power of labor unions? (4) How workers, labor organizations, communities, and governments respond to the restructuring process. These questions are developed in more detail in chapter 3 and the appendix, which contains the questionnaire that was the basis of the survey research, and in the five separate chapters on the Asian NIEs.

While there is much to be reported in each case, it is clear from our research that the Asian NIEs have entered a period of sustained economic transformation and industrial restructuring. How their firms respond to the changing economic imperatives of global competition will profoundly affect each economy's long-term growth and relative position in the global economy. Our goals for this book are twofold: first, we aim to illustrate the significance of this issue by placing the recent experience of the Asian NIEs in a broader international context; second, by using our original empirical material we aim to help understand the patterns and processes of Asian industrial restructuring, recognizing the distinctiveness of each economy's response. Throughout the book, there is a continual interplay between international economic imperatives and the dimensions of corporate response at the local level. As such, the book reflects the interdisciplinary and international scope of the research team as well as the logic or method of comparative analysis deployed in the original research design.

To appreciate what is implied by our comparative perspective, it would be useful for the reader to understand the status of commonalities and differences between the various case studies. The research project began with the assumption that all four Asian NIEs are now facing an increasingly hostile and competitive global economy. How and why this is so and the dimensions of global economic competition crucial for the performance of the Asian NIEs are the topics of the first part of the book. To begin at that point is not meant to suggest that the logic of global economic competition is so all-embracing that the four Asian NIEs are now caught within a common strait-jacket, individually and collectively overwhelmed by the imperatives of competition. While we do think that the future of the Asian NIEs will be determined, in part, by the responses of NIEs' firms to global economic competition, we do not expect that those responses need be the same, nor do we expect that the consequences of those responses for the future performance of each of the NIEs need also be the same. Although the project begins at what we think are a set of shared and significant conjunctural economic events (in the 1980s), we believe that understanding the strategies and consequences of corporate responses to those events requires a detailed appreciation of the institutions and social and political practices of each Asian NIE. In essence, the case studies of part 2 were written with these overarching presumptions in mind. Note that we do not deny the virtues of direct comparisons or cross-economy statistical analysis (the focus of part 3). Rather, it is a matter of sustaining the interplay between scales of analysis (international and local) and the significance of the context of corporate decision making.

To facilitate comparison between the four NIEs and the case studies of industrial restructuring and corporate strategy, the research project began with a set of accepted commonalities. As noted above, the most important shared beginning point was the realization that the NIEs are now facing increasing competition in those labor-intensive industries that were once the driving force behind their separate and distinctive paths of export-led economic growth. To compare the dimensions and consequences of that realization for the Asian NIEs, a common group of labor-intensive industries was chosen to be the empirical focus of the research project, and a questionnaire was designed to be the basis of firm-based research in each economy. We sought to keep constant or common between the case studies of industrial restructuring and corporate strategy the focus of the study (the local response to global competition), the type of industries (labor intensive), the empirical framework (the type of questions asked), the analysis of the data (the coding of responses), and even the timing of the fieldwork. The case studies exhibit some differences in industry focus, reflecting in part differences in economy, industrial statistical categories, official terminology, and data availability. As will be apparent in part 2, participants in the research project were also encouraged to writeup their results using a common format. However, it will be apparent that each case study has its own narrative logic and its own story to tell, set within these accepted commonalities. In the case of Hong Kong, the story is about disorganized capitalism, in the case of Singapore, neo-colonial corporatism, and so on. The quality of each chapter and the whole book is a product of joining the analytical framework with the distinctiveness of each story. Likewise, an important contribution of the book is its original research results conceived within a common research framework (see part 3).

All cross-country, cross-economy comparative projects inevitably involve (directly or indirectly) deeper questions about the relative status of countries' histories, geographies, and cultures. Any comparative project that does not recognize this could be thought naive, be accused of being misleading, or, perhaps worse, be extraordinarily functionalist in orientation. Clearly, we do not accept the idea sometimes advanced in the social sciences that the scope of agents' behavior (in this case, firms' strategies and responses) is simply a function of their host economies' stage of development. Likewise, we do not accept the idea that the significance of institutions like the state, markets, and firms are also solely determined by economic imperatives. The deeper dimensions of distinctiveness of each Asian NIE are, in large part, crucial to our understanding of the character and scope of firms' responses to industrial restructuring. Thus, the case studies reflect upon, and draw upon, those deeper dimensions. To the extent to which our common empirical framework allows us to better understand the interplay between global economic competition and the nature of local response, then, the project will have contributed to a richer understanding of the contemporary circumstances of the Asian NIEs and their possible futures.

One final qualifying point regarding the nature of comparative,

cross-country analysis should be recognized. In her critical analysis of
the use of Western theory in understanding the culture and institutions
of China, Zhang Longxi (1992) notes that the translation of a work
from one culture to another is always and necessarily relative to the location of the translator. She cites (107) approvingly a comment made
by Friedrich Schleiermacher, a German language scholar and theolo-
gian of the early eighteenth century, to the effect that "the translator
of a foreign work can either ask the reader to go to the foreign author
or bring the foreign author to the reader back home." Longxi is very
concerned about the use of translation (of Western theory into Chinese
and its transportation home) and about the political implications of
translation, where one culture appropriates another's texts for specific,
if often hidden, motives. We are not so concerned about the political
implications of our work (though perhaps we should be). Rather, the
point is we are similarly engaged in a project of translation. By anal-
ogy, the research reported in this book basically aims to bring the subject (industrial restructuring and corporate strategy in the Asian NIEs)
to the Western reader. Because of the methodological stance taken in
the research, the common empirical framework, and the focus of
analysis, it is apparent that East Asian industrial restructuring is portrayed in terms consistent with Western research and economic and geographical concepts. Reinforcing this apparent choice of portrayal are
the backgrounds, training, and experience of our colleagues—the team
of researchers recruited by the East-West Center to participate in the
project. While our collaborators have different disciplinary perspectives, it is clear that they share common analytical perspectives. A more
ambitious research project would map out the implications of our
translation of the recent experience of the Asian NIEs and perhaps even
compare it with the analytical focus of any related research project,
which would ask the reader to go to the foreign lands. One implication, however, of Schleiermacher's argument is, of course, that the
choice of analytical focus is an exclusive choice. That is, we either take
the reader to the foreign lands or bring the foreign lands to the reader.
There can be no in-between analytical strategy. We chose the former
strategy over the latter, recognizing that the alternative exists for future research.

Acknowledgments

Many institutions and organizations contributed to the project and to the book. With the leadership of Dr. Won Bae Kim, the Program on Population of the East-West Center was the initial host and sponsoring institution of the project. The center provided financial and organizational resources that made the project possible and contributed to its overall design. The East-West Center also sponsored the final conference of the project and the publication of the book. The Center for Advanced Studies of the National University of Singapore also contributed significantly to the project, hosting an interim meeting of the research group in 1992. Similarly, resources were provided by the United Nations' Center for Regional Development (Nagoya), the Wakayama Prefecture Government, and the Japanese Ministry of International Trade and Industry and Ministry for Foreign Affairs, for another, later meeting of the research group.

With respect to the economy-specific survey research, we would like to thank the Seoul Development Institute and the Project on Regional Industrial Economics (PRIE) at Rutgers University, where Professor Park completed his research, for research facilities, as well as the Korea Research Foundation; the National Science Council, the Industrial Development Bureau, and the Bureau of the Census, all of Taiwan; the National University of Singapore; and the Chinese University of Hong Kong. Preparation and publication of the book was supported, in part, by Monash University's Monash Asia Institute and assisted by Michael Mackay and Wayne Caldow. Corrie McKee provided able and imaginative word-processing expertise.

We would also like to thank researchers from the East-West Center and academics from the University of Hawaii for their critical interest

in the progress of the project. In particular, we would like to acknowl-
edge the support of Dr. Lee-Jay Cho and Dr. Bruce Koppel (vice pres-
idents of the East-West Center), Dr. Andrew Mason (director of the
Program on Population), and Dr. John Bauer, Professor Burnham
Campbell, Dr. Pearl Imada, Dr. Shelley Mark, Dr. Manuel Montes, Dr.
Chungsoo Kim, and Mr. Byung-Joo Lee (all of the East-West Center)
for very useful and insightful comments on papers presented at various
meetings in Honolulu. Professor Reginald Kwok, Professor Michael
Douglass, Professor Alvin So, and Emeritus Professor Fred Hung, all
of the University of Hawaii, also made significant intellectual and critical contributions to the project.

Finally, we would like to thank Professor Ezra Vogel, of Harvard
University, and the Harvard University Press for permitting us to quote
a passage from his recent book as the epigraph to our book. Professor
Vogel also provided words of encouragement and enthusiasm at just
the right stage of the project.

Abbreviations

ASEAN 4	Association of South East Asian Nations (Indonesia, Malaysia, Philippines, Thailand)
CAD	Computer-aided design
FDI	Foreign direct investment
FEER	*Far Eastern Economic Review*
FMS	Flexible manufacturing systems
GATT	General Agreement on Tariffs and Trade
GDP	Gross domestic product
GLCs	Government-linked companies (Singapore)
IFR	Industry for rationalization (Korea)
IMF	International Monetary Fund (Washington, D.C.)
MITI	Ministry of International Trade and Industry (Japan)
NAFTA	North American Free Trade Agreement
NIEs	Newly industrialized (or industrializing) economies
OECD	Organization for Economic Cooperation and Development (Paris)
OEM	Original equipment manufacturers (Korea)
PRC	Peoples' Republic of China
R&D	Research and development
SIC	Standard industrial classification
SME	Small and medium enterprises

PART I

Global Economic Forces

Introduction

Gordon L. Clark and Won Bae Kim

This book is about industrial restructuring in the Asian newly industrializing economies (NIEs) of Hong Kong, Korea, Singapore, and Taiwan. We might have used the word "industrialized," rather than "industrializing," because in many respects the former term captures the
reality of the situation in the 1990s. Compared with many smaller
OECD (Organization for Economic Cooperation and Development)
countries, the Asian NIEs are indeed industrialized; the mix of employment between agriculture and manufacturing in Korea and Taiwan, for example, is now similar to the industry composition of many
of the industrialized OECD countries around 1960 and 1970. Of
course, for Hong Kong and Singapore the word "industrialized" is
clearly passé; those two economies are rapidly becoming postindustrial
economies with significant and growing international finance and service sectors. The pace of economic growth in these economies has been
nothing short of miraculous. In a recent book, Chow and Kellman
(1993) note that the four Asian NIEs have been able to defy the vicious
circle of poverty over the last quarter century and have shown remarkable resilience and durability despite the turbulence of the global
economy. Indeed, the International Monetary Fund (1993) notes that
what they term as "outward-oriented" growth strategies have generated more efficient use of resources than normally suggested by conventional models of resource allocation. In this respect, there can be no
doubt that the Asian NIEs' export-based growth over the past few
decades has become a major reference point for other developing nations wishing to join the ranks of the developed nations. Even Western

industrialized nations are now reconsidering their own industry and trade policies in the light of the Asian NIE's extraordinary growth (see, generally, World Bank 1993a, but compare with Krugman and Lawrence 1993).

Whereas many economic analyses of the Asian NIEs concentrate on the nature and logic of export-oriented or export-led economic growth strategies, often emphasizing the role of state policy and the linkage effects of international markets, this book goes a step beyond that story of growth and development and considers the contemporary circumstances facing the NIEs. Here, our interest is in how the Asian NIEs are responding to the costs of success—escalating costs (commodity, land, and wages), slowing rates of productivity growth, and increasing competition in the markets they have exploited over the past decade. In particular, the book is a series of economy-based case studies focused upon the patterns and consequences of corporate restructuring in labor-intensive industries like the garment, footwear, and electronics industries. These case studies use a common empirical framework to identify and evaluate corporate restructuring strategies while being also cognizant of the role and status of state policy in fostering economic adjustment to each NIE's particular and changing place in the global economy. Thus, unlike many studies of the Asian NIEs, our primary focus is upon firms and firm strategy. Why? For a couple of reasons. For a start, the issue of firm strategy in the Asian NIEs has been somewhat neglected in favor of issues of more general interest, like the relationship between states and markets. It is also possible that firm strategy will be more important than state policy for the economic performance of the NIEs through the end of this century than it has been over the past two decades. Through the various case studies, the book explores the dimensions and contemporary significance of corporate strategy with reference to industrial restructuring.

Notice, again, that the empirical focus of the book is on restructuring in labor-intensive industries. These industries have been very important to the NIEs over the past few decades; they have been essential to their export-led growth strategies and have often played an important (though less recognized) role in promoting sectoral and social transformation. Now, however, these industries are facing fierce competition from China and Southeast Asia. At the same time, their economic significance in each NIE is relatively declining as other industries take their place as the engines of economic growth. Their share of total employment is declining, and their contribution to total income is also on the decline. Perhaps not surprisingly, as labor industries grapple with changing competitive circumstances, the connection between state policy and corporate strategy is increasingly tenuous and uncomfortable. This introductory chapter outlines the contemporary realities facing the Asian NIEs and sketches out our approach to corporate strategy in relation to state policy.

Asian NIEs in the 1990s

Much of the current research on Asian NIEs stresses the economic success of these countries; the historical record of economic growth, international competitiveness in middle and high-value-added traded commodities, and technological development are the standard reference points of this literature. Notwithstanding the many obvious and subtle differences between the Asian NIEs, for many European and North American countries the success of the NIEs has been nothing short of miraculous. Just twenty years ago, the hegemony of the United States, for example, was unquestioned. Just twenty years ago, the rank order of developed economies in terms of their rates of growth and standards of living seemed impervious to change. Only Japan was given a chance to break into the world "league tables." But behind Japan have come the Asian NIEs. In an era where productivity, real wage rates, and rates of investment have stagnated in the West, export-led development has become the new model of growth. Recognizing that few nations except Germany can aspire to the economic power of the United States and Japan, many of the smaller Western nations have come to believe that the experience of the Asian NIEs provides a workable strategy for future development.

The success of the Asian NIEs has challenged all kinds of notions about the long-term status of Western industrialized countries as well as the plausibility of conventional economic growth theories. An indication of just how important this model has become is to be found by comparing Bardhan's (1988) survey of alternative approaches to development economics with Ariff's (1991) edited volume on the patterns and diversity of Asian economic growth around the Pacific Rim (including Australia, the United States, Japan, the Asian NIEs, and the ASEAN 4). In the space of just a few years, the institutions and policies of the Asian NIEs have been taken from the fringe of economic theory (grouped with Marxist and related so-called radical theories of development) to the very center of the field.

Clearly, the lessons of Asian NIEs' growth for Western countries are being hotly debated. At the same time, however, the Asian NIEs are facing new problems and challenges. At the most aggregate level, the Asian NIEs have found their new positions in the world and Pacific economies challenged on two fronts. The accelerating economic and political competition between the United States and Japan and integration of the European economies have combined to effectively crowd out the NIEs from direct access to the major centers of world economic policy making. Asian NIE country-specific development policies are no longer sufficient, given the competition for world markets and the development of macroregional trading blocs. At the moment of their success, some Asian NIE policy makers believe their future is imperiled by the political economy of world trade. Their apparent vulnerability to the actions of the major world economic powers has been exacerbated by competition from below: the ASEAN 4—Indonesia, Malaysia, the Philippines, and Thailand—and China are also growing very strongly, manufacturing products at prices that compare competitively with the Asian NIEs. Over the coming decade, the now favorable economic position of the Asian NIEs will be increasingly squeezed between the interests of the major world trading partners and new competition from below. The future of the Asian NIEs' success is more problematic than often acknowledged (see Easterly 1994).

Within each Asian NIE, economic success has brought its own costs and problems. Most obviously, labor shortages have affected each NIE, albeit in different ways, depending on the cultural and historical particularities of each economy. Labor shortages have accelerated real wage increases, drastically altered the desired configuration of capital investment, and exacerbated internal competition for labor between sectors. The local future of Asian NIEs' labor-intensive industries is now an open question. If they remain located at home how can the Asian NIEs' labor-intensive industries compete over the long-term, when the ASEAN 4 nations and China are increasingly technologically competitive at much lower real wages? Apparent solutions like further capital investment may not deliver long-term success. The diffusion of new technology in many of these industries is quick and relatively inexpensive for the ASEAN 4 competitors. On the labor side of the equation, new sources of local labor supply, the upgrading of labor skills, even the importing of labor have been proffered as useful solutions. Even so, the alternative is also quite clear. Instead of retaining production at home, corporations are increasingly segmenting and separating functions, locating lower skilled and most labor-intensive functions elsewhere in Southeast Asia. This strategy is well documented in the West and is normally described in the literature as the international division of labor. Notwithstanding the apparent value of such a strategy for individual enterprises, in some Asian NIEs sending labor-intensive production offshore goes against the recent history and community expectations of sharing the benefits of national economic growth.

In Michael Webber's survey (chapter 2, this volume) of the economic forces shaping the competitive positions of the Asian NIEs during the 1990s, he emphasizes the interaction between two related forces. With respect to export-led economic growth, he argues that this "engine of growth" is losing its potency as imports of inputs to the production process (like oil) and consumer goods (including lower-value-added, labor-intensive commodities) begin to take up an increasing share of NIEs' trade with the rest of the world. As the relative contribution of exports to economic growth wanes (as the value of imports and exports approximate one another), the rate of growth of each Asian NIE is increasingly dependent upon the internal level of real wages (consumption) and the rate of investment. But as real wages have increased, reflecting, in part, the demand for labor and the rising costs of urban life in the NIEs, individual firms in labor-intensive industries have been forced to restructure production, including shifting to overseas sites of production. By doing so, however, the rate of growth of imports may increase again at a time when investment (which is necessary to maintain the rate of exports) is being increasingly diverted offshore. Webber suggests that this interactive economic process, involving structural accounting (the balance between exports and imports) and what could be termed the manifestations of economic success (the rate of increase in real wages), reflects the transition of the Asian NIEs to a more "mature regime" of growth, one increasingly reliant upon regional rates of consumption.

The prospects for economic growth in the Asian NIEs have been affected by other factors, particularly global economic turbulence. In their *World Economic Outlook,* the International Monetary Fund (1993b) noted that economies' capacity to respond to unexpected shocks has been a crucial determinant of their long-term growth rates. After reviewing the evidence for and against the value of Asian NIEs' industry policies (in particular, Korea and Singapore), the IMF concluded that these policies had mixed success (in terms of efficiency) and variable impact across time and across economies. What they did suggest to be important in terms of government policy contributing to long-term growth were the creation of a stable macroeconomic environment and an outward-oriented trade strategy and interventions that complimented the market rather than attempted to replace the market. These conclusions are not universally accepted, nor is the evidence as clear as the IMF would like to imagine. Furthermore, the first few conclusions could be accepted without necessarily subscribing to the last pair. Nevertheless, on the basis of the studies presented in this book, we do believe that the adjustment potential of government policy with respect to macroeconomic stability and the adjustment capacity of corporations with respect to changing international circumstances are vital to the growth of trading economies in general, and to the Asian NIEs in particular.

For example, currency revaluation in the Asian NIEs in the late 1980s may have profound effects on the ability of the NIEs to hold their local labor-intensive industries during the 1990s. Their dependence on export-led growth has made them vulnerable to currency revaluation as well as other kinds of financial shocks; notwithstanding the Asian NIEs' past resilience, an autonomous and unanticipated currency shock can radically, and, adversely, alter the international competitiveness of their industry. Those industries with a high labor (wage cost) component are particularly vulnerable, especially where shortages of labor are such that real (with respect to internal costs and productivity) wages are rising rapidly. This appears to be the recent experience of Korea and Taiwan. In chapter 3, Gordon Clark extends this analysis by reconsidering the status and significance of global economic turbulence for Asian economic growth. He argues that the responsiveness of firms and states to this variable (or set of variables) is an increasingly important determinant of long-term growth, given the relatively declining significance of export-led growth. In this respect, the vulnerability of the Asian NIEs to those same forces now affecting Western economies' economic performance is further evidence for Webber's thesis that the regime of Asian growth is in transition, perhaps moving toward the regime of growth that typifies many OECD countries.

Here, and in other chapters, we are conscious that a generation-long period of economic growth and structural stability has raised social and political expectations for increases in the social wage (welfare). Whereas in the past real wages were kept low through a variety of institutional and coercive forces, the costs of growth in terms of the lives of individual workers (pollution, congestion, housing, etc.) have become such that extensive social investment has become a political necessity. Offshore relocation of labor-intensive industries may be a useful social strategy for minimizing public investment in a higher social wage but may also bring into the open issues related to the welfare of ordinary workers. It remains to be seen whether the Asian NIEs can adjust internally to these forces as they were able to adjust to the demand of external markets.

External and internal pressures on Asian NIE's competitiveness and relative economic position in the global economy have prompted industrial restructuring. The East-West Center project was conceived to articulate in more detail the causal links between economic growth and industrial restructuring, drawing on the experience of these economies to examine the process of restructuring and identify the particularities of each economy. Interest in articulating the causal mechanisms of restructuring has also prompted an interest in the experience of other countries, such as the United States and the countries of Western Europe that have gone through a sustained period of restructuring. While there may be lessons to be learned about the success of the Asian NIEs with respect to other countries' growth strategies, uncertainties about the likely patterns and logic behind industrial restructuring has led researchers in turn to ask about the restructuring experience of Western economies. In general, the focus of this research is on enterprise-based restructuring strategies in labor-intensive industries, paying particular attention to the various strategies used to control labor costs and encourage labor flexibility. As is well appreciated in the Western literature, these strategies are intimately and inevitably geographical. Thus, the research project is about both industrial restructuring and regional adjustment, in the sense that firms' strategies are explicitly about reconfiguring the inherited structure of production and are explicitly linked with questions related to the current and possible future locations of production (see Markusen 1994).

States and Markets

It is tempting to treat the Asian NIEs as an undifferentiated group, somehow inextricably bound together by common measures of their economic success during the 1970s and 1980s. The West, having already witnessed the extraordinary economic growth of Japan since about 1950, now seems ready to cloak the Asian NIEs with a distinctive oriental model of development. Deyo (1987) and Wade (1990a), among others, suppose that this model (and that part of the world it supposedly represents) is based upon an unmatched (in the West) relationship between the state and markets. It is also tempting to treat the NIEs as so successful that their future growth and relative development is assured (again, see Easterly 1994). By this analysis, the means of their success may be worth emulating in the West, given forecasts of slow to negligible long-term growth for so many OECD countries. But if we were to treat the Asian NIEs as an undifferentiated group, we would lose sight of the many distinctive features of each economy and the problematic place of each (for different reasons) in the global economy of the 1990s. This is not meant to imply that there are no commonalities between these four economies; after all, they are relatively small economies (compared to Japan, the United States, and the European Community) and are overwhelmingly dependent upon export-led external demand for economic growth and development. Rather, it is to emphasize individual differences so as to better understand the general situation. As we have noted, one major contribution of this book is its examination of the interplay between the commonalities and differences of the Asian NIEs.

One way of distinguishing between the NIEs is to emphasize their very different spatial configurations. The fact that Singapore and Hong Kong have been for many years virtual city-states, whereas both Korea and Taiwan were agricultural economies for much of the twentieth century (before becoming city-centered industrial economies), is an obvious distinction. At first sight, this distinction creates a twofold typology that neatly matches their different physical situations. But there are significant differences between Singapore and Hong Kong, just as there are significant differences between Korea and Taiwan (see also Young 1992). In chapter 4, Stephen Chiu and Tai-lok Lui show that Hong Kong's development has been, in part, chaotic and relatively unorganized (compared to Singapore), being dominated by small, locally financed (and often undercapitalized) firms connected to the rest of the world by spatially extensive trading networks. By contrast, K. C. Ho (chapter 5) emphasizes the multinational corporate structure of Singapore and the extraordinary level of government intervention in local factor markets, consumption, and production. Whereas Chiu and Lui's story is one of neocolonial unorganized capitalism, Ho's story could be construed as an oriental democratic version of corporatism. Robert Barro (1992) suggests, as is analyzed in detail in chapter 3 of this book, that the Hong Kong model is superior to the Singapore model in that

Hong Kong has not overinvested in capital—a problem he attributes to Singapore. Quite clearly, he questions the efficiency of Singapore's development strategy and lauds the limited role of the Hong Kong state.

Allowing for their differences, Chiu and Lui and Ho both show that Hong Kong and Singapore now face serious problems in accommodating to their rapidly changing positions in the global economy. In Hong Kong, escalating land, building, and labor costs threaten the viability of labor-intensive commodity production, while on the market side of the equation volatile international demand for their products has made it difficult to sustain investment in new local plant and equipment better able to cope with these competitive pressures. What are common strategies of corporate restructuring? Chiu and Lui identify three: (1) reduction of local commodity production and concentration on product-oriented research and development; (2) concentration on trading rather than on local production; and (3) expansion of capacity by relocating commodity production to China. Notwithstanding the uncertain political future of Hong Kong, all three strategies use Hong Kong's connections to China as a means of remaking Hong Kong's place in the world economy. In this respect, their conclusions are consistent with Leung's (1993) comprehensive analysis of subcontracting networks and relationships between Hong Kong and China. If successful, these strategies promise to remake Hong Kong into a commercial trading and financial center for China, bridging the development strategies of special economic zones and the outside world. In his chapter, Ho shows that Singaporean firms are facing similar cost pressures and uncertainties. The three strategies identified for Hong Kong are also important for Singaporean firms, in this instance, though, assuming geographical scope by firms' expansion into southern Malaysia and close regions of Indonesia.

There are, of course, some significant differences between the strategies of Hong Kong and Singaporean firms. Their very different industry structures, firm sizes, and relationship to international corporations make a significant difference (for example) to the relative significance of technology-oriented strategies in the two NIEs. In Singapore's case, Ho shows that state-based, technology-oriented investment strategies have been an essential feature of restructuring. Whether or not these strategies have been successful, or more or less successful than different strategies taken in Hong Kong, is difficult to judge. It is apparent from Ho's research, however, that the long-term nature of these technology strategies is very different from the short-term focus of Hong Kong firms' strategies. Also, notice how problematic is the Singaporean state's role with respect to restructuring: at one level, Ho reports on the frustration of firms with the government's unwillingness to add to the stock of available local labor (with foreign workers), whereas, at another level, the state is significantly adding to the stock of labor by promoting the growth triangle. The Singaporean state is now, in effect, an economic agent, a regional developer, and an entrepreneur. By contrast, the Hong Kong state seems preoccupied with collective consumption and infrastructure provision, leaving matters directly related to production processes to local firms and their partners across the border. The colonial administrators are, of course, also preoccupied with 1997 and the coming incorporation of the city-state with China.

When we turn to the second pair of the set of four Asian NIEs, other stories intrude to disturb the easily made presumptions of preordained economic growth and continued success. The essays by Park, on Seoul, and Lim, on Pusan, suggest different economic worlds within a single country. Since the early 1970s, the Seoul metropolitan region (including Inchon and Kyonggi) has dramatically increased its share of national economic growth. According to Michael Douglass (1993), the region's share of all Korean manufacturing firms increased from about 35 percent in 1973 to more than 60 percent in 1990. He argues that corporate restructuring in the 1980s resulted in further spatial centralization of the nation's economy, as capital investment and corporate control were concentrated in the Seoul region while outside regions bore the brunt of plant closings. Park's analysis (chapter 6) is of the internal (to the Seoul region) patterns of growth and change, emphasizing the suburbanization of the electronics industry and the changing gender composition of employment in the garment industry. Both industries rely heavily on export markets, but their strategies of restructuring in the face of severe labor shortages and rising wage costs are very sensitive to firm size. Small firms in the garment industry tend to depend upon external labor sources, whereas small firms in the electronics industry tend to rely on internal strategies to retain their labor force. Park's survey results suggest that, to the extent that new technology is a strategic option in corporate restructuring, it is an option more related to product quality and market profile than to savings in labor costs.

Compared to the Pusan footwear industry, however, the Seoul region's electronics and garment industries seem likely to survive, albeit

in different ways and forms. By Lim's account (chapter 7), the Pusan
footwear industry is in serious trouble. Given the significance of this
industry to Pusan over the past few decades, this is both an economic
and a political crisis (a situation familiar to many in the Western world:
see Hayter and Harvey 1993). Footwear manufacturers are caught between pressures brought by international brand-name owners for
lower costs of production (compared to other sites of production in
China and the ASEAN 4) and their existing investment in local plant
and equipment. Michael Douglass (1993) characterizes the Pusan
"problem" as a problem common to Fordist manufacturing in general.
That is, the large size of existing plants and the inflexible nature of capital equipment and work practices have, in combination, meant that
local firms are both profoundly uncompetitive in terms of the price of
production of a standard footwear commodity and dependent on the
inherited configuration of production, which has become an important
barrier to in situ restructuring. In essence, the sunk costs of production
(defined in Clark 1994 as those costs that could not be recovered even
if production were to cease) are an incredible burden on the restructuring process. This is not just a problem of relative prices (comparing
Pusan against sites of production in Indonesia, for instance); it is also
a political problem, in that the loyalty of local manufacturers to the
community is now in doubt. International brand-name owners have
put considerable pressure on Korean firms to export their expertise to
Southeast Asian sites of production, while at the same time requiring
Pusan production (and employment) in the industry to wither and die.

Park's analysis of the Seoul metropolitan region and the suburbanization process emphasizes the role that government policy has played
in facilitating the recent development of Inchon and Kyonggi. He argues that industry policy tied to land development policy has transformed the structure of the electronics industry, even if the central government appears to have been indifferent to the development (or
otherwise) of the garment industry. In effect, if not deliberately, government policy has created an electronics industrial district, a spatial
configuration of industry now thought by many analysts to be a necessary ingredient for an effective industry policy (Markusen and Park
1993 have published a paper on Chanwon based on this supposition).
But what should be the role of the state with respect to restructuring,
as opposed to industrial development? It is apparent that there is enormous debate and disagreement about this issue in Korea. One line of
argument goes as follows: the more exposed an industry is to interna-

tional competition, the more innovative it is, and the more competitive it is in the global economy. There comes a point, however, or so the argument goes, where its natural comparative advantage is exhausted and external competition comes to dominate local firms in that industry. By implication and argument, the state cannot (and should not) protect local industries. If this means that Pusan's footwear industry is destroyed and that Seoul dominates the economy (one possible scenario), then that is an inevitable, if not entirely desirable, result of a policy regime aimed at maximizing national economic growth.

This is not the only argument made about the proper role of the state with respect to industry competition. Some economic policy makers would deliberately facilitate restructuring and industrial transformation even if this means that the traditional functional characteristics and employment base of an industry and region are radically altered as a consequence. They would argue that this kind of policy is consistent with the goal of maximum national economic growth yet does not require acceptance of the notion that industries grow and die on the basis of fixed natural comparative advantage. In the case of Korea, this second argument has extra weight because of the interregional rivalries and politics of growth that have marked the Korean state since the late 1950s. The politics of regional advantage and disadvantage are also connected to the politics of urban middle-class aspirations and democracy, suppressed for so many years by military and technocratic elites. Deeply embedded, then, in the Korean debate about the proper role of the state with respect to restructuring are political questions about the relative status of past sacrifices made (and sometimes obtained by force and coercion) in the name of national economic success. In this respect, the state-sponsored policy of industrial restructuring targeted on the Pusan footwear industry has a particular political role to play, even if its economic effectiveness is open to doubt.

Underlying the Korean debate about the proper role of state policy is some uneasiness about the economic future of Korea. The declining competitiveness of labor-intensive industries, the increasing importance of foreign direct investment for firms' overall competitiveness, the increasingly fierce competition for market share, and the increasing market overlaps between Japanese, American, and Korean manufacturers have all contributed to doubts about the continuing viability of past government policies and business practices. In Taiwan, though, the issue is starker and perhaps more profound. At issue is the extent to which Taiwanese firms' interests are now consistent with the interests of the state and its citizens.

Robert Wade (1990a, chapter 4) begins his account of the growth of Taiwan with the Japanese occupation of the island from 1895 to 1945. He suggests that, by 1945, it was one of the most advanced trading provinces of China, with a history of high agricultural productivity, literacy, and manufacturing growth. The lack of a local capitalist elite and the history of suppression of dissent thus (according to Wade) provided the Nationalist party with an economic base and an opportunity to sustain its state-led path of industrialization. Subsequent liberalization of trade by the Nationalists in the late 1950s provided Taiwanese firms an opportunity to use their locally acquired expertise to generate higher rates of profit than would have otherwise been possible. Wade's story about Taiwanese growth and development during the 1960s and 1970s is a story of state policy and market expansion, the former reinforcing the latter on a virtuous path of capital accumulation. His story about the late 1970s and 1980s, though, is more complex; industrial policy is more involved (for instance, linking issues of innovation with intellectual property), just as the interaction between internal and external markets is more problematic (for instance, reconciling the advantages of export competition with the potential harmful effects of dramatic shifts in global relative prices). In the end, Wade's conclusion is that "the Taiwan economy can be thought of as containing both the Hong Kong paradigm and the Korean or Japanese paradigm" (306).

Ching-lung Tsay's research (here and elsewhere) for the industrial restructuring project does not directly challenge Wade's conclusion. He does, however, identify a set of issues that are important for the current performance of Taiwanese firms (see chapter 8, this volume). In doing so, he indirectly raises questions about the continuing viability of some state policies previously thought essential for development. Tsay suggests that labor supply, technological innovation, and foreign direct investment are three important factors affecting the formation and implementation of corporate strategy. As currency exchange rates have moved against Taiwan, as external markets have become more competitive and politically contentious and as land prices have escalated, many firms' competitive positions in relatively low-value-added, labor-intensive industries have been eroded. For some firms, employing illegal immigrant labor has been an option; for other firms, women and part-time employees have been preferred; and for yet other firms, overseas production sites have been the chosen option. Foreign direct investment, often linked to the coastal provinces of China, has become a major problem in that innovation in operating capital (plant and equipment) is increasingly located overseas rather than on the island. At the same time, many commentators believe that local firms have not been as successful in developing market-edge product innovation as they expected. State policies restricting imports of capital equipment seem to have restricted the ability of local firms to keep up with market leaders at the high-value-added end of international markets.

Tsay's research stresses the internal dynamics of industry competition and corporate strategy. It is also argued by some commentators that the Taiwanese political economy is undergoing radical transformation, aided and abetted by a profound cultural upheaval related to the nature and value of work in Taiwanese society. This story is not easily attributed to just one author. Its elements are, nevertheless, easily identified. The transformation story goes as follows: with the overwhelming success of Taiwanese firms in Western markets during the early 1980s and the subsequent revaluation of currency exchange rates, the Taiwanese economy accumulated massive foreign exchange holdings. In Taiwan, these reserves contributed to massive rises in land and stock prices, and currency speculation. By this logic, the bubble economy, sustained and encouraged by financial speculation by many of the middle class, overwhelmed the commodity-producing economy. At the same time, the small relative size of the local economy coupled with escalating input costs encouraged massive capital outflows, some of which were directed to commodity production in the rest of Asia (especially China) and some of which were directed to U.S. financial and property markets. Thus, the apparent shortage of labor may be thought indicative of a shift in social values, commodity production being devalued in the face of financial opportunities (employment and income).

Clearly, Tsay's research is more narrowly focused on questions of labor supply, technological innovation, and overseas investment. Still, the cultural transformation story is a useful addendum to what could be otherwise imagined to be simply an issue of relative costs and prices. But consider the implications of Tsay's empirical research coupled with the cultural transformation story. Whereas it might be supposed that in the recent past (according to Wade, at least) corporate interests were coincident with social interests—the growth of employment, income, and opportunities for future generations—that coincidence may no longer be an essential ingredient defining collective interests. Indeed, commodity-based exporting firms could justifiably suppose that their interests are better served by relocating to sites of production where wages are much lower and workers' commitment to work and productivity are much higher than in Taiwan. To the extent that state policy is currently a barrier to world-defined "best practice" technological innovation, then firms' interests are also different from the state's interests in local development. To the extent that local commodity-based firms have been remade into finance and asset management firms, then again firms' interests are less consistent with state interests, even if consistent with elements of the local middle class.

What is the role of the state? Will the development state as described by Amsden (1989), Wade, and others survive the 1990s? And what of the future of the Asian NIEs? This last question is addressed in detail in each economy-specific paper and in the conclusion to this book. With respect to the first question, the role of the Taiwanese state seems both more problematic and more profound. It is more problematic than allowed for by most commentators because of the apparent social divisions within Taiwanese society over the nature and value of work. It is more profound in the sense that the Taiwanese state seems to be the only institution capable of setting out a viable regulatory framework that could go beyond the short-term imperatives associated with the bubble economy. But this is a most ambitious role; it presumes that the state—its managers and policy makers—is aloof or at some distance from the opportunities represented by the bubble economy. Nevertheless, as is the case with the Korean state, the 1990s represent a real threat to the Taiwanese state's prerogatives and powers. Not surprisingly, there are internal arguments about the proper role of the state with respect to markets: Some factions support a reduced role of the state, limited to maintaining access to international markets and sustaining market efficiency rather than intervening in local markets to set the agenda for a new round of industrialization. In this respect, the Taiwanese state may retreat to a role commonly attributed to the Hong Kong state.

One implication to be drawn from this project is that the Asian development state, so essential to arguments about the distinctiveness of the NIEs' development, may not survive the 1990s. Let us be clear at the outset about the bases of this claim. For a start, it should be apparent from this project that the Asian development state as described by Amsden, Wade, and others is actually limited in application to Singapore, Korea, and Taiwan. In light of Lui and Chiu's research it is difficult to sustain an argument that the Hong Kong state has been anything more than preoccupied with housing and social services. It might be argued, of course, that assuring collective consumption is a vital ingredient for development and, as a consequence, the Hong Kong state could be thought to have been a development state in a different guise. But Amsden's and Wade's development state is more than simply the agent of collective consumption. By their reckoning, the development state was the architect of industrial structure. In any event, it is not clear at all that in the case of Hong Kong collective consumption was a necessary condition for development; collective consumption could be equally thought to be the result of development. A slightly different argument, sometimes made on behalf of the Singaporean state, is that the state played a vital role in facilitating the development process by using the benefits of growth to minimize political opposition and ensure political stability. We would accept this point but would also suggest that this role is now more difficult than ever before.

By our assessment, the architectural, or industrial structure, role attributed to the development state may be difficult to sustain for three reasons. First, the coincidence of interests between major corporations and the state, so essential for the power of state policy making during the 1960s and 1970s, may not be as obvious as it was a couple of decades ago. Industrial restructuring by corporations in labor-intensive industries has brought about a common realization that: (1) the state does not depend on those sectors for employment growth and export income as it once did; (2) viable options for restructuring often involve foreign direct investment; and (3) the growing geographical reach of Asian NIEs' corporations has transformed many economy-dependent corporations into international production *and* trading companies. In essence, neither the state nor labor-intensive industries have the same mutually dependent relationship. A second reason for the likely decline of the development state is related to the first; that is, to the extent that industry structure is now more than ever vulnerable to international economic forces, state policies of selective investment and targeted growth may face considerable opposition from within the historical elite networks that were essential for the power of state policy making. The rise of the financial sector in all the NIEs is, in part, a political challenge to the power of older elite networks. A third reason for the likely decline of the development state is closely related to the second reason: that is, the growth but fragmentation of interests of the middle classes is likely to increase demands for cultural consumption of all kinds. To sustain political legitimacy, the development state may become the "overloaded" state, argued by many to be typical of the West.

This is not to suggest that the state will be any less important to the development of the Asian NIEs. Rather, it suggests that the coherence and comprehensiveness of industry policy will be replaced by partial policies of selective investment, justified by reference to the individual NIEs' strategic place in the global economy. It also suggests that the state will be more important on the side of collective consumption, its scope matching the diverse interests of its middle-class clientele. Neither role will be easily reconciled with the past, and neither role need draw the kind of support that the state was able to orchestrate in the past. The state will also be more heavily involved in industrial regulation—competition within and between industries—rather than the planning of industrial growth. The separation of interests between the state and corporations could mean closer scrutiny of corporate decision making with reference to the national interest (however defined in particular circumstances), rather than automatically supporting the interests of firms. At the same time, the development state is likely to be drawn into the international regulation and management of trade. To protect their collective welfare, to protect firms against exclusion from the world's emerging supraregional trading blocs, the development state may be forced to negotiate policies of trade equalization and trade reciprocity. Instead of treating the global economy as a free good, the Asian NIEs will be increasingly held accountable for the bilateral consequences of their firms' actions. Accommodating international claims may, however, compromise the development state's political alliances with many of the industries that were essential to the maintenance of power over the past quarter century. It is just as likely that these same industries will develop their own alliances outside the Asian NIEs.

Looking Forward

The so-called Asian development states now face a complex agenda: the transformation of their economies, including the increasing significance of the financial sector, will make management of middle-class aspirations, industry restructuring, and international trade an extremely complex process, certainly less coherent and less comprehensive than that identified by development theorists to have been the past practice of some Asian states. Whereas the growth and development of the Asian NIEs with respect to the markets of the Western economic world was guaranteed for decades by the cold war and the pivotal place of the NIEs and Japan in Asia, the collapse of the U.S.S.R. and eastern Europe has made the Asian NIEs less significant to the West. Indeed, as the Cold War is replaced by trade wars, the Asian NIEs are peculiarly exposed to the competition for markets between the large trading blocs. In this sense, the focus of the development state on internal growth through exploiting international trade may be politically impossible to sustain at the same time as economic maturity narrows the gap between imports and exports. As a consequence, the future of the development state and the Asian NIEs in general is now very much an open question.

In the last part of the book, we look at two issues that have great significance for the future of the Asian NIEs. Won Bae Kim (chap. 9, this volume) collates and compares in a statistical manner the results of the common cross-economy empirical framework. He expands upon these observations about the contemporary circumstances of the Asian NIEs. In the promised new world of managed trade and limited trade between rival trading blocs, it is no longer sufficient for economies to be simply competitive with respect to price and quality. Restricted access to markets, bilateral trading regimes designed to equalize the benefits of trade, and mutual protection against common trading adversaries seem to be just as likely as a GATT-based expanded free trade system. To orchestrate the appropriate industry response at the local level will be a vital task of governments. And yet, as Kim observes, the authority and bureaucratic capacity of the Korean development state, in particular, seems to be ebbing as increasing social and political demands conspire to redirect the state's attention toward equally compelling issues of equity and justice. In this context, Kim suggests that the policy-making initiative may well fall to enterprises at home and overseas. His comparison of enterprise strategies in the Asian NIEs emphasizes both the diversity of responses and the necessity for innovation at the higher-value-added end of production.

Yet, even as firms struggle to adjust and respond to the new competitive pressures and global turbulence with new modes and techniques of production, an alternative set of opportunities threatens to profoundly alter the mode of adjustment. That is, with the astounding rate of development of China, local enterprises could just as easily (and perhaps more easily) use the emerging financial sector of Asia to restructure the form of the enterprise so as to become a trading enterprise rather than a production enterprise. This is clearly a possibility suggested by Chiu and Lui's work and is a strong possibility for enterprises whose primary focus has been labor-intensive production (see chapter 10, this volume). If this is a common long-term response to the new global trading order and the extraordinary competitive pressures posed by the new Asian dragons, then the rate of industrial restructuring will accelerate, and the rate of growth of the Asian NIEs will decline faster than previously imagined. The Asian NIEs will, of course, remain comparatively rich economies. But whereas in the past their success was based upon export-led growth, their future growth over that allowed by the level of real wages will depend on the repatriation of profit from investments in China. In this sense, the future of the Asian NIEs seems more likely to be consistent with similarly sized economies of the OECD than with the growth path of Japan.

TWO

Changing Places in
East Asia

Michael Webber

In the past forty years, the Asian newly industrialized economies (NIEs) of Hong Kong, the Republic of Korea, Singapore, and Taiwan (the Republic of China) have changed dramatically. From being relatively poor they are now entering or challenging to enter the ranks of the rich industrialized market economies. From being economically and politically dependent on outside hegemonic or colonial powers they are now—except Hong Kong—substantively independent and wield at least regional power. Their peoples are increasingly well educated and urbanized and enjoy a widening range of citizenship rights.

With this maturity have come new challenges and new priorities. The international political order changed as U.S. influence in East Asia waned and that of Japan grew; as the North American and European markets became themselves more integrated and apparently inward looking, as the ASEAN 4 countries began their push to industrialize and develop, and as China opened its doors to global commerce and politics. The economic power of NIEs has grown, and the range of industries in which they compete internationally has broadened. As people within NIEs have become richer, so their priorities have begun to broaden from growth to quality of life, from material to political development. The changes in economic policies and corporate strategies that are needed to respond to the new challenges and to react to the new priorities are collectively labeled restructuring.

These changes in political and economic conditions within NIEs have been widely observed. ADB (1991) and UN (1991) have commented on the restructuring that is needed in NIEs in response to changes in competitiveness and the global political economy. W. B. Kim (1993a) has observed these impulses and the forms of industrial restructuring that have occurred. International conferences have explored both the reasons for restructuring and the emerging patterns of industrialization and regional trade and investment: the Institute of Economics in Academia Sinica examined Taiwan's new role in the emerging Asia-Pacific region in 1988; the German Foundation for International Development investigated the situation and plans for NIEs in relation to Europe in 1989; the East-West Center organized conferences on restructuring in the NIEs in 1991, 1992, and again in 1993. Politicians such as Taiwan's Minister for State Shirley Kuo have been drawn into conferences on the changing role of NIEs in the Asia-Pacific region (Kuo 1993).

What are the sources of the impulse to restructure? How are we to interpret what has been going on? First, after a quarter century of rapid growth of output and exports, the last few years have witnessed increasing concerns about the prospects for continued growth as the whole pattern of growth is changing. Exports and imports are now growing at approximately the same rate, which imposes entirely new relationships among growth, local real wages, and capital flows. This change from a model in which exports grew faster than imports to one in which exports grow at about the same rate as imports is the object of restructuring. At heart, restructuring is the process whereby economies shift from one model of growth to another, establishing a new growth pattern.

Second, the NIEs have been forced to change their pattern of growth because their very success has altered the conditions under which they grew. The relations between corporations in the NIEs and other corporations are changing as the global political economy itself evolves. So NIE corporations must deal with currency revaluations and protectionism from Europe and North America. Furthermore, growth has prompted changes in the internal class structure of NIEs that have altered the balance of class forces and so the objects of social and economic policy. Consequently, NIE corporations face shortages of labor and rising wages. These on-the-ground manifestations of the changing conditions of growth—currency revaluations, protectionism, shortages of labor, and rising wages—have forced the rate of growth of exports down, and it is to these manifestations that corporations and governments have now to react by changing strategy.

Third, rising wages and the concomitant offshore investment reflect corporations' adjustments to the new pattern of growth. They are also the means by which the pattern is achieved. Firms are evolving new strategies that use technology and labor in different ways as the rules of their games are altered. Fourth, strategic adjustments to achieve this new pattern of growth are, however, occurring under altered political economic conditions as corporations take more responsibility from the state to orchestrate change; the stories of the reactions by corporations comprise the empirical basis for this book.

Growth: Enter the Dragons

In the years since 1960, the dragons emerged as world industrial powers. What have been the dimensions of this change? And how is it to be explained?

The Evidence

In the 1970s and the early 1980s, real gross domestic product (GDP) per capita in each country grew at about 6.5 percent each year (7.4 percent in Singapore); their real GDPs were growing at 8.3–9.3 percent per annum (table 2.1). Unlike virtually all other developing economies, the NIEs have been catching up with the advanced economies. In international prices, per capita gross domestic products that were in 1960 9, 14 , 17, and 21 percent of the United States level in Korea, Taiwan, Singapore, and Hong Kong respectively had risen by 1984 to 25, 34, 49, and 64 percent (Summers and Heston 1991). Exports increased even faster: measured in current United States dollars, exports grew on average 7–8 percent each year in Hong Kong and Singapore and 10–12 percent in Korea and Taiwan. Except in Hong Kong (where invisibles have become increasingly important), rates of growth of exports comfortably exceeded rates of growth of imports. And except in Hong Kong, this growth was accompanied by industrialization: by 1984, about half the GDP of Korea and Taiwan, and 43 percent of that of Singapore, originated in industry.

The industrial specializations of the four dragons changed during this period of growth. In Hong Kong, manufacturing declined in rela-

Table 2.1   Growth of the Asian NIEs, 1970–1984

	Hong Kong	Korea	Singapore	Taiwan
GDP per capita[a]				
1960	2,210	907	1,710	1,382
1970	4,456	1,688	3,155	2,387
1984	10,710	4,056	8,519	5,651
1990	14,410	6,209[b]	10,965	8,510
Rate of growth 1970–1984[c]	6.46%	6.46%	7.35%	6.35%
Rate of growth 1984–1990[c]	5.07%	8.89%	4.30%	7.06%
GDP				
1970	18	54	7	35
1984	58	164	23	107
1990	84	263[b]	33	175
Rate of growth 1970–1984[c]	8.84%	8.27%	9.31%	8.33%
Rate of growth 1984–1990[c]	6.43%	9.93%	6.35%	8.46%
Exports[d]				
1970	2.0	0.8	1.6	1.5
1984	17.6	29.2	24.1	30.5
1990	29.0	64.8	52.6	60.6[e]
Rate of growth 1970–1984[c]	7.0%	11.8%	8.9%	9.8%
Rate of growth 1984–1990[c]	3.75%	5.9%	5.8%	7.7%[e]
Imports[d]				
1970	2.9	2.0	2.5	1.5
1984	28.6	30.6	28.7	22.0
1990	82.5	70.0	60.7	49.7[e]
Rate of growth 1970–1984[c]	7.4%	8.8%	7.9%	8.6%
Rate of growth 1984–1990[c]	8.0%	6.2%	5.6%	9.3%[e]
Percentage of GDP from industry				
1970	36.3	32.3	32.5	34.1
1984	30.9	48.3	43.0	52.8[f]
1990	26.2[b]	50.3[b]	40.1	35.3[f]

Sources: GDP data are from the Penn World Table (Mark 5.5) (Summers and Heston 1991). Trade and industrial composition data for Hong Kong, Korea, and Singapore are from World Bank (1993b); for Taiwan, from Economic Daily News (1986, 1992), Taiwan (1991b), and Economic Planning Council (1986, 1992).

[a] 1987 $US, international prices (GDP are in billions of dollars).

[b] 1989 data.

[c] Compound rate of growth, percentage per annum.

[d] $US billions, current; customs basis.

[e] 1988 data.

[f] Percentage in manufacturing, not industry.

tive significance after the 1960s (28 percent of GDP in 1971; 18 percent in 1989), being replaced by wholesale and retail trade, restaurants and hotels (20 percent in 1971; 24 percent in 1989), and finance, insurance, real estate, and business services (11 percent in 1961; 20 percent in 1989) (Lui and Chiu 1993). Equivalent changes occurred in Korea. In 1970 the leading industries were the textiles, clothing and leather industries, with 31 percent of persons employed in manufacturing, but this declined to only 26 percent by 1987. By 1987 the leading industries were fabricated metal products, machinery, and equipment, which accounted for 34 percent of manufacturing employment in 1987, from 17 percent in 1970 (Park 1993a). In Singapore an early concentration on food, beverages, and tobacco and, to a lesser extent, on paper products (which in 1961 combined to produce more than 50 percent of Singapore's manufactured output) gave way to a reliance on petroleum refining (37.7 percent of manufactured output in 1975) and then on electronic components, chemicals, and pharmaceuticals (47 percent of manufactured output in 1988) (Ho 1993). Paralleling this development has been a declining contribution of commerce (33 percent of GDP in 1961; 18 percent in 1988) and a growing role for finance and business services in the Singapore economy (2 percent of GDP in 1961; 28 percent in 1988—almost equal to the contribution of manufacturing) (Ho 1993). In Taiwan a sustained decline in agriculture has been matched by an equivalent relative growth of manufacturing: from 19 percent of GDP in 1960, manufacturing accounted for 29 percent of GDP in 1970 and almost 40 percent by 1986. More recently the finance, insurance, and business services sector has begun to grow rapidly: after contributing less than 10 percent of GDP until the mid 1970s, this sector now provides over 20 percent of GDP (Taiwan 1992c).

Fueling the performance of industry have been high rates of investment and rapid increases in productivity. With rates of gross domestic investment between 25 percent (Korea and Taiwan) and 30 percent (Singapore) of GDP, the NIEs comfortably outperformed most other developing economies between 1960 and 1984 (World Bank 1993a; 42). (Hong Kong's rate of 22 percent was about what would have been expected from its level of per capita income.) These high rates of investment and high levels of enrollment in education contributed to relatively high rates of growth of output per worker in the four NIEs (World Bank 1993a, 52–53). However, in addition to increases in factor inputs there have been rapid rates of growth in total factor productivity: the average rates of growth of total factor productivity of 3.5–4.5 percent per annum between 1960 and 1989 in Taiwan, Hong Kong, and Korea are three of the four highest rates in the world—and Singapore's rate of 1.6 percent is still in the top third of all developing economies' rates (World Bank 1993a, 55–57).

Growth was not smooth. In the aftermath of the oil price rise of 1974, the rate of growth of exports from the dragons slowed—especially from Hong Kong, Korea, and Taiwan. The rate of growth of exports again slowed in the late 1970s and early 1980s: this time Hong Kong suffered more than the others. Singapore's exports grew only slowly between 1981 and 1985. Employment in manufacturing rose slowly in Hong Kong and Singapore after the first oil price rise; the early 1980s saw a more severe slowdown of growth in employment in manufacturing in Korea and Taiwan, where readjustments included measures of trade and financial liberalization (Corbo and Suh 1992; Lau 1990). Still, these slowdowns only temporarily interrupted a sustained and dramatic economic transformation.

There were also episodes of restructuring in NIEs during this period. In Singapore, the government pushed wage increases in the early 1980s as a way of encouraging firms to restructure away from labor-intensive to more knowledge- and capital-intensive forms of activity. The Taiwanese government has attempted to promote high-technology industry since the late 1970s to reduce the island's dependence on labor-intensive exports. More spectacularly, the Korean heavy and chemical industrialization of the late 1970s was designed to circumvent the perceived threat to Korea's exports from protectionist sentiment in North America and Europe and from competition from low-cost producers in China and the ASEAN countries (SaKong 1993, 35, 41).

To these impressive data on the growth of output and exports, the World Bank (1993a) adds two more characteristics. First, paralleling the growth of output in industry have been high rates of growth of productivity and output in agriculture in Korea and Taiwan. We pay little attention to agricultural change in this book, but changes on the land have been as dramatic as those in industry—at least in the economies with significant land resources. Second, among the developing countries, the NIEs exhibited relatively low (and declining) levels of income inequality, early declines in fertility, and a persistent attention to education (World Bank 1993a, 38–46). Again, these social characteristics do not figure large in the stories that follow, but they are important indications of the success of growth.

Although the dragons are sometimes portrayed as a group of economies with common characteristics, they have taken somewhat different paths. Hong Kong in particular has become quite different from the others. Its employment in manufacturing rose more slowly than in other NIEs, its commodity exports have grown more slowly than its commodity imports, the commodities that it exports have not changed greatly over the years, and its GDP comes increasingly from nonindustrial sources. Whereas Korea, Singapore, and Taiwan have been industrial, commodity-exporting countries—and becoming more so—Hong Kong has been on a different path, to specialization in trade and finance. Now Hong Kong's manufacturing is largely small scale and labor intensive, relying on flexible uses of labor and investment within China to compete within international networks of subcontractors (see chapter 4, this volume). The active, interventionist states in Korea, Singapore, and Taiwan have also created quite different kinds of industrial structures: contrast an industrialization based on large domestic conglomerates funded by government-controlled international finance capital in Korea, the relatively large subsidiaries of foreign direct investors in Singapore, and the combination of relatively small indigenous enterprises and state-run monopolies in Taiwan. Even within these economies, garments and electronics have evolved differently (compare chapters 5, 6, and 7, this volume). Often, these emerging differences seem hidden by common economic success; yet they condition the different responses of Asian NIEs to the new demands of the late 1980s and 1990s.

Neoclassical and Revisionist Accounts

Orthodox versions of the dragons' story revolve around theories of comparative advantage—the neoclassical story. A central feature of the neoclassical account is its emphatic claim that governments have played limited roles in these four economies, providing rather a stable macroeconomic environment in which prices were right (see, for example, the characterization in World Bank 1993a, 82–83). When prices are right, according to the theory of comparative advantage, growth depends on relative cost advantages derived from patterns of factor abundance. (In the theory of competitive advantage, relative cost advantages may also derive from conditions other than factor abundance.) In these views, NIEs faced lower costs of production than traditional manufacturing countries and, therefore, outstripped them in world market competition. Flows of capital from advanced capitalist countries to NIEs reflected cost—and, therefore, profitability—differences and were the means by which NIEs achieved high rates of economic growth.

Revisionist accounts question the significance of cost advantages to the growth of NIEs. Capital flows do not necessarily advantage countries with lower costs, and, therefore, faster rates of growth do not imply higher rates of profitability (Webber 1987). In any case, comparative advantage cannot explain different rates of growth—only different specializations. Among political economic historians and geographers, Mandel (1978) and Harvey (1982) argue that NIEs have grown in part because of the slowdown in the advanced capitalist countries, employing capital that is produced but cannot be profitably invested there. Thus, the comparative advantage explanation is far too simplistic.

Growth in most NIEs has not been determined by cost advantages, neither in its rate nor in its direction. Asian NIEs certainly benefited from the relatively open global trading regime of the 1960s and 1970s, when world trade in manufactured commodities grew far faster than world production. The economies of Hong Kong and Singapore have been relatively open, and those of Korea and Taiwan oriented to exports. But that does not imply that Korea, Singapore, and Taiwan were market-directed and liberal economies (Bradford 1990). Even the Hong Kong government has promoted exports in foreign countries, provided training to small entrepreneurs, and altered factor market conditions by immigration policy, housing policy, and its promotion of the finance sector (though the effects of these policies can be disputed; see Liu and Chui 1993). In most NIEs, including Korea and Taiwan, competitiveness was irrelevant to growth: industries were set up independently of their competitiveness—they became competitive through continued growth (Webber 1994). Subsidies, tariffs, and distortions in the price of capital directly rebut the view that cost advantages have controlled the pace and direction of growth. Rather, comparative advantage has been deliberately crafted, working off a process of internal firm dynamics that can be shown to be analogous to Scott's (1989) new model of economic growth.

Industrialization in NIEs—except possibly in Hong Kong where growth has increasingly tended to favor the financial and service sectors—also exemplifies the importance of various forms of local, state initiatives. Like corporations (see chapter 3, this volume), states have strategies that are not bound by the structure. What happenes in one country differs from what happens in others; but each history demonstrates a local power to act. Successful NIEs have acted in ways different from the prescriptions of orthodox economics through the fashioning and implementation of local policies. The state is in social context, whence it derives the will and the strength to create industrial policy. The fact that industrialization in the Third World has been selective implies that the traits of individual places influence economic change, so development is not purely structural: the individuality of development in NIEs reflects the inherited social structure and states' attempts to shape the pace and pattern of industrialization. States have used many powers to influence industry and investment: investment incentives; employment and labor policies; state ownership of assets; government procurement policies; institutional structures; environmental and health regulations; foreign direct investment, either outward investment by domestic firms or inward investment by foreign firms; tariff and nontariff barriers; and export policies.

States have promoted investment and growth. In turn, investment and growth have been the principal means to enhancing firm and industry competitiveness. New investment carries improved technologies; continued production and larger scales of production offer the opportunity to learn by doing; and growth of output provides economies of scale. In Korea, Singapore, and Taiwan especially, exports have been the principal method of achieving competitiveness, enlarging the scale beyond the domestic market and inducing additional investment and new techniques (see evidence on economies of scale in Chen and Tang 1990; Ohno and Imaoka 1987), which is why global economic conditions have been so important to the emergence of NIEs. The crucial controls over growth in Korea, Singapore, and Taiwan have been through national accumulation strategies and nationally directed investment policies—within the context of a global economy awash with overaccumulated (financial) capital. In Korea, Singapore, and Taiwan the state has exercised a political will to develop, reflecting local class structures and perceptions of geopolitical forces. Certainly Korea, Singapore, and Taiwan have used the capital produced in the center to finance their development programs, but the programs were indigenous, not driven by foreign direct investment. The central role of state investment strategies in determining rates of growth explains why capital has flowed to only some Third World countries. (Hong Kong, where class structures were different and state policy less interventionist, is inconsistent with this story; but its outcome has also been quite distinct.)

In sum, the revisionist account argues that the industrialization of NIEs reflects conditions within the global economy that provided surplus capital after the early 1970s and the actions of local states that made investment in NIEs profitable (Singapore) or permitted investment to become profitable (Korea and Taiwan). In Hong Kong, growth has followed a different path, largely outside industry, under positive nonintervention (Lui and Chiu 1993).

A Middle Road

The World Bank (1991, 1993a) has attempted to reconcile its leanings toward neoclassical theory and the evidence that has been produced by the revisionists. It argues that rapid growth in the NIEs has been associated with effective but limited government action: governments have got out of the economic arenas in which they do harm (mainly production) but have intervened in areas where markets are not effective. These areas are the fundamentals: providing macroeconomic stability, investing in human capital, opening the economy to international trade, and encouraging private investment and competition (World Bank 1993a, 84–85). In particular, the World Bank has provided what it calls a "functional approach" to growth (1993a, 87–102).

Choices had to be made over three arenas of policy:

- *the fundamentals:* macroeconomic stability, human capital investment, openness to the international economy, limited price distortions, and agricultural development policies;
- *selective interventions:* export push incentives, financial repression that permitted states to direct credit to favored activities, and selective promotion; and
- *institutions:* technocratic insulation, high-quality civil service, and monitoring.

The World Bank insists that a central facet of the success of the East Asian NIEs has been the imposition of a competitive discipline on corporations, even in arenas where governments were intervening. As argued by neoclassical theory, the fundamentals are most important in promoting one form of competitive discipline: market competition. However, markets sometimes fail, especially in providing information and credit and in circumstances where external economies argue for interfirm cooperation. So other forms of competitive discipline have been invented: in particular, states have put the corporations in situations where they compete among themselves for export credits, investment funds, and information. These state organized competitions are called "contests" by the Bank. By and large, the yardstick used by governments to judge performance in these contests was exports. The referees in the contests were sometimes private corporations (e.g., the banks, in the case of export credits) but more commonly state institutions; thus, the quality of personnel and their insulation from corporate and populist pressures have been vital to both the quality of monitoring and the impartiality of the contests.

Together the two forms of competitive discipline have organized the central growth functions. The World Bank (1993a) identifies three of these functions:

- *accumulation:* increasing human capital, high savings, and high investment;
- *allocation:* effective use of human capital in the labor market and high returns on investment; and
- *productivity change:* productivity-based catching up and rapid technological change.

In turn, these three functions have generated rapid and sustained growth under conditions of relatively equal distribution of income—outcomes that in turn have fed back into policy choices and growth functions.

Certainly, these more recent arguments of the World Bank do recognize many of the criticisms made of the neoclassical account by the revisionists. They recognize that the state has played a substantial role in assisting and directing the growth of the NIEs. However, these arguments are about growth: the question for the NIEs now really concerns restructuring.

A New Model of Growth

Restructuring is a change in the relations between the elements of an economy that alters its character (Webber et al. 1991). This change occurs as a country, industry, region, or firm switches from one accumulation strategy or pattern of growth to another. An accumulation strategy is an economic growth model, with its preconditions, and a strategy for its realization (Jessop 1990, 197–206). At the level of a national economy, industrialization through export promotion or adding increased value to products are accumulation strategies. In a corporation, differentiation or specialization are accumulation strategies (Clark 1993b). Industrial restructuring includes the transitions from import replacement to export promotion in the 1970s in Korea and Taiwan or from export-led growth to growth led by domestic demand in Japan in the 1980s. It also includes changes in the strategic directions taken by corporations. Restructuring, therefore, involves a struggle between different industrial sectors and between ruling and subordinate classes to determine the balance of interests that are satisfied in the new strategy.

Restructuring occurs after it has been realized that the existing strategy of accumulation no longer delivers material benefits or does not satisfy the long-term interests of a new dominant industrial sector. Restructuring entails conflict and struggle between industrial sectors and between ruling and subordinate classes over the way and the degree to which their interests are represented in the new strategy. Restructuring also involves the constructive use of language: to idealize the past or other places; to allocate blame for the breakup of the past; to apportion the costs of economic change; and to justify changes in the place of the economy, industry, or region in the broader world.

Restructuring in Asian NIEs has become an object of stories in other countries. As Clark (see chapter 3, this volume), notes, the structure of state involvement in, and the economic performance of, Asian NIEs have become raw material in arguments about government intervention in development and industry policy. The experience of the Asia-Pacific Rim is said to be crucial in testing new theories of economic growth that emphasize human resources (Ogawa, Jones, and Williamson 1993). In Australia the experience of East Asian NIEs is variously interpreted in debates about competitiveness, environmental policy, and government intervention in the Australian economy (contrast Garnaut 1989 and Webber 1991, 1994).

Asian NIEs have in the late 1980s and 1990s entered just such a period of restructuring: their model of growth or strategy of accumulation has faltered as global and domestic circumstances have changed. A new model of growth is being set in place. Thus, warnings have begun to sound that the basis of growth in NIEs has been eroded. Certainly rates of growth have slowed (table 2.1). Rates of growth of real GDP per capita that were 6.5 percent or higher have fallen to 4–5 percent in Hong Kong and Singapore. Rates of real GDP growth are lower in Hong Kong and Singapore than they were (6.5 percent compared to

9 percent or more). Korea and Taiwan, at least until recently, escaped this slowdown in aggregate growth: in 1992 Korea's rate of GDP growth was only half that of 1991 (*FEER* 15 March 1993). Corporations in all four economies have experienced or expect slowly growing output (see chapters 4, 5, 6, and 7, this volume). In all four dragons, exports are now growing more slowly than they were: more slowly than or at about the same pace as imports. The aggregate slowdown is paralleled by the performance of individual industries such as textiles and garments (Lui and Chiu 1992) and regional economies such as Pusan (Lim 1993b). To the extent that exports composed the engine for growth of NIEs, this slower growth of trade presages more fundamental changes. This concern itself reflects a fundamental shift in the pattern of growth in NIEs. The dragons are shifting from an export-dominated economic structure to one that is more mature. As the upper part of figure 2.1 displays, corporations in NIEs are required to adopt strategies that both reflect and implement this shift to a new model of growth. In that shift, wages, currency values, and the relation between exports, imports, and investment are changed.

To illustrate the significance of this shift, consider the standard decomposition of gross domestic product:

$$O = C + I + E - M \tag{1}$$

where O denotes output; C, consumption; I, investment; E, exports; and M, imports. The output of governments is allocated by function to these four categories.

This identity is taken to be a long-term structural equation that constrains a society, rather than merely a description of what happens over short-term fluctuations. Denote the rate of growth of the components of output by O^*, C^*, I^*, E^* and M^* respectively (e.g., $O^* = 1/O \cdot dO/dt$). And let c, i, e, and m denote respectively the share of consumption, investment, exports and imports in gross national product (e.g., $c = C/O$). Then equation (1) implies:

$$O^* = cC^* + iI^* + eE^* - mM^* \tag{2}$$

Equation (2) indicates that the rate of growth of output depends on the rates of growth of consumption, investment, and net exports—all weighted by their relative shares in the economy.

For a variety of reasons—canvassed in the previous section—

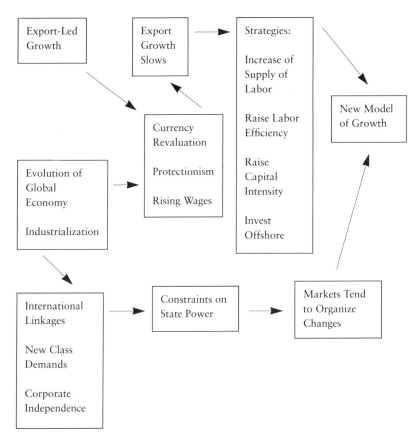

Figure 2.1 Political economy of industrial restructuring.

corporations in the NIEs were able to maintain high and rising rates of investment. These rates of investment, in turn, permitted the corporations of the newly industrialized economies of Hong Kong, Korea, Singapore, and Taiwan to embody new technology, learn by doing, and reap economies of scale. The corporations were therefore able to create cost advantages (or to reduce cost disadvantages) that permitted exports to grow faster than imports and both to grow faster than aggregate output. The crucial fact about export-led growth is that exports grow faster than imports. It is not important that the level of exports exceeds the level of imports—only Taiwan was recording a surplus in its commodity trade by the 1980s. The growth of output had in this model of growth been disconnected from the growth of in-

Table 2.2 Components of Economic Growth 1970–1990

	Hong Kong	Korea	Singapore	Taiwan
Rate of growth of output				
1970–1984	8.8	8.3	9.3	8.3
1984–1990	6.4	9.9	6.4	8.5
Share of consumption in output				
1970–1984	0.74	0.72	0.66	0.65
1984–1990	0.74	0.63	0.56	0.62
Rate of growth of consumption				
1970–1984	8.9	6.9	6.6	7.4
1984–1990	6.4	8.1	7.3	9.4
Share of investment in ou;ut				
1970–1984	0.21	0.31	0.47	0.33
1984–1990	0.21	0.38	0.44	0.34
Rate of growth of investment				
1970–1984	9.4	10.2	9.9	8.3
1984–1990	5.4	13.9	3.0	8.6
Share of trade in output				
1970–1984	0.98	0.27	1.37	0.40
1984–1990	1.19	0.34	1.75	0.48
Rate of growth of net exports				
1970–1984	–0.4	3.0	1.0	1.2
1984–1990	–4.3	–0.3	0.2	–1.6
Error [a]				
1970–1984	0.6	–1.1	–1.2	0.3
1984–1990	5.7	–0.8	0.7	0.5

Source: Calculations on the data in tables 2.1 and 2.2

[a] Error is the difference between the measured rate of growth of output and the measured contributions $cC^* + iI^* + 0.5(e + m)(E^* - M^*)$. In the terms of equation (2), the rows represent, in order O^*, c, C^*, i, I^*, $(e + m)/2$, and $E^* - M^*$.

ternal consumption: NIEs could grow, even if internal consumption was stagnant.

Table 2.2 illustrates the components of equation (2). In the 1970s and the early 1980s, rates of growth of consumption were high but— except in Hong Kong—well below the rates of growth of output. The rates of growth of investment were as high as or slightly higher than the rates of growth of output. The difference between the rates of growth of consumption and the rates of growth of output was largely remedied by the faster growth of exports than of imports (again, except in Hong Kong). In the 1960s and 1970s, $(eE^* - mM^*)$ was high and rising. In Korea, the rate of growth of exports less that of imports between 1970 and 1984 was 3.0 percent per annum; in Singapore, 1.0 percent each year; and in Taiwan, 1.2 percent per year (table 2.1). Only in Hong Kong was this not true: there, the rate of growth of imports was 0.4 percent per annum less than the rate of growth of exports (bear in mind that these data refer to commodities). Investment has induced the cost changes that have permitted exports to grow, which in turn has meant that growth has not had to rely on rising consumption (that is, on rising real wages).

Such a pattern of growth could not continue. In practice, no country's exports can grow faster than its imports indefinitely. As Japan has been attempting to follow the same strategy, the four dragons have faced the inevitable fact that their export success is causing rates of growth of output in other parts of the capitalist developed world to fall. This fact is mere accounting: in other countries, $eE^* < mM^*$. The export success of NIEs and Japan necessarily implies the import success of other countries. Therefore, a continued policy of export-led growth has drawn forth protest in the form of rising protectionism and the demand that the currencies of NIEs and Japan be permitted to appreciate. In the late 1980s, the dragons' economies essentially shifted to a pattern of growth in which either exports and imports grow at approximately the same rate and are approximately in balance or imports grow at a faster rate than exports (see table 2.1): in Hong Kong, exports are growing 4.3 percent per annum more slowly than imports; in Korea, exports are growing 0.3 percent per year more slowly; and in Taiwan, 1.6 percent each year. Only in Singapore are exports growing slightly more quickly than imports (by 0.2 percent annually). This is the fundamental change from an export-led regime of growth to a mature regime of growth: in a mature regime, equation (2) has $eE^* = mM^*$. Restructuring can be understood as the attempt by the state, corporations, and workers to change institutions and modes of behavior from those appropriate to an export-led pattern of growth to those appropriate to a more mature one.

The nature of the changes can be identified from equation (2). Since NIEs have arrived at a state in which approximately and over the long run exports grow at the same rate as imports and are in balance ($eE^* = mM^*$) equation (2) becomes:

$$O^* = cC^* + iI^*. \tag{3}$$

That is, the rate of growth of output now depends on the rates of growth of internal consumption and investment, weighted by their relative sizes in the economy.

Table 2.2 indicates the magnitude of the change. For Korea and Singapore, the shift from a model in which exports grow faster than imports to one in which imports grow at least as fast as exports has the effect of tending to reduce the rate of growth of output by about 1 percent each year; in Taiwan the effect is 1.25 percent annually; and in Hong Kong the effect is 4.7 percent each year (though Hong Kong's trade in invisibles must make up much of that difference). Therefore, either the rate of growth of output falls (as in Hong Kong and Singapore) and/or the rate of growth of consumption rises (as in Korea, Singapore, and Taiwan) and/or the rate of growth of investment rises (as in Korea).

To see the implications of equation (3) even more clearly, consider the determinants of consumption and investment. The total level of consumption depends on the real wage (D) and the number of workers in the economy (L): $C = DL$. Therefore, the rate of growth of consumption is equal to the sum of the rates of growth of the real wage and the labor force: $C^* = D^* L^*$. Suppose, furthermore, that the rate of growth of domestic investment depends on the rate of growth of output, with a coefficient of proportionality a, and on exogenous influences (I^+): $I^* = aO^* + I^+$. Therefore,

$$O^* = c\,(D^* + L^*) + i(aO^* + I^+)$$

or

$$O^* = (1 - ia)^{-1}\,[cD^* + cL^* + iI^+]. \tag{4}$$

Evidently the rate of growth of output is now constrained by the rate of growth of the real wage and the rate of growth of the labor force, unless exogenous investment can be increased rapidly. The pressure to increase consumption is evident in table 2.2.

The central issues of restructuring in the four dragons are raised by the differences between equation (2) and equation (4). The impulse to restructure comprises those changes that have caused the growth of exports to slow. Figure 2.1 identifies these in an immediate sense as currency revaluation, protectionism, and rising wages (chapters 4 through 8 add labor shortages, land costs, and social unrest in particular places or industries). These are the means by which NIEs have been forced from export-led growth to a mature pattern of growth. In this mature pattern, the rate of growth of output is constrained internally by the rates at which real wages and the labor supply grow (D^* and L^* respectively) and externally by offshore investment (I^+).

The old model of growth has become unstuck. NIEs are in a state of flux between one model and another: the structure is no longer fixed. As Gordon Clark (see chapter 3, this volume) points out, a period of uncertainty about structure makes corporate strategy all the more important. Corporations must decide what a new model of growth might imply—indeed, it is their decisions that in aggregate create the new structure. Corporate strategies must be created to discover new industries, to find new technologies or ways of using labor or new locations, perhaps even to leave production for the world of finance. In particular, for corporations, the supply of labor now constrains growth (for competition argues against wage rises); for the economy as a whole, labor supply and the level of wages both constrain growth. Therefore, firms seek new forms of labor or economize on its use; the state is more willing to sanction rising real wages, as well. Some of these strategies are listed in figure 2.1; they are described in detail in chapters 4 through 8.

The central tensions in growth are obvious too, reflecting the reality of the new strategy of accumulation. The rate of growth is raised in the short run if real wages are raised and corporations invest offshore; but both strategies reduce the competitiveness that is required to keep exports growing at about the same pace as imports. Equally, the benefits of wage rises flow to all corporations (in the form of increased demand), whereas the costs are born only by those firms that raise wage rates—so each corporation wants all others to raise wages but none has an incentive to raise wages individually.

Restructuring in Practice

NIEs are being forced to embark on a new growth model as exports no longer provide the engine for accumulation that they did in the 1960s, 1970s, and early 1980s. This underlying shift is identified in the upper portion of figure 2.1. The impulse to restructure—the need to adopt a model in which exports and imports grow at about the same rate—derives from structural changes in the political economy of NIEs. Two changes are fundamental. First, NIEs are now inserted in the global economy in quite a different way: corporations overseas and other nations are reacting to NIEs as major players. Second, development has wrought a quite different structure of classes and industrial sectors from what once existed, bringing new demands and new concerns that were previously unvoiced. The most obvious manifestations of these changes are new demands for economic and political liberalization. These sources of change, and some of their consequences, are identified in the middle portion of figure 2.1. Moreover, the various forms of restructuring occur in a new political environment: it is not clear that the state-dominated institutions of growth are those that are orchestrating the response to changes since 1985 (see chapter 1, this volume). The evolution of new political conditions within NIEs is identified in the lower portion of figure 2.1.

The Global Economy

The global political economy has changed since the 1960s. The economic, political, and sometimes military struggle between one alliance centered on the United States (which included Hong Kong, Korea, Singapore, and Taiwan) and another centered on the Peoples' Republic of China (PRC) and the U.S.S.R. is no longer a central feature of world political relations; the price of capital has risen; NIEs themselves are now important global actors; and corporations now link economies in novel and stronger ways. Such changes drive new corporate responses to NIEs. They amount to deep-seated changes in the structure of the global political economy over the past thirty years.

NIEs are no longer in the forefront of the campaign to contain communism and the PRC. Thus, Korea and Taiwan, especially, but also Singapore, no longer receive special treatment from the United States and the European Community, while Hong Kong is about to be reintegrated with China. The aid and military purchases that flowed in the aftermath of the Korean War and that remained so important in the 1960s and during the Vietnam War no longer flow. Woo (1991) describes this and other aspects of the changing international environment to which the Korean state has sought to respond (see also Cumings 1988).

The cheap capital that was ranging about the world in the middle and late 1970s is now expensive (Daly and Logan 1989). The debts incurred in the 1970s have to be repaid, and new debts have to be paid at higher interest rates than formerly: both reduce levels of domestic demand. Because new investment projects have now to earn higher rates of profit before they can pay both interest and a premium for risk, investment rates are reduced, too. At the same time, NIEs have themselves become important sources of foreign direct investment: in 1989, NIEs provided nearly a quarter of foreign direct investment into Indonesia, nearly half of that in Malaysia, over a third of that in the Philippines, a quarter of that in Thailand, and over half of that in China (W. B. Kim 1993a).

The trade relations between Japan, NIEs, other Asian countries, and the traditional manufacturing economies of North America and Western Europe have altered substantially in the past two decades. NIEs have become one of the vehicles by which Japan has diversified its trade surplus: Japan has a trade surplus with NIEs, which in turn run a surplus with North America and the European Community. And as NIEs' offshore investment is partially directed to East Asia, so too is an increasing proportion of their trade. Thus, whereas 10.5 percent of Taiwan's exports were sent to Hong Kong, Korea, and Singapore in 1984 and nearly 3 percent to the ASEAN 4, those proportions had doubled by 1991 (Taiwan 1992b). Equally, in 1985 Korea sent 18.5 percent of its exports to China, ASEAN countries, other NIEs, and South Asia; in 1991 that proportion was 26.6 percent (SaKong 1993, 233). Thus, it is important to recognize the evolving patterned nature of trade relations as well as the emergence of currency blocs. In this respect the linkages between Japan, the Asian NIEs, the ASEAN 4, and China argue for a new currency regime, maybe a yen bloc (Frankel 1992).

NIEs have become more significant actors in the global economy, and corporations elsewhere and other states are responding to the challenges that NIEs pose for them. At the level of the state, the European Community and North America have responded by protectionist measures and pressures on currencies that seek to restrain the flow of imports (SaKong 1993, 130–34, briefly describes Korean-U.S. trade relations; World Bank 1984 provides examples of nontariff barriers to imports into North America and the European Community). The European Community, and especially the United States, have pressed NIEs to institute more liberal and less regulated economies. Such trade disputes have also entered such arenas as agricultural policy, intellectual property rights, insurance, and advertising (EIU 1989). Trade disputes and state responses to them in East Asia, North America, and Europe threaten to escalate into the formation of distinct trade blocs (see

Japan 1990 and chapter 3, this volume). The response of outside corporations has two elements. On the one hand, Japanese corporations
especially—but also U.S. ones—have become far more careful than
they once were about transferring advanced technology to corporations in NIEs, or they license technology only if the licensee agrees to
limit exports (*FEER* 12 November 1992): Nippon Steel does not sell
or license its latest technology to POSCO (personal communication,
Nippon Steel, October 1991); Bello and Rosenfeld (1990, 148–52)
quote similar examples about the electronics industry. On the other
hand, European and North American corporations have themselves cut
costs and raised product quality by a series of process and product innovations, for example, in textile manufacturing (World Bank 1984)
and auto production (*FEER* 17 August 1989, 64).

The strategies, forms of organization, and modes of operation of
global corporations have all altered while NIEs have been growing.
The larger corporations in Korea, Singapore, and Taiwan—and some
of the medium ones—are all integrated into this evolving network of
global producers, sometimes as wholly owned subsidiaries or joint ventures, sometimes as more or less independent subcontractors or original equipment manufacturers, sometimes as licensees of technology
(see, for example, the story on Nike in *FEER* 5 November 1992). Even
the smaller corporations in Hong Kong remain closely connected with
global commercial networks while they develop their new links with
the Pearl River Delta (Sit 1989). International business now transcends
national boundaries and limits the effectiveness of nations as economic
units (Japan 1990). As the strategies and operations of the global corporations alter so must also the strategies and operations of the linked
corporations in NIEs. The histories of process and product changes in
the electronics industries of NIEs illustrate these changing linkages
(Bello and Rosenfeld 1990), as do the tribulations of the auto industry
in Taiwan and Korea (Bello and Rosenfeld 1990, 260–65; *FEER* 12
November 1992)—not unlike those of Australia's auto industry. At this
level of analysis, the corporations located in Hong Kong, Korea, Singapore, and Taiwan have changed from being independent entities
chipping away at the low-cost end of the markets of the advanced industrial economies to being producers integrated into global production networks and seeking to enter higher technology and so higher
profit markets.

NIEs are now important players in the global economy. The rest of
the world is responding to their success: the practical manifestations of

this response include protectionism and pressure on NIEs to revalue their currencies. Corporations have also changed over the past forty years, becoming increasingly global in their scope. The change is observable in new forms of corporate linkages that reduce the significance of national boundaries and increased care over technological competition (see, generally, Harrison 1994).

Emerging Class Structures

Economic growth through industrialization and urbanization brings forth new class structures. The process of accumulation itself alters the class characteristics of societies. When the pace of accumulation has been fast, as in NIEs, the pace of change of class structure is also fast. But as the balance of classes alters in a society, their relative strengths and their impact on economic structure and social relations also change. A second impulse to restructuring in Asian NIEs derives from such changes in the balance of class forces: restructuring can be impelled by a change in the relative strength of classes even if the pace and form of accumulation has not changed. The formation of a capitalist class in the four dragons is described by Hamilton (1983); the evolving alliance between the state and that class is described in Park (1990), Gold (1988) and Winckler (1988), among others. More recently, in the 1980s capital-state alliances became weaker in Korea and Taiwan (see, for example, the corporations' evaluation of state policies in chapters 6, 7, and 8, this volume), and there have emerged stronger oppositions to the form and path of accumulation in all four NIEs.

Accumulation and industrialization have produced a working class in Hong Kong, Korea, Singapore, and Taiwan. From less than 10 percent of the workforce in the 1950s, the industrial working class has expanded in Korea and Taiwan to encompass over half the workforce and in Singapore over a third. In Hong Kong, Korea, and Singapore, these workers are highly concentrated in large cities; in Taiwan they are more spread out over the landscape. In all four societies, the state has suppressed working-class organizations: in Singapore, the People's Action Party emasculated trade unions in the 1960s; in Korea, the United States destroyed socialist organizations in the 1940s and early 1950s, and the Koreans themselves have continued to suppress working-class demands since; in Taiwan, the kumintang (KMT) infiltrated workers' organizations and diverted them to peripheral issues (Lau 1990; Park 1990); in Hong Kong, the opposition to and periodic immigration from the PRC has weakened workers' organizations (Lui and Chiu 1993). Nevertheless, as workers have become more numerous and more powerful, so their protests over working conditions have become louder, more effective, and—in Korea at least—more violent. The nitty-gritty world of the expanding interests of the emerging industrial working class in countries like Korea questions the coherence and logic of holist notions of race and religion so crucial to those, like Huntington (1993), who foretell a coming economic conflict between the East and the West.

In all four economies, labor disputes have become more numerous in the 1980s. Hong Kong has witnessed relatively few strikes in the 1980s, but the number of disputes has risen: there were 50 percent more disputes annually between 1978 and 1986 than between 1968 and 1977, and the annual number of grievances trebled between 1974 and 1977 and between 1983 and 1986 (Turner, Fosh, and Houg 1991, 71–72). In Korea there were thirteen times as many labor disputes each year from 1987 to 1989 as from 1980 and 1984 (*FEER* 23 May 1991). In Taiwan, the number of disputes doubled between 1980 and 1986 and again by 1988, and the number of disputes over wages increased fivefold (see also Hsiao 1992). In Singapore the People's Action Party (PAP) has been able to keep the industrial peace more effectively (EIU 1992a).

Protests have not simply been over wages. In Hong Kong only about 20 percent of strikes, disputes, and grievances have concerned wages: other conditions of employment, such as job security and claims against dismissal, have been far more important (Turner, Fosh, and Houg 1991, 71–75). In Korea the treatment of women in factories, enforcement of labor laws, industrial safety, land prices, income distribution, and especially political liberalization have all figured in strikes and riots (Ogle 1990). In Taiwan, too, claims about dismissal and layoffs, arrears of wages, and injury compensation caused over 60 percent of the disputes between 1981 and 1988 (Hsiao 1992, 159).

With economic development has come a middle class: doctors, engineers, journalists, public officials, scientists, teachers. People in these occupations have developed skills in organization and publicity and, with higher incomes, an interest in issues other than those of factory working conditions: land prices, political liberalization, social welfare, and the environment, especially (Cho and Kim 1991; Lau 1990). In Taiwan the local protest movement against pollution began in 1980, the natural conservation movement in 1982, and the movement op-

posing nuclear power in 1988 (Hsiao 1992, 153–54), and by 1986 the
environment movement was strong enough to prevent Du Pont from
making what would have been the largest single foreign investment in
Taiwan's history (Bello and Rosenfeld 1990, 212; see also Williams
1992). Middle-class people are voting with their feet by emigrating
from NIE societies: most of the Taiwanese who enter the United States
to study for higher degrees remain there, and nearly 1 percent of Singapore's population emigrates each year (*Asian Wall Street Journal
Weekly* 14 April 1989, 16 October 1989; EIU 1992a). Emigration
from Hong Kong rose after the 1984 agreement between China and the
United Kingdom and particularly after the massacre in Tiananmen
Square.

Thus, in all four NIEs—with the partial exception of Singapore—
oppositions to authoritarian forms of corporatist states have emerged.
These oppositions have taken a variety of forms and ranged over a variety of issues, from the environment through consumers' and women's
movements to racial movements. An important source of opposition
has been workers' revolts against established working conditions and
wages. Perhaps the most fundamental demand, though, has been for
more open and democratic forms of government. Not surprisingly,
these movements have prompted some commentators in the West to
raise questions, more generally, about the justice of Asian economic development (see Collingsworth, Goold, and Harvey 1994).

Concrete Effects

Gradually emerging during the period of rapid growth in the 1970s
and early 1980s but now evident through the early years of this decade
have been a pair of new circumstances: externally, new forms of global
political and economic organization, and internally, new social structures. These new conditions have prompted currency revaluations and
protectionism under pressure from North America and the European
Community and rising real wages under pressure from stronger workers' organizations. These effects have themselves fueled the slowdown
in growth (UN 1991) and are the real or concrete changes to which
corporations respond.

The first and most commonly identified cause for concern is a shortage of labor and consequent rise in relative wages. In Hong Kong and
Singapore, rapid industrial growth had eliminated urban unemployment and underemployment by the mid-1960s, and in Korea and Tai-

wan surplus labor from rural areas had been absorbed by the end of the 1960s. Since then, rapid industrial growth has fueled increasing shortages of labor. And with shortages of labor comes a demand-side pull for higher wages as firms compete for whatever labor is available.

The concern about rising real wages has been voiced in all four dragons (see chapters 4 through 8, this volume). In Hong Kong, real earnings per employee rose between 1984 and 1988 at 2.6 percent each year (World Bank 1993b). In Korea, the annual rate of real wage increase was 5.5 percent between 1970 and 1975 but 15.6 percent between 1976 and 1980 and 18.5 percent between 1988 and 1990 (Lim 1993a): in 1992 the government imposed a 5 percent ceiling on wage increases (*FEER* 3 December 1992). In Singapore wages have also risen. Between 1973 and 1978 real average earnings rose at 1.7 percent each year, well below the 2.7 percent per annum rate of real productivity growth; by 1982–84, however, real wage growth at 8.3 percent per annum was nearly double the rate of real productivity growth (Ho 1991), and in 1989 and 1990 wages again grew faster than productivity (EIU 1992a). Taiwan is also experiencing a labor shortage, reflected in rising real wages (Tsay 1993): real wages began to rise faster than productivity in the 1970s (Liang and Liang 1988a, 337) and in the 1980s real domestic wages doubled. In thirteen of the twenty two-digit manufacturing industries in Taiwan, the ratio of labor costs to total expenses increased between 1976 and 1986. By the end of the 1980s, average monthly wages in Korea, Singapore, and Taiwan were three to five times those in Indonesia, Malaysia, and Thailand (Kim 1989), and wages per hour in the textile industry were six to ten times higher.

In Singapore, though, the relationship between real wage increases and restructuring is not simple. The orthodox interpretation argues that rises in real wages prompt restructuring. In practice, the recommended pay increases of the National Wages Council (NWC) have come to be accepted as the norms that firms and unions follow (EIU 1992a). The recommendations take into account not only local conditions but also such long-term goals as international competitiveness. By deliberately increasing wages through the NWC, the government of Singapore tried to force many firms to modernize or shift production out of the country (Reiger and Veit 1990). In other words, the state's desire for restructuring prompted wage increases.

The second factor about which commentators are concerned is the rise in the value of domestic currency relative to the currencies of the United States and Japan (chapters 5 through 8, this volume). Korea,

Singapore, and Taiwan either experienced surpluses in their balance of trade or were increasing exports much faster than imports. More particularly, their trade surpluses with North America and the European Community were large and increasing (UN 1991). Under these circumstances, sustained pressure from the European Community and the United States has led to currency revaluations (EIU 1992b). These tend to make imports cheaper and exports more expensive, reducing the competitiveness of local manufactures in domestic and international markets. A parallel pressure has seen some import barriers reduced in Korea and Taiwan (Han 1990; Liang and Liang 1988a).

Currencies have recently been revalued in the dragons. Hong Kong's dollar has been falling in value relative to that of the United States—from HK$4.93 in 1980 to HK$7.81 in 1990—but has recovered to HK$7.74 in 1993. (All data in this paragraph are from Access Economics Pty. Ltd., and refer to averages for the first quarter of the year nominated.) After a long period of trade deficits during which the value of the Korean won fell, the trade surpluses of the late 1980s and U.S. pressure induced a corresponding rise in the value of the won. The won has risen from a rate of 885 per U.S. dollar in 1986 to 672 per U.S. dollar in 1989 before falling back to 794 per U.S. dollar in 1993. Since the Singapore dollar began to float in 1973, it has steadily appreciated against the U.S. dollar. In 1980, S$2.17 was worth US$1.00 and in 1987 the rate was little different; by 1993 that rate had fallen to S$1.65. The strength of the Singapore dollar contributes to the country's image of financial strength—important to the encouragement of its financial industries—and reduces the rate of inflation (Ho 1991). The Singapore government has encouraged its dollar to revalue throughout the 1970s and 1980s: there is nothing especially new about the experience of the late 1980s. Similarly, the Taiwanese dollar was fairly stable through the 1970s but in response to American and European pressure has more recently been revalued (Tsay 1993), rising from about NT$35.69 per US$1.00 in 1987 to NT$25.17 per US$1.00 in 1993. In Korea and Taiwan, then, the late 1980s have witnessed a new change as local currencies have revalued; in Singapore, there has been a long term revaluation of the Singapore dollar; there has been only slight and very recent revaluation of the Hong Kong dollar.

Actually, the significance of revaluation for export-oriented manufacturers is limited in two respects. First, the Japanese yen has also been revalued against the U.S. dollar. Whereas each dollar was worth Y360 in 1970, the dollar had fallen to Y237.5 in 1984 and again to Y144.8

Table 2.3   Asian NIEs' Currencies in Relation to Yen, 1970–1990

	Hong Kong	Korea	Singapore	Taiwan
1970	1.69	86.28	0.86	11.14
1984	3.28	339.36	0.88	16.67
1990	5.39	488.81	1.24	19.75

Source: World Bank (1993b).
Note: Units of local currency per 100 yen.

in 1990. The changes in local currencies in relation to the yen are shown in table 2.3. In every country, the currency has appreciated against the yen, even in the late 1980s. Exporters that sell to Japan or sell through Japanese trading companies have been insulated against the revaluation of the local currency. Second, currency appreciation reduces the price of imports. Firms that import machinery and raw materials and consumers who buy imported goods have all benefited from the revaluations of the 1980s. The effect of currency appreciation is diminished by cheaper imports—especially important since imports comprise well over 40 percent of GDP in all four NIEs.

A third cause for concern has been a rising sentiment for protectionism in North America and the European Community. (Haggard 1988 describes the politics of American trade policy in the 1980s.) Huge trade surpluses are, in the opinion of Liang and Liang (1988a), the major structural economic problem Taiwan faces. As exports from the NIEs take ever larger shares of the markets of the advanced industrial countries (U.N. 1991), they are being pressed in the same manner as Japan by the threat of quotas and tariffs. Imports of cotton textiles from Taiwan were limited by the United States in 1963, and imports of synthetics after 1971; the European Community followed suit in 1975 (Liang and Liang 1988b). After demanding a range of voluntary export restraints, in 1989 the United States revoked the NIEs' access to duty-free imports under the General System of Preferences. The United States and U.S. corporations have also restricted trade in intellectual property, demanded royalty payments from computer companies, and threatened trade sanctions unless copyright laws are enacted and enforced (*FEER* 3 December 1992). Not that exports to the European Community or to Japan have proved any easier (*Financial Times* 2 April 1990). Thus, corporations may find it easier to export to the advanced industrial nations from China or from one of the ASEAN countries and to serve China and Southeast Asian markets from sites within China and Southeast Asia. (See Hamilton 1983 and W. B. Kim 1993b.)

In Hong Kong, Singapore, and Taiwan, a fourth cause of concern has been the property market boom (see chapters 4, 5, and 8, this volume). In the 1980s factory rental rates more than doubled in Hong Kong (Lui and Chiu 1993). This factor has also been cited in Taiwan (Tsay 1993) where it has been commented that speculation in property markets and finance is attracting the middle classes and capital away from production (see also chapter 3, this volume). Singapore's land prices are also causing concern (see chapter 5, this volume).

Implications

This argument is summarized in the central portion of figure 2.1. The underlying forces that prompt restructuring are changes in global economic conditions (including overseas responses to export-led growth) and changes in social structure induced by industrialization and economic growth. These forces have prompted the concrete, on-the-ground changes that are the immediate concerns of the states and corporations of East Asian NIEs: currency revaluation, rising protectionism in the markets of the European Community and North America, and faster wage increases.

In turn, the strategies followed by the restructuring corporations reflect these forces (see the details of specific nations in chapters 4 through 8, this volume). The main directions of restructuring involve: (1) strategies to increase the supply of labor by importing labor (including illegal migrants) and encouraging women and older people into paid employment (EIU 1992a; Ho 1994; Tsay 1993); (2) strategies to raise the efficiency with which labor is used by increased subcontracting, outworking, and other forms of "flexibility" (Lui and Chiu 1992; 1993; Tsay 1993); (3) strategies to increase the relative weight of capital-intensive industries at the expense of labor-intensive forms of production (Han 1990; Ho 1994; Liang and Liang 1988a; Lim 1993b; Lui and Chiu 1992; Park 1993a; Webber 1994); (4) investment in China and the ASEAN countries: to access pools of unused and cheaper labor, access the markets and raw materials of those countries, and avoid protectionism against the NIEs (*FEER* 18 March 1993; Ho 1993,

1994; Lui and Chiu 1993; Schive 1988; Tsay 1993); and (5) investment behind actual or threatened tariff barriers in North America and the European Community (Lui and Chiu 1993; Tsay 1993).

Together these strategies are having the effect of shifting NIEs into a pattern of growth in which exports grow at about the same pace as imports. This structural change can be implemented by different combinations of these five strategies. As the case studies that follow make clear, different corporations and states have different strategies. Part of the story of restructuring in the NIEs, therefore, concerns the reasons why these differences between economies and corporations occur.

Conclusion

In restructuring, a conscious attempt is made to change the pattern of accumulation in order to redistribute the benefits of growth to one or more groups within society. The current bout of industrial restructuring in the Asian dragons can be understood at several levels. The political economy of NIEs has been realigned as the manner in which NIEs are inserted into the global economy has changed and the balance of class forces within each NIE has altered. This realignment is forcing a shift from a pattern of accumulation that depended on exports for its dynamic to a strategy of accumulation that is more heavily dependent on the growth of the internal market (and perhaps on capital exports). As this shift occurs, output and real wages must move in tandem, except to the extent that investment can be directed overseas. The changes in wage levels, currency values, and conditions in the export market all reflect these fundamental changes in political economy and patterns of accumulation. NIEs are entering an era in which the problems of economic management become those of profitability and stability—just as in the countries of the OECD.

However, the forces that induced restructuring have also produced other changes—liberalization, new class powers, and new levels of corporate independence from the state—that combine to reduce the power of the state to orchestrate the changes in economic relations that are required to shift to the new model of growth: many of the new aspects of restructuring are being organized by markets. (This is the third level of figure 2.1.)

New sources of power have arisen in the NIEs as new social and political movements have arisen from the new structures of classes. The authoritarian state has been losing legitimacy (Moon 1988). Political liberalization has proceeded furthest in Korea, where, since 1988, the opposition has held the majority of seats in the National Assembly (Cho and Kim 1991), and former dissidents have become cabinet ministers since the election of Y. S. Kim (*FEER* 11 March 1993). In Taiwan, martial law was lifted in 1987, and bans on new political parties and newspapers revoked (Lau 1990); the representation of mainlanders in the National Assembly and Legislative Yuan has been reduced (EIU 1992b; *FEER* 12 November 1992); and even the KMT is being modernized and made more democratic (*FEER* 15 April 1993). In Hong Kong, too, new forms of participatory democracy have been pressed on the colonial government, especially since the massacre at Tianmen Square. Least progress to openness and participation has been made in Singapore, but even there the People's Action Party is garnering a decreasing share of votes (EIU 1990), and since Lee stepped down as prime minister in 1990, the government seems to be taking a softer line on political dissent and criticism (EIU 1992a).

The voices of workers and the new middle classes are now beginning to be reflected in a range of government policies. The state increasingly has to mediate labor-capital disputes rather than simply operating as an enforcement arm of the corporations (*FEER* 23 May 1991, 23 April 1992, on Korea; *Asian Wall Street Journal Weekly* 10 April 1989 and Lau 1990, on Taiwan). Particularly in Korea, the reliance of the government on popular electoral support means that "insatiable political demands overpowered economic logic that was politically rather unpopular" (SaKong 1993, 5; see also 179). Likewise, as corporations have become larger and more independent, so they rely less on the state, and the hegemony of the state is reduced on both sides. Together with pressure from the United States and European Community to deregulate and liberalize the economy, changes in the structure of classes and in the independence of corporations have reduced the power of the state to orchestrate the changes that are now needed in NIEs: restructuring relies on the market to a greater extent than growth once did.

THREE

Corporate Strategy and Industrial Restructuring

Gordon L. Clark

Notwithstanding arguments made in previous chapters, it may seem odd that this book is concerned with corporate strategy. After all, much of the debate about the causes of the recent growth of the Asian NIEs (compared to the OECD countries and Africa) has been about the role of the state in fostering the spectacular performance of these economies since 1960 (Wade 1990a is an example). In part, this debate has had a narrow focus, being preoccupied with evaluating competing ideological positions about the proper role of the state in market economies. Thus, the economic performance of the Asian NIEs has been used as the raw material in arguments for and against government intervention in the development process. In particular, at issue in the United States and elsewhere in the West is the degree to which the experience of Japan and the Asian NIEs can justify trade and industry policies (see Tyson 1992). More specifically, Amsden's (1989, 63–64) research on Korea suggests a strong role for the state in fostering development, though recognizing that this role was not a deliberate policy choice but rather the inevitable consequence of past economic and social practices. Her research emphasizes the long-term commitment of the Korean state and its political and economic partners to a distinctive path of development, rather than the market-oriented strategic actions of particular corporations.

While it is useful for purposes of argument and debate to treat the Asian NIEs as a distinct class of economies (separate from OECD countries, for example), there are actually many significant differences between the NIEs. For instance, the Hong Kong economy is clearly driven by international market imperatives, articulated through extensive networks of small to medium enterprises located in Hong Kong and China. Commodity production systems are relatively undercapitalized; low-value-added products are the staple of Hong Kong's international commerce; and state development policies have been rather unimportant over the past few decades. In recent years, restructuring of the economy has been fashioned on an ad hoc basis with individual firms utilizing opportunities in China to respond to international competition (Lui and Chiu 1994). By contrast, the historical importance of multinational firms to Singapore has been identified as a constraint on development, limiting the access of smaller firms in a variety of sectors to finance and political power. Companies outside these older established networks have had to develop their own responses to the harsh realities of international competition (Ho 1993). Even in Korea, it appears that the institutions of economic development have not been particularly important in coordinating or implementing industrial restructuring (Amsden 1989). The work of Park (1993a) and Lim (1992) on Korea suggests that restructuring is increasingly a corporate responsibility. Indeed, it appears that past industry development policies are less relevant to the forces of industrial transformation now surging through the Korean economy (something also apparent in Taiwan; see Tsay 1993).

The diversity of industrial restructuring in the Asian NIEs and the extent to which industrial restructuring has become a corporate responsibility rather than a state responsibility are, of course, the essential topics of this book. The point I wish to make here has three parts. First, general claims made about the relative significance of the state compared to the market in fostering economic growth in the Asian NIEs often ignore the diversity of firms' experience within and between the NIEs; second, such claims tend to focus on the institutions of economic growth rather than the NIEs' different patterns and processes of industrial restructuring since the 1985 G7 Plaza Agreement; and, third, the future of the Asian NIEs depends, in part, upon the capacity of their corporations to respond to the new sources of international market competition. It is too often presumed that the institutions of growth will be the institutions of industrial restructuring, even though there is a great deal of anecdotal evidence, in Korea, for example, that the state has increasingly relied upon the market to orchestrate an economic response to the events of the post-1985 era. The appreciation of NIEs' currency values, chronic labor shortages, and the vulnerability of their labor-intensive industries to price competition all belie the coherence of previous state-based growth policies. Our project presumes that there is a significant role for corporate strategy in restructuring, although we also demonstrate that corporate strategy varies between the Asian NIEs and even within the Asian NIEs.

Global Economic Turbulence

For many analysts, one source of international volatility is to be found in market turbulence: in particular, the large and unpredictable fluctuations in currency exchange rates that have occurred since 1973. Frankel and Mussa (1980, 378) note generally that "the period since 1973 [has] witnessed great turbulence in the world economy and great uncertainty about the future course of economic events." For Frankel and Mussa, turbulence appears to have significant social costs, especially centered on asset holders (like firms with plant and equipment) and wealth holders (individuals with savings and land holdings). As well, they note that turbulence may affect the pricing system in ways that lead to a misallocation of resources between assets and between production and consumption. While they focus on currency exchange rates, there are other equally important aspects of international finance to be considered when understanding the recent performance of the Asian NIEs. For example, the International Monetary Fund (1993) believes that countries' differential abilities to accommodate market turbulence (broadly defined) has been an important factor contributing to differential growth rates.

Thus, the relation between a nation's economic growth and market turbulence is a matter of considerable significance for all countries. Indeed, it is an issue of considerable importance for the Atlantic economies, Japan and now Eastern Europe. Chinloy and Stromsdorfer's (1987) edited book on the adjustment potential of Pacific economies' labor markets (including Canada, the United States, Mexico, and Japan) to fluctuations in the exchange rate is indicative of the scope of the issue. More specifically, Wade's (1990a) commentary on the performance of the Taiwan economy over the 1970s and 1980s makes much of the impact of the 1973 and 1979 oil shocks, demonstrating the vulnerability of small export-led economies to price fluctuations in "key intermediates" (97). In the first instance, Wade notes

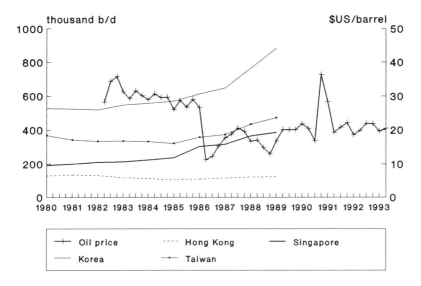

Figure 3.1   Oil consumption by country and oil price.

that the quadrupling of oil prices drastically suppressed the rate of economic growth (real GNP grew by only 1 percent in 1974, as opposed
to about 10 percent per annum over the previous ten years), led to
massive short-term inflation, and blew out the trade deficit. In response, the Taiwanese government used a combination of monetary
policies and commodity pricing policies to stabilize prices and then
used fiscal policies to stimulate the economy. While the 1979 oil shock
did not have as significant effects on real activity, it is apparent that the
need to accommodate exogenous price fluctuations has prompted a series of rounds of industrial restructuring in Taiwan.

It might be suggested, of course, that having endured the oil price
shocks of the 1970s, the real economies of the Asian NIEs have adjusted to the pattern of relative prices and have prospered as a consequence. It might also be thought that as the real price of oil (U.S. dollars per barrel) has declined over the 1980s, the Asian NIEs are
increasingly insulated from the effects of international commodity price
shocks. But the data presented in figure 3.1 makes sich a general conclusion difficult to justify.[1] Although oil prices have declined in real
terms (absolutely and with respect to local exchange rates measured
against the U.S. dollar), they remain volatile, and consumption is growing in all NIEs, except Hong Kong, at a rapid rate. In Taiwan's case,

oil consumption declined through to the mid-1980s and has since been growing at an increasing rate. In Korea's case, oil consumption leveled off in the early 1980s but now appears to be growing at an exponential rate. Here, it is important to make three specific points before a more general claim: (1) if the NIEs' industry structures are now more oil-efficient, economic growth has nevertheless increased their dependence upon imported oil; (2) the lack of local mineral resources means that the Asian NIEs are very reliant upon intermediate commodity producers; and (3) the combination of small size and export dependence means that the NIEs are probably more vulnerable than Japan to international price fluctuations. In this sense the Asian NIEs, like Japan, are very vulnerable to what the Japanese External Trade Organization's (Japan 1990) *White Paper on International Trade* describes as the turbulence of the global economy.

The 1990 *White Paper* distinguishes between the economic events of the 1980s and the new currents that promise to remake global economic relationships. With respect to the 1980s, the *White Paper* identifies many factors as having contributed to the turbulence of the global economy, including the transition to floating exchange rates, the oil crises, and high real interest rates. These, in combination, have exacerbated trade tensions between the developed economies (including Japan and now including the Asian NIEs) and between the developed and developing economies of the world. Throughout the 1980s, Japanese commentaries published in the yearly *Economic Survey* were obsessed with international trade tensions between the United States and Japan. In the early years of the decade, the high relative value of the U.S. dollar—the global economy's basic unit of exchange—was the major source of tension between the trading partners. After the 1985 G7 Plaza Agreement, which orchestrated the rapid appreciation of the yen in relation to the U.S. dollar, the terms of dispute changed to become more focused on market access and barriers to trade. In effect, however, the appreciation of the yen and the devaluation of the U.S. dollar significantly altered the relative standing of Singapore and Taiwan in global currency markets and demonstrated to Hong Kong and Korea how vulnerable they were to third party bilateral agreements regarding currency values (see figure 3.2 for details of currency exchange rates over the 1980s and early 1990s).

With respect to the new currents of the global economy, the *White Paper* identifies three forces that promise to remake the international economy of the 1990s. The first is the globalization of business: "In the

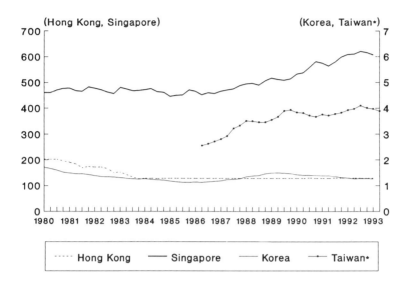

Figure 3.2 Exchange rate, in US$s/1,000 national currency units. *Taiwan is 100 national currency units.

1980s, the frontiers of corporate activities were rapidly expanded and the business world scrapped the old perception of countries as economic units to engage in international business spanning national boundaries" (5). The report notes a series of related indicators of this trend, including increased rates of foreign direct investment, especially in the Asia-Pacific region, the geographical relocation of employment, the relocation of industry and technology, and the promotion of inter-business linkages between economies. The second is the polarization of the global economy: the relative decline of the United States and the growth of Japan and the Asian NIEs promise to polarize the "free" economies into a set of distinct blocs rather than being focused around just one economy. The report also mentions Germany, the ASEAN 4, and China. In retrospect, it now appears that polarization may be less significant than segmentation into trading economies based in Asia and those based elsewhere. The third factor is new trade regimes and rules: sustaining the polarization of the global economy are trading blocs and the multilateral process of trade regulation. In fact, the *White Paper* suggests that market integration into trading blocs "should be complementary to a multilateral process of deregulation" (5). Whether this is actually possible remains to be seen. Indeed, important sources of

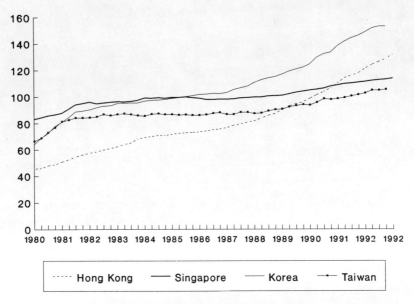

Figure 3.3 Consumer price index.

global economic turbulence are the manifest consequences of the political tensions inherent in what may actually be opposing forces: market integration and trade deregulation.

Intermediate commodity price shocks, exchange rate volatility, and
the political economy of trade are all factors contributing to economic
turbulence. Also important, though, are internal factors that now lie
outside the control and authority of the development state. Control
over internal wages and prices seems increasingly difficult to maintain
in the Asian NIEs. Figures 3.3 and 3.4 show the patterns of consumer
prices and real manufacturing wages in the four economies since about
1980. While there are clear differences between the economies on both
counts, notice how significant consumer price inflation has been in
Hong Kong and Korea since the mid-1980s. Notice also how successful the governments of Singapore and Taiwan have been in moderat-
ing consumer price inflation over the same period (although Taiwan
experienced significantly higher price inflation during the early 1990s)
(fig. 3.3). Overlapping price inflation has been the fact that real manufacturing wages have grown significantly in all NIEs since 1980, accelerating most markedly in Korea and Taiwan since 1987 (fig. 3.4).

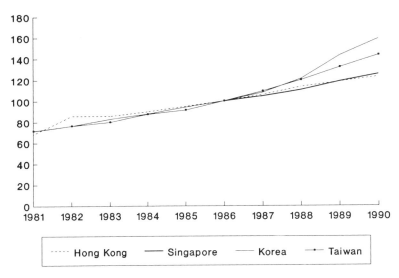

Figure 3.4   Real wage index, manufacturing.

These two economies have also experienced the most marked increases in currency values relative to the U.S. dollar over the same period of time (see figure 3.2). In effect, Korean and Taiwanese international competitiveness in manufacturing industries has been doubly disadvantaged: dramatic increases in real wage rates being amplified by adverse shifts in currency exchange rates. For individual Korean and Taiwanese manufacturing firms, internal trends in prices and wages represent another, practically uncontrollable set of factors that add to the external turbulence of economic life.

Confounding, even resulting from, these identified patterns of wages and prices, trading conditions, and currency exchange rates has been the rise of the financial sector in all four economies. At one level, it might be supposed that the financial sector is simply a necessary condition for globalization. Without adequate financial services of all kinds, offshore trade and investment (hence economic growth) would be impossible. Thus, to the extent that each Asian NIE is dependent upon the global economy for markets, it has a financial sector that at least matches (in size and complexity) and facilitates (through its various functions) the demand for services apparent in economy-to-economy commodity trade. This argument supposes, however, that the financial sector is just an intermediary between the producers and

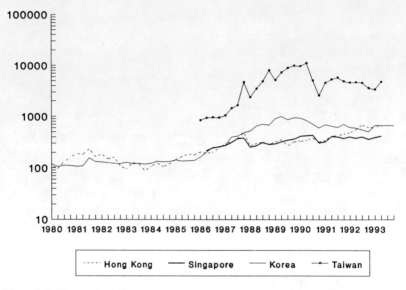

Figure 3.5   Share price index.

consumers of commodities (wherever located). It supposes that the value of the finance sector is to be found in its services. In fact, the financial sector has become more important to all four Asian NIEs than this simple proposition would seem to allow. While it is far beyond the scope of this chapter and the book to assess the scope and determinants of the growth of Asian NIEs' financial sectors, it is clear that speculative finance has played a significant role in each NIE since the mid-1980s. Figure 3.5 displays the rates of change of the stock market indexes of all four economies. (The vertical axis is scaled using logarithms to reflect the rate of changes rather than levels).

Taiwan, having experienced an extraordinary wave of stock speculation and trading before and after the October 1987 crash, is a special case. But the Korean stock market is also quite volatile, as are the Singaporean and Hong Kong markets (in that order). This kind of volatility is not just an issue of economic turbulence. Reports about recent events in Taiwan, the most extreme case, suggest that stock market turbulence has been an important social force, representing real shifts in the expectations of citizens for greater wealth set against their commitment to commodity-based trading and economic growth. It has also been suggested that part of the wealth generated by exports during the 1980s has been diverted into stock market and money market speculation sustained and encouraged by the limited set of opportunities for investment in Taiwan. If turbulence in the stock market and money markets has had real effects (economic and social), turbulence is also a source of business for trading houses whose income depends on the rate of turnover in those markets. In this respect, an increased rate of speculation could generate employment in the finance sector, just as the collapse in stock prices in Taiwan in 1990–91 caused significant economic dislocation in employment and income. By this account, the financial sector is now more than simply a service sector reflecting the needs of commodity producers. The finance sector has grown to such significance that it is an alternative source of income and employment. Thus, financial turbulence has been factored into economic expectations (IMF 1994).

The role and significance of finance for the development of the Asia-Pacific economy should not be underestimated. In the Ministry of International Trade and Industry's (MITI) 1989 commentary on international trade (published in the Japan Institute of International Affairs's *White Papers of Japan*), much was made of the close relationship between Japanese capital flows and Asian NIEs' rates of growth. MITI observes that the economic links between Japan, the NIEs, the ASEAN 4, and China were such that the Asia-Pacific region was increasingly internally focused, rather than externally focused on the United States and Western Europe. In schematic form, the authors of the MITI report sketch out a model of regional integration and growth based on capital flows and the deepening division of labor in the Asian NIEs. Their model begins with an industrialized nation that stimulates the industrialization of other linked economies by virtue of the expansion of the first nation's domestic markets; as other economies grow by virtue of the transfer of capital and employment opportunities, those economies, in turn, stimulate the industrialization of other nations through secondary transfers of capital and employment opportunities (and so on). This favorable cycle of industrialization is only possible through the smooth operation of the price mechanism—specifically, the mobility of capital and the international division (and redivision) of labor. In this respect, one of the most important roles identified by MITI for the Japanese government is the enhancement of the Asia-Pacific trading system.

At this point, there is no reason to dispute the logic of the MITI model of Japanese-led Asian industrialization. It is clear that regional economic integration is accelerating, driven, in part, by Japanese and Asian NIEs' investment in Southeast Asia and the growing significance of China as a consumption market, not simply a site for industrial production. It is also clear, however, that the turbulence of the global economy may be a significant impediment to the smooth operation of market-led economic integration and growth. Moreover, it is important to recognize that, whereas MITI's model is a model of whole economies and their interrelationships, in fact the institutions that are the bridging forces between economies are actually firms, not governments. Indeed, the MITI model is quite clearly dependent on the putative efficiency of factor markets in allocating firms' production among regions based on relative labor costs (wages discounted by labor productivity, exchange rates, etc). In this context, the nature and scope of industrial restructuring in each of the Asian NIEs is an essential ingredient in any comprehensive understanding of the patterns of growth in the Asia-Pacific region. This is why appreciating the nature and scope of the restructuring of the Pusan footwear industry, for instance, in the context of rapid shifts in the global economy is so important for understanding the long-term structural configuration of the Asia-Pacific region.

To the extent that governments have a role in the turbulent world of the 1990s, that role is perceived to be one of facilitating the adjustment of industries to their changing relative competitiveness in different economies and ensuring that capital switching within industries and between regions is relatively efficient. Essentially, the mercantilist development state is to be replaced by a state whose interests are best served by market stability and market integration. Those interests may also be best served by international firms rather than the state or firms loyal to local communities. Clearly, this is an idealization of the market, its agents, and its institutions. Nevertheless, it reflects a vision of the world in which roles and responsibilities are increasingly defined by the market rather than the standard story attributed to the Asian development state. In this setting, firms, their actions, and their strategies are very important for the sustenance of the MITI vision. Similarly, while the state remains a vital part of the architecture of the future growth of the Asia-Pacific region, its role has been redefined and narrowed around market imperatives. While it may be less focused than implied by MITI and more responsible for a wider range of functions and ambitions than desired by MITI, the future of the development state is bound up with the putative efficiency of markets and firms. The turbulent world of the 1990s is a world of markets and states, increasingly held together by corporate strategy.

Asian Growth and Market Dependence

In his empirical analysis of the correlates of economic growth, Robert Barro (1991, 437) states that "given the level of initial per capita GDP (real gross domestic product), the growth rate (of nations) is substantially positively related to the starting amount of human capital." His empirical research was based upon some ninety-eight countries for the period 1960–85, using data derived (in part) from Summers and Heston's (1988) comparative international database of real national accounts. The lumping together of many different countries from all regions of the globe, their particular circumstances in 1960, and their very different trajectories of change through to 1985 immediately raise doubts as to the extent to which Barro can reasonably draw inferences about the determinants of growth for any one country or group of countries. He notes, for example, that "the results leave unexplained a good deal of the relatively weak growth performance of countries in the sub-Saharan Africa and Latin America" (437). Nevertheless, he claims to show empirically that per capita growth of GDP is also: (1) negatively related to the ratio of government consumption expenditure; (2) negatively related to price distortions; (3) unrelated to the quantity of government investment; and (4) negatively related to political instability.

What countries might be thought to represent the kind of success (growth in GDP) implied by these results? Crudely speaking, if all these results are factored into the identification process, successful countries over the 1960–85 period were those that may have begun poor but had a tradition of mass education, limited government consumption expenditure, used the market to sustain growth (and industrial transformation), and pursued political stability (minimized dissent). This profile is nothing less (and nothing more) than a version of the ideal market-driven laissez-faire economy; by Barro's account, the protection of private property rights is an essential ingredient to growth. This ideal type need not have been democratic, nor would it have had a significant social welfare component. So, what country represents this ideal? In a brief op-ed comparative analysis of Singapore and Hong Kong, Barro (1992) suggests by implication that Hong Kong is close

Table 3.1   Growth of Asian NIEs, Australia, Japan, and the United States 1960–1989 (percentage of growth)

	Hong Kong	Korea	Singapore	Taiwan	Australia	Japan	United States
Real GPD							
1960–1973	11.3	9.2	11.3	9.1	3.4	13.5	3.2
1973–1984	4.5	9.7	4.7	4.5	0.7	1.4	0.5
1984–1989	9.7	13.5	6.3	9.7	2.7	5.2	3.2
GDP per capita							
1960–1973	10.4	8.9	10.4	8.3	3.3	12.7	2.9
1973–1984	4.0	3.8	4.1	4.1	0.5	1.4	0.3
1984–1989	9.4	12.9	5.8	9.0	2.4	4.7	3.1
GDP per worker							
1960–1973	10.5	7.8	8.8	8.3	2.6	12.2	2.4
1973–1984	3.3	3.5	2.5	3.8	0.2	1.6	−0.2
1984–1989	8.6	11.6	5.4	8.3	2.1	4.7	2.8

Source: Penn World Table (Mark 5.5) (Summers and Heston 1991).

to the ideal type, whereas Singapore seems to have overinvested in public infrastructure and has introduced distortions into the market that have compromised its rate of growth.[2] Table 3.1 compares per capita and per worker GDP growth rates for the Asian NIEs, Australia, Japan and the United States. Actually, until 1984 Singapore's average yearly real GDP growth was at least equal to Hong Kong's, though the biggest differences are between the Asian NIEs and the other countries. Still, Barro concluded that Singapore's industry policy has been too active and that companies have failed to capitalize on potential production efficiencies that could be wrung out of the existing industrial structure.

There do appear to be significant differences between Hong Kong and Singapore on the issue of investment. Using Summers and Heston's (1991) Penn World Table (Mark 5) and its June 1993 supplement (Mark 5.5) (which allows for a direct comparison between countries' real GDP), table 3.2 compares the four Asian NIEs, Australia, Japan, and the United States in terms of the relative shares of expenditure distributed among private consumption, investment (public and private), and government consumption. A feature of Summers and Heston's (1991) approach is that national accounts are calculated in "a common set of prices in a common currency so the *real* international quantity comparisons can be made both between countries and over time"

Table 3.2 Estimates of Growth and Expenditure of Asian NIEs, Australia, Japan, and the United States 1960–1988 (current prices)

	Hong Kong	Korea	Singapore	Taiwan	Australia	Japan	United States
Population (millions)	5.6	41.9	2.9	19.9	16.5	122.6	246.3
Real GDP per capita ($US 1,000)	14.8	6.3	10.3	8.5	16.4	15.2	19.5
Expenditure (% of GDP)							
Consumption	69.0	56.0	53.8	47.4	62.2	53.8	66.4
Investment	20.3	33.0	32.2	27.0	31.7	38.5	23.6
Government	5.1	8.0	7.6	19.6	10.6	7.4	11.7

Source: Penn World Table (Mark 5.5) (Summers and Heston 1991).

(327). Remarkably, Hong Kong's private consumption share of total expenditure is similar to that of Australia and the United States; these are relatively wealthy economies by a number of different quantitative and qualitative measures. By contrast, Singapore's consumption share of total expenditure is quite low, equal with Japan, lower than Korea, but higher than Taiwan. It is clear from the data that Singapore has spent an enormous amount of its income in public and private investment. By contrast, Hong Kong's investment share of total expenditure is lower than all other countries including the United States and is overwhelmingly private in character.

Are these differences as significant as Barro claims? Notwithstanding the comprehensiveness of his empirical analysis, some features of his approach are open to dispute. For a start, his empirical analysis is about the internal, supply-based factors of growth. These factors are thought to push economic growth. By implication, market-led growth is less important. In part, his emphasis on supply-based factors is a product of his predisposition toward neoclassical growth theory. If markets are assumed to be complete (geographically comprehensive), efficient (regarding the allocation of resources), and adaptive (in terms of the flexibility of prices), then the "demand side should have little effect on real variables" (Durlauf 1992, 124). Barro might suggest, of course, that supply factors including the extent of market distortions are a constraint in the rate of market-led growth, not a substitute for market-led growth. But even if this qualification is accepted, his analysis does not recognize the fact that for the Asian NIEs, external, market-led growth was a key determinant of economic growth over the period from 1960 to 1985. In essence, it could be suggested that Barro does not take his own argument far enough; he fails to take account of the constraints on the growth of Asian NIEs imposed by market distortions in the principal international markets of the economies he analyzes. On the other hand, by theoretical assumption, he does not allow for the possibility that regulated and restricted internal markets may have been a precondition for some Asian NIEs' success in international markets. One way or another, by Barro's analysis, commodity markets are of little consequence over the long term.

With respect to Hong Kong and Singapore, Barro's (1992) comparison of the two economies ignores the issue of external markets and seems to assume equivalent industry structures. Different international markets, by geography and product niche (assuming equivalent industry structure), would presumably result in different investment profiles as would different industry structures. Even if Singapore and Hong Kong shared the same markets and industries, differences in industry organization (firm size, ownership, competitive position, and market strategy) would surely make a difference to economies' capital needs. Indeed, all factors would surely differentiate (by volume and type) each economies' investment share of total expenditure. Of course, these factors may be insufficient to explain all differences between Singapore and Hong Kong in terms of their consumption and investment shares of total expenditure. The separate work of Ho, on Singapore, and Chiu and Lui, on Hong Kong, reported in this book (chapters 5 and 4 respectively) and elsewhere make it plain that even if industry structure is held constant, there are striking differences between these economies in terms of markets, industry organization, and internal structure. Moreover, there are remarkable similarities *and* differences between the economies in terms of their corporations' responses to the economic events of the post-1985 era. To the extent that such similarities and differences can be explained by reference to initial resource endowments (supply-based factors), Barro's analytical perspective is relevant. But, in fact, we would also argue that demand factors have also been important—something not easily rationalized within his theoretical perspective.

At issue here is the distinctiveness of Asian economic growth. While it is obviously true that long-term supply factors are important, it is clear (to us, at least) that the success of the Asian NIEs has been premised on market demand factors as well. Of course, for Hong Kong, Singapore, and Taiwan, their internal markets (bounded by their governments' jurisdictions) have been less important than their external markets. Long-term success in international markets has given the corporations of all three small economies a chance to develop economies of scale, capitalize on learning-by-doing, and combine new methods of production (or new sites of production) with product innovation. In this respect, the 1960 base level of education (human capital) seems to have been less significant than the targeting of investment in related skills and training over the period from 1960 to 1985, given very different inherited industry structures and organizations. For Korea, which began the period at a point of virtual economic chaos, growth has been the complex product of interaction between domestic and international markets, state institutions and private corporations, and local and international sources of product innovation. Protected local markets have been very important for developing the requisite production efficiency later deployed in international markets. All four economies have had quite distinctive and different relationships between the state and markets, large and small corporations. Indeed, the variety of those relationships is so complex that it is impossible to simply summarize each economy and its differences. It is misleading to talk of a single, distinctive model of Asian economic growth, even if compared as a class against the OECD countries (see Helliwell 1992).

At the same time, acknowledging that the growth of the NIEs has been contingent, in part, on their companies' performance in the market *and* the performance of markets themselves means also that their economies have become increasingly sensitive to the volatility of global markets.[3] For over two decades, the growth of each economy was closely tied to and structured by the growth of the North American, European, and Japanese economies with little competition from elsewhere in the global economy. Success reinforced state policy (particularly in Korea and Singapore) and private commitments (particularly in Hong Kong and Taiwan). However, the contingency of economies' growth on global markets was exposed with the slowing growth rates of core markets, the G7 Plaza Agreement, and the concomitant penetration of international markets by low-priced, more flexible competitors from the ASEAN 4 and China. These observations about the vulnerability of the Asian NIEs to market factors is related to an empirical point made by Durlauf (1992). Examining a selected group of OECD countries, he shows that there is a significant stochastic component in those countries' output series and that their long-term growth is determined, in part, by the capacity of domestic institutions and local corporations to respond to unanticipated market events.[4] While his empirical analysis is not as comprehensive as Barro's, he also shows that countries' output series are not cointegrated—an essential condition for any argument that would assume market performance is ephemeral compared to supply-based factors. Oddly, Barro has considered this issue in work with Sala i Martin (1990), which allows for the possibility of random disturbances (perhaps even market volatility) having a long-term impact on countries' rates of economic growth.

Durlauf's point, which we endorse, is that the stochastic component of market conditions combined with the adjustment potential of domestic institutions (including corporations) can have a profound affect on the path of national economic growth. In some cases, those institutions may promote growth by incorporating unanticipated events into the market strategies of governments and corporations, whereas in other cases local institutions may be unable to successfully accommodate unanticipated economic events. In this respect, the future of the Asian NIEs (separately and together) depends upon their corporations' capacity to restructure in the face of global market competition and all it entails.

Corporate Strategy and Market Structure

By this analysis, there is a vital and necessary role for corporate strategy. While we could argue that corporate market-oriented strategy always has been important in each economy (although with different dimensions), it is apparent now that state institutions and policies may be less relevant than in the past. The events of the post-1985 era have forced greater reliance on corporate market strategy (especially in Korea and Singapore) and have expanded even further (especially in Hong Kong and Taiwan) the possible scope of market strategies. But what is corporate strategy, and how does strategy relate to the inherited structure of institutions and industry? Use of the term *strategy* in this context refers to the chosen actions of corporate agents taken with respect to the anticipated actions of others whose own actions may in turn affect the possible payoffs of all related agents' actions. Normally, definitions of strategy refer to rationality and the idea of winning contests.

For example, Schelling's (1960) seminal book depicts strategy as artful and sophisticated sets of moves and countermoves based on calculated self-interest and consistent rules of decision making regarding agents' interests and the interests of others who are directly involved in competition. Clearly, Schelling's definition was informed by game theory. Indeed, much of the literature on corporate strategy is likewise informed by game theory; goals and objectives (interests) are specified and policies and plans (the ingredients of strategy) are chosen to achieve those objectives (see Andrews 1971, on corporate strategy). But like many corporate strategy theorists and practitioners, we use the notion of strategy here as a heuristic device for explicating the logic of calculated action in the context of the anticipated actions of competitors, rather than in the formal analytical sense used by most game theory advocates.

The term *structure* is used here to refer to market structure, in particular, and more generally to the antecedent circumstances and behavioral imperatives associated with the organization of markets. In theory, it is often presumed that structure has three overlapping dimensions with respect to agents' autonomy.[5] First, structure is assumed to be beyond the capacity of corporate agents to immediately affect and may be outside the capacity of many agents to affect over the long term. Consequently, in the short term, structure (like the inherited configuration of production—what could be termed the history and geography of a firm) can be thought of as a constraint on action (the second dimension). But more subtly, structure can also be defined as a systematic set of incentives and disincentives conceived by the state to elicit over the long term particular actions and outcomes (the third dimension). In combination, these dimensions of structure presume that it is identifiable (albeit at a cost), to corporate agents who share similar market locations, and systematic, in the sense that agents commonly understand one anothers' options with respect to antecedent circumstances and the pattern of shared incentives and disincentives. Like the term *strategy,* however, we should be wary of assigning too much in the way of logic and internal coherence to the notion of structure. There are limits to the coherence of structure, limits that corporate agents may exploit in their strategic interaction with others.

Structural explanations of market behavior dominate the economics literature. For example, neoclassical economic theories of location assume that in perfect competition the imperatives of comparative advantage and relative economic efficiency by region are sufficient to determine corporate location and product decisions. Actions that deviate from the logic of those imperatives would be, by definition, inefficient. Given the efficiency-oriented assumptions of such models, deviations would be "naturally" corrected or firms would go out of business. By this logic, strategy is either irrelevant, if consistent with market imperatives, or irrational, if at odds with market imperatives. Emphasis on structure in explaining corporate behavior translates into studies of industry-level market competition and the economic attributes of home nations and regions. Thus, corporate strategy, including decisions about the nature and efficient location of labor-intensive production (the topic of this book), is assumed derivative of more general structural determinants of behavior, which are applied to all relevant firms in an industry. This kind of modeling procedure is thought to have a couple of virtues. In particular, by focusing on structural determinants, the particularities of firms and strategies are eschewed for parsimonious predictions of normal behavior. However, like Collis (1991), we would argue that firms are in some sense always unique, given their particular histories (investment profiles) and geographies (locations of production and markets). And, in any event, it is the interaction between strategy and structure that is so important for understanding contemporary patterns of corporate restructuring in the Asian NIEs.

It is not the case, however, that structural models of economic behavior are unrelated to strategic behavior. In fact, strict game-theoretic versions of strategy place a high premium on structure. The nature and scope of strategy in their account of economic behavior derives from structure; such strategies are *structure-dependent* strategies. For Shubik's (1982) kind of strategy, a priori structural conditions are necessary to define the boundaries of competition, the rules of competition, and the potential set of payoffs. Without structurally defined parameters defining the margins and rules of competitions, solutions to competitive games may be impossible to compute and actions a priori indeterminate. Without structure, strategists could not "provide for all contingencies that could arise" in playing a game (34). A more liberal model of strategy, one that allows for autonomy and some measure of discretion, could be termed *structure limited*. Here, it is presumed that corporate planners have scope for independent action not strictly or exclusively defined by structure. This means there may be a greater variety of plans, moves, and countermoves taken with respect to corporate managers' own interests, and the anticipated interests and actions of others, than implied by structure-dependent strategies. At the margin, however, variety is limited by structure in the sense that structure provides a powerful set of rules and conventions that can not be violated without incurring stringent penalties. This type of strategy and structure has much in common with spatial metaphors of structure and behavior. It is consistent, for example, with related arguments to the effect that structure provides the stage for action (in the horizontal plane) or the floor and ceiling for action (in the vertical plane). These metaphors have close legal and regulatory analogues (Tribe 1989).

There are three ways of accounting for variety within limits. (1) Structural indeterminacy: notwithstanding the significance of market-based economic imperatives, those imperatives may not provide unambiguous recipes for action. By virtue of their generality or their connections with other elements of economic structure, in some circumstances it may be impossible to find the best and most complete set of competitive strategies relevant to those situations. (2) Cognitive limits: corporate agents may not be able to compute the global best set of strategies. Given many agents and many interests, they either know less than they need to or are unable to factor into their own decisions all the relevant information, given the complexity implied by system-wide competitive accounting. Instead, recognizing their cognitive limit, agents may settle on partial solutions to strategic dilemmas, which they then adapt to changing circumstances. (3) Path dependence: having chosen partial strategies consistent with their local situations and immediate reference points (other competitors), their chosen actions may be reinforced by their superior knowledge of the local situation (compared to those outside the situation and in other situations). Adaptation may be dependent on the trajectory of prior actions (investment and production) and may not be easily reversed if sunk costs are a significant portion of fixed costs (see Clark and Wrigley, forthcoming). This model of the relation between strategy and structure has the advantage of being relevant to the world in which firms have distinct histories and geographies and face the prospect of failure if their strategies are poorly conceived. Otherwise, it is hard to understand why firms would be different within industries or could fail in structure-dependent models of strategy.

So far, strategy has been treated as benign toward or at least tolerant of market structure. But another model of strategy and structure takes the relationship into the world of takeovers, mergers, and acquisitions (corporate restructuring). Specifically, some strategies are *structure-focused*—strategies that focus on the margins of the rules of competition and take advantage of the special position of some agents with respect to industry competition and government policy. This model of strategy and structure makes two assumptions. First, it is assumed that corporate agents are self-conscious, being aware of their own interests and the need to strategically represent those interests in their interactions with others. Second, it is assumed that agency costs are a significant, if not a dominant, part of firms' cost structures. Put very crudely, there may be a profit to be made by acting outside the rules of market competition (violating the structure of competition and regulation). How is this possible? Some corporate agents may use the trust of others in their best intentions to take advantage of them in ways that are difficult to discern. If there is an asymmetry of intentions, on one side an intention to deceive and on the other side an intention to trust, and if it is costly to observe underlying motives as opposed to stated intentions, then some corporations may effectively subvert the rules of the game in their own interests. If subversion finances the transformation of these agents into other areas of competition, even other industries, then reputational checks on such behavior may not be effective (compare Rose-Ackerman 1991). In this manner, structure may be both the object of strategy and the means of hiding illegitimate motives.

Why would firms be interested in operating at the margins of markets? Here, there are two obvious explanations. (1) Profit opportunities: at the margins of competition there may be opportunities for excess profits—more than the profit available within the existing configuration of industry competition. Profit opportunities at the margins of competition (and the rules of competition) may occur for any number of reasons. The introduction of new technologies may suddenly offer a chance to make a profit in markets that were previously outside the normal boundaries of industry competition. Similarly, new financial instruments and new modes of corporate organization and control may enable firms to widen the scope of market opportunities outside the normal boundaries of competition.[6] Such strategies may be legal (for example, using genetic engineering to create new products) but may be illegal (for example, using new techniques to produce and market refined heroin). (2) Inertia and incumbency: having made significant nonrecoverable investments in certain products and production systems (sunk costs), firms may come to believe that the only way of overcoming their mistakes is to find a way to shift the burden of their mistakes to others. This may involve actions that deliberately go outside the normal boundaries of private responsibility. This may also involve advocating new interpretations of the existing rules of competition and their applicability, including legal strategies designed to shift the boundaries of competitive games. Such structure-focused strategies have been particularly apparent in bankruptcy situations in the United States (and elsewhere, including Korea).

If we were to subscribe to a structure-dependent model of strategy, the kinds of actions of corporations described immediately above could be thought either irrelevant to the overarching logic of structure (would make no difference to the profound effects of structurally based economic imperatives) or simply representative of opportunism (would be cured with sufficient enforcement of the boundaries of games). Alternatively, it might be argued that when such actions occur, structure has been somehow distorted by inappropriate external interests (like public policy). One way or another, structurally based economic imperatives would remain transcendent. By contrast, we would argue that structure-focused strategy is the inevitable result of allowing structure-limited games of strategy. That is, once discretion is introduced, once the structural imperatives of market competition are shown to be inexact and difficult to apply to specific circumstances, then the integrity of the inherited market structure is at risk to corporate strategists who do not share common assumptions or norms of behavior or who use the fact that some observe such norms as an advantage in their strategic actions. Realization of the scope of discretion available to economic agents in the Asian NIEs is one reason we should be more focused on corporate strategy than state policy.

Corporate Restructuring and Strategic Options

One of the most important points to come out of the previous discussion about strategy and structure has to do with the scope of firms' strategy—the discretion available to corporations in responding to changing circumstances. Clearly, if the rules of market competition are comprehensive and stable, few firms have the capacity and opportunity to act outside of those boundaries. Only larger firms with relatively more resources than average firms have the capacity to implement competitive strategies outside of normal competition. But, just as clearly, it seems to us that the post-1985 era has seen the slow demise of the inherited growth-oriented rules of market competition and the fracturing of state institutions and regulatory policies, which were conceived to deal with very different circumstances. Thus, even small firms in the structure-dependent domain face the prospect of widening discretion and scope for corporate strategy. Indeed, the increasing irrelevance of structure-dependent strategy and the apparent necessary reality of structure-limited, even structure-focused, strategy has forced even small firms into a world of many more options and often unknown possibilities. Of course, this project is not focused on case studies, though some of the results reported in subsequent chapters often rely upon so-called representative firms to illustrate empirical conclusions. As a consequence, there is no direct analysis of the styles or types of corporate strategy. Rather, we begin with a presumption that the firms surveyed in each economy are in the worlds of either structure-limited or structure-focused strategy.

Another important implication to be drawn from the preceding discussion of strategy and structure is that the size, ownership, and control of firms matters a great deal in the formation of strategic policy. From single-industry, owner-managed firms through to multiindustry, management-controlled conglomerates, ownership and control are essential beginning points in any understanding of the dimensions of strategy. Few single-industry, owner-managed firms have the scope of the latter kind of firm, whatever the inherited economic or social circumstances. The sheer resources of multiindustry, management-controlled firms encourages the formation of strategy aimed at the very margins of market competition. Part 1 of the survey sought information on ownership and size of firms in each Asian NIE and each industry (see appendix). Ownership data includes reference to local and foreign ownership, whether the enterprise is independent or part of a larger organization, whether it is owner managed, whether it operates through subcontractors, and the size of the enterprise (including sales, assets, and employees). Notice, of course, that detailed assessment of particular corporate strategies is not the principal focus of this analysis. Rather, the issue of strategy and structure is addressed in a general manner, allowing for comparative analysis between economies and industries.

A final implication to be drawn from the preceding discussion regarding both the relationship between strategy and structure and the significance of markets in the post-1985 era concerns the focus of the data analysis. Here, unlike many previous studies of the Asian NIEs, we emphasize firms' market strategies rather than state policy. This is, of course, a partial view of the complex interplay between markets and social and economic structures. Like Wade (1990a), we are willing to accept that state policy can and does affect market structure and, hence, the options and scope of corporate strategy. But care must be taken not to overemphasize the power of structure; it is apparent that few Asian NIE corporations operate in the world of structure-dependent strategy. However, the very different circumstances and institutions of each Asian NIE guarantee that we can only partially address these very complex issues. In this respect, focus on firms' market strategies using common industries and a common research design is intended to complement our understanding of the contemporary performance of the different Asian NIEs.

The empirical analysis of firms and industries is premised on a set of general observations made about the contemporary situation of the Asian NIEs in the global economy. As has been stressed in this chapter, state planning for long-term economic growth seems to be now less important than corporate restructuring in the face of internal and external market pressures. Thus, parts 2 and 3 of the research framework attempt to situate firms' labor market strategies in this context. Recognizing the Asian NIEs' labor-intensive industries of footwear, garments, and electronics have been driven in the past by export demand, the data collected allows connection between the size of the firm and the distribution of its employees among various categories (full-time or part-time, managerial or clerical, etc.) and the export focus of the enterprise, including broad identification of markets and shares of total exports going to different markets. Most importantly, the empirical framework allows for the surveyed enterprises to report qualitative judgments about the changing nature of business conditions, providing a comparative assessment of changing conditions since 1989. These qualitative assessments are then linked to a series of variables affecting the economic performance of Asian NIEs' enterprises. With respect to domestic labor market situations and external conditions, firms were asked to order in importance the impact of factors like higher wages, higher raw material costs, currency fluctuations, and competition in product markets. As a means of connecting changing economic circumstances with issues of strategy, the firms were then asked about strategic initiatives taken over the past few years (e.g., product diversification and investment overseas in plants and production facilities, where those investments were made, and the principal reasons for overseas investment).

In effect, questions about overseas investment in plants and production facilities match in substance commonly noted Western corporate strategies of geographically segmenting production—that is, a spatial division of labor driven by escalating real wages of labor (relative to competitors' prices, the productivity of labor, and shrinking wage differentials between different classes of workers at common domestic sites of management and production) (see Clark 1981). In part 4 of the survey, individual enterprises were asked about wage costs in relation to total production costs, how wage costs have changed over the past few years, the rate of turnover in the enterprise, and the extent to which turnover affects the skill and age profile of the enterprise. Previous work by Ho (1993) on Singapore, Lui and Chiu (1993) on Hong Kong, and Park (1993a, 1993b) on Seoul, Korea (for instance) have together pointed to the significance of the spatial division of labor as a strategy for controlling labor costs. These strategies do vary considerably, however, between the Asian NIEs. In Singapore, corporations have developed strategies of spatial management of production based on the so-called golden triangle involving sites in Indonesia, the Malay Peninsula, and Singapore. There is considerable evidence that Singaporean companies retain close control over ownership of land, plant, and equipment, whereas Hong Kong companies subcontract a great deal of their production from independently owned sites in southern China. Korean enterprises seem to have made significant investments in new production sites in countries like Thailand and Malaysia, while Taiwanese firms appear to have become the financiers of local investment in China.

With respect to managing labor costs, other relevant strategies were identified by the survey. For example, questions were asked about the rate of introduction of new technology, the kind of technology, and the reasons for introducing technology (part 5). This was followed by a series of detailed questions about contracting out work and the use of part-time and shift labor (part 6). Here again, the management of labor costs was an important issue linking decisions made about the sourcing of labor with the various determinants of those actions. As is apparent from the individual case studies, contracting out work is sometimes a local phenomenon and sometimes an international phenomenon, undertaken in Singapore and Korea, for instance, for less skilled labor tasks at lower wages. With respect to temporary workers, many of whom are believed to be illegal immigrants in Singapore, Hong Kong, and Taiwan, it is also clear that this source of labor is increasingly important to labor-intensive enterprises in those economies. Their availability allows some enterprises to maintain existing production facilities without necessarily investing in technology or pursuing a strategy of spatially dividing tasks and production functions. For many enterprises, the use of temporary workers seems to be a short-term expediency driven by the lack of alternatives.

The survey also asked enterprises about redundancy, retraining, and retention strategies, noting the various factors that were important to the firms in retraining (for example) (part 7). Enterprises were asked about the role and status of unions in their decision making (part 8). Finally, enterprises were asked about the role of the public sector in facilitating or hindering the process of corporate restructuring over the past few years (part 9). All these questions are about the interaction between corporate decision making and state policy. These questions are not about industry policy in the sense commonly understood; that is, nothing was asked about targeted public investment in particular sectors or firms, and nothing was asked about special incentives for investment or disinvestment (compare with Johnson's 1982 seminal study of the Japanese Ministry of International Trade and Industry). Rather, the issue embedded in all questions was the extent of management discretion in using labor (or disposing labor) and the extent of discretion in responding to competitive pressures over the past few years. Here, the issue is simply and profoundly what are the limits of management capacity to deal with the changing circumstances of labor-intensive industries in the Asian NIEs? To what extent can the supposition that the economic growth of the Asian NIEs is different from that of the West be sustained on the basis of their separate experience with respect to industrial restructuring?

Conclusion

In his review of recent events (post-1985) in Taiwan, Tsay (1993) suggests that one impediment to industrial restructuring is public policy. In particular, he suggests that continued protection of domestic markets is limiting the capacity of firms to acquire foreign resources and capital equipment. As a consequence, the competitiveness of many Taiwanese firms that now operate in international markets is being harmed by state policies that were relevant for an earlier era of protected economic growth. This is not to say that Tsay suggests that state policy ought to be dispensed with or that state policy is now irrelevant. Quite the contrary. He notes that state policies ought to facilitate technological innovation and technological transfer, both speed restructuring and ameliorate the effects of restructuring, and encourage financial markets to respond to the new competitive circumstances of corporations. Whatever the significance of his observations about the patterns of economic restructuring in Taiwan and his recommendations for public policy, his general point about the necessary focus of state policy deserves emphasis. That is, the increasing importance of corporate strategy in the Asian NIEs does not deny the significance of state policy in general; rather, it questions the value and virtues of previous specific growth policies.

Interestingly, Tsay advocates a stronger role for government spending on infrastructure and research and development. This would presumably mean increasing the proportion of expenditure going to investment and perhaps decreasing government consumption expenditure (see table 3.2). Compared with other Asian NIEs and with Japan, the United States, and Australia, Taiwan has a low rate of (public and private) investment. He also suggests a specific facilitating role for state policy, linking U.S. sources of technology with Taiwanese producers, a kind of policy akin to industrial development policy without significant subsidies on capital investment. These kinds of policies are not exhaustive of the new role for state policy in Taiwan, nor do they represent a recipe for state policy in the Asian NIEs. Clearly, however, they are policies that enhance market competition, open markets to imports, and sustain firms' competitive strategies. In this sense, one role for state policy in the new world of global competition is to broaden the scope of corporate strategy and develop opportunities for new forms of alliances between companies in the Asian NIEs and elsewhere. The fact that Taiwan has historically relied upon small to medium enterprises for economic growth means, of course, that such policies would have to be particularly sensitive to the structure of industrial organization. There remains, as implied by the previous discussion about strategy and structure, a close connection between the scope of strategy and the structure of markets.

Three criticisms are often made of strategy-oriented models of corporate economic performance. One is to be found in neoclassical economics: that, for all the energy and ambition of corporate executives, if their chosen strategies go against market imperatives those strategies (and companies) do not survive. In essence, the metaphor of survival of the fittest is invoked to weed out aberrant behavior (see Alchian 1950). But this model of behavior only works if market imperatives are well known and coherent. In fact, that does not seem to have been the case in the Asian NIEs since 1985. Another objection comes from institutional economists: that models of strategy are too "clean," too "precise," for "the complex, imprecise, and fumbling way by which human beings have gone about structuring human interaction" (North 1990, 15). Clearly, we do not mean to suggest that competitive strategy is as North describes it; in fact, we make a point of distinguishing corporate strategy from formal game theory in the earlier sections of this chapter. Still, North makes an important point. It may be the case that the increasing significance of market competition and the increasing scope for corporate strategy in the Asian NIEs is a temporary phenomenon to be brought back under consistent rules of market competition through new (internal and external) regulatory regimes. At best, we are agnostic about this possibility. Finally, it could be argued (as it is sometimes suggested in the comparative literature) that talk of corporate strategy is vacuous given the profound cultural differences between the West and the Asian NIEs and between the Asian NIEs. Amsden's (1989) book is one of many that suggest the Asian NIEs are so special that their institutions (rules of social end economic life) are not plausibly translated into Western concepts of markets and corporate strategy.

There are obvious important differences between the West and the Asian NIEs and within and between the Asian NIEs. At the same time, corporations' market performance, and the performance of markets in general, have become very important for the long-term welfare of the Asian NIEs. The Asian NIEs are now an integral part of the global market system. It is no longer appropriate to treat them as separate and insulated from the forces affecting the economic performance of other major economies of the world. That is the point, after all, of this project. We wish to test out the significance and scope of corporate strategy in the context of industrial restructuring in the four different economies and their rapidly changing markets.

Notes

1. Much of the data for what follows was provided by Access Economics (Melbourne). Data on oil consumption come from Table A6, *1990 Annual Oil*

Market Report, published by the International Energy Agency. Oil prices are based on west Texas crude U.S. dollars per barrel at the nearest quarterly contract. Share price indexes are based on end-of-quarter prices—the All Share Index (Singapore), the Composite Stock Market Index (Korea), the Total Market Stockmarket Index (Hong Kong), and the Stock Exchange Weighted Index (Taiwan). Currency exchange rates (in terms of U.S. dollars) are taken at the end of quarter (Korea and Taiwan) or are the average quarterly exchange rates (Singapore and Hong Kong). Quarterly consumer price indexes are based on all items, for all four economies. The real wage index is yearly data based on all manufaturing sectors, for all four economies (1986 = 100), taken from the ILO *Yearbook of Labor Statistics* (1991). Won Bae Kim provided the wage data.

2. One of the ironies of Barro's (1991, 1992) work is that his empirical analysis is actually quite limited with respect to Hong Kong. Because of data limitations, Hong Kong was not included in the comprehensive models of country economic performance.

3. In their review of the growth prospects of Japan, the Asian NIEs, the ASEAN 4, and China over the next few years, the Australian Department of Foreign Affairs and Trade (Australia 1993) notes that their growth rates are likely to be significantly higher than their OECD countries. Most countries will grow at about 6 to 7 percent over 1993 and 1994. Export growth rates have been maintained in part by shifting toward Chinese markets, as expanding domestic demand has fueled internal growth as well. However, it is also noted that countries dependent on the West for markets have suffered some decline in growth and have been increasingly affected by upward pressures on the value of their currencies. For instance, Singapore's dollar is now one of the strongest in the world.

4. Durlauf also takes his quarterly output data from Summers and Heston (1988), concentrating on the performance of just six closely related OECD countries—Canada, France, West Germany, Japan, the United Kingdom, and the United States—for the period 1950 to 1985. Some doubts could be raised about his time-series methods, particularly his use of regression without an explicit attempt to control for autocorrelation. While "detrending" is a common approach in these circumstances, it is not as efficient as other time-series methods, such as Box-Jenkins, which make the stochastic component the object of statistical analysis (see Clark, Gertler, and Whiteman 1986 for an example in the regional context).

5. Structure is normally explained in the social science literature through a biological metaphor or systems theory. That is, structure is assumed to define the underlying fixed or formal relations between units of an organism. So, for example, in international relations it is often assumed that the underlying structure of power (resources, economic capacity, and geographical position) between countries determines their interests and actions with one another (see

Stein 1990). In this chapter, the term *structure* is most often used to refer to that part of a firm's capital or market position that is outside its immediate control; this is an agent-centered definition of structure, which supposes a certain plasticity of structure over the long run.

6. Hovenkamp's (1991) study of the breakdown of the classical tradition in American law over the period from 1836 to 1937 is indicative of the fragility of structure. His historical analysis emphasizes the rapid transformation of markets and the startling changes of corporate form that combined to effectively destroy the traditional regulatory structure. He argues that during this period head-to-head competition, the staple of structure-dependent strategy, proved to be ruinous competition. Only at the margins of the economic and legal systems did companies have a chance to make extra profits. But those actions inevitably brought about the decline of the integrity of the classical regulatory system.

PART TWO

Dimensions of Corporate Strategy

FOUR

███████

Hong Kong: Unorganized Industrialism

Stephen W. K. Chiu and Tai-lok Lui

After almost four decades of unbridled growth, Hong Kong's manufacturing industries have reached a critical turning point. Beginning in the mid-1980s, both the soaring domestic costs of production and the emergence of low-cost foreign competitors posed formidable challenges to the further development and, indeed, survival of Hong Kong's manufacturing industries. The garment and electronics industries, the two leading industries in Hong Kong, have employed a number of strategies to restructure their operations. These strategies are related to a broader institutional context of unorganized industrialism that shapes the calculus of individual firms.

Hong Kong Manufacturing in the World Economy

From modest beginnings in the 1950s, Hong Kong's manufacturing sector grew rapidly and, by 1961, it accounted for 23.6 percent of GDP and 43 percent of total employment (Zheng 1987, 123; Hong Kong 1982, 138). Many factors were conducive to Hong Kong's industrialization. Such rapid industrial growth was brought about by factors including entrepreneurship, particularly management and skills from emigrant entrepreneurs from mainland China (S. L. Wong 1988; J. Wu 1988); the economic culture of the population (S. L. Wong 1986); a 'positive non-interventionist' government that promotes a laissez-faire economy and contributes to the provision of the infrastructure for economic development (Haddon-Cave 1984; Friedman and Friedman 1980, 54–55; but see Schiffer 1991 for a critical review of the colonial government's intervention in economic activities); and the supply of a hard-working and flexible labor force (see, for example, Lethbridge and Ng 1984, 96). Without denying or understanding the importance of all the above factors to Hong Kong's industrialization, it is unmistakable that the international economy played a significant role in stimulating export-led industrialization in East Asia in general and Hong Kong in particular. The spectacular growth of the Hong Kong economy through export-led industrialization was essentially conditioned by the restructuring of the world economy in the early postwar years (Chiu 1992; Dicken 1992; Froebel, Heinrichs, and Kreye 1980; Landsberg 1979; So 1986).

The restructuring of the global economy brought about a change from the previous international division of labor, which was based on a small core of industrialized and developed capitalist countries trading with the raw material producing developing Third World countries. In effect, there has been a spatial relocation of manufacturing productions in the world economy. During this process of relocation, some developing economies emerged as the sites for export manufacturing. This reorganization of the international division of labor was the precondition for Hong Kong's industrialization. The emergence of the international subcontracting network has facilitated the incorporation of Hong Kong into the global manufacturing system through the network of transnational corporations (Dicken 1992; Germidis 1980; Chu 1988). Hong Kong was also well suited to take advantage of the opportunities in the world market due to the abundant supply of labor in the early postwar years, which allowed for the development of labor-intensive production of consumer goods. Furthermore, the preexisting network of commercial transaction evolved from the entrepot years fostered an easy integration of Hong Kong's manufacturers into the international subcontracting system.

Similar to other industries in Hong Kong's manufacturing sector, both the garment and the electronics industries are export-oriented and fast growing. In terms of the contributions to employment, gross output, and domestic exports, they have been the top two industries since the 1960s. The garment industry developed rapidly in the 1950s and had overtaken the textile industry as the leading export earner and employer among other manufacturing industries by the 1960s. Compared with garments, the electronics industry was a late starter—it began in

Table 4.1   Development of Garment and Electronics Industries, by Number of Enterprises and Number of Employees, Selected Years 1950–1991

	Garments				Electronics			
	Enterprises		Employees		Enterprises		Employees	
	No.	%[a]	No.	%[a]	No.	%[a]	No.	%[a]
1950	41	2.8[b]	1,944	2.4	—	—	—	—
1955	99	4.1	4,261	3.9	—	—	—	—
1960	970	18.1	51,918	23.8	4	0.1	183	0.1
1965	1,514	17.5	87,454	25.6	35	0.4	5,013	1.5
1970	3,491	21.1	158,025	28.8	230	1.4	38,454	7.0
1975	8,047	25.9	257,595	37.9	490	1.6	53,833	7.9
1980	9,499	20.9	275,818	30.9	1,316	2.9	93,005	10.4
1985	10,307	21.4	292,789	34.5	1,304	2.7	86,115	10.1
1986[b]	10,392	21.4	299,932	34.5	1,823	3.7	103,796	11.9
1987	10,556	20.9	298,377	34.1	1,949	3.9	106,835	12.2
1988	10,412	20.6	286,659	33.9	1,939	3.8	109,677	13
1989	9,672	19.4	274,732	34.2	2,009	4.0	99,455	12.4
1990	9,746	19.9	251,746	34.5	1,815	3.7	85,169	11.7
1991	8,837	19.1	224,925	34.4	1,633	3.5	71,466	10.9

Source: Hong Kong (1991b, 42, 57).

[a] Percentage share of all manufacturing industires in the respective year.

[b] Figures from 1986 to 1991 include electronic watches and clocks, previously classified under the watch industry.

the late 1950s, and only in the 1970s did it experience rapid growth. But once established, the electronics industry developed rapidly, and by the late 1970s it had secured its place in the manufacturing sector next to the garment industry.

The garment industry reached its peak in the mid-1970s. In 1975, there were 8,047 establishments in the industry (25.9 percent of the total number of manufacturing establishments), employing 37.9 percent of the manufacturing workforce (table 4.1). Since then, the industry's growth has slackened compared to other manufacturing industries, but it continued to grow in absolute terms until 1987–88. From 1988, both the number of establishments and the number of persons engaged dropped sharply. Between 1988 and 1991, the number of establishments and persons engaged declined by 15.1 percent and 21.5 percent respectively. The electronics industry grew rapidly between 1975 and 1985, with an average annual growth of 10.3 percent in establishment numbers (Hong Kong 1990, 48). Thereafter, the industry experienced a lower rate of annual growth until it reached its peak in 1988. The number of persons employed fell from 109,677 in 1988 to 71,466 in 1991, a dramatic culling of about 35 percent of the workforce.

That the two leading industries began to run out of steam in the 1980s was largely a result of changes in the business environment. Simply put, by the 1980s, industries in Hong Kong found it increasingly difficult to maintain their competitiveness by continual reliance on labor-intensive manufacturing. First, labor costs have been increasing in both real and nominal terms since the 1980s. Average daily money wage in manufacturing more than doubled from HK$73 in 1982 to HK$184 in 1990, while average real wage in 1982 prices increased from HK$73 in 1982 to HK$101 in 1990 (Hong Kong 1991a, 22). This poses serious problems to Hong Kong's manufacturers, because such increases would make it difficult for them to compete with producers in other NIEs who still have the advantage of low labor costs. Second, the rising wage rate is only one among many issues related to organizing labor for production. Equally pertinent is the question of labor shortage (Joint Associations Working Group 1989; Ng, Chan, and Wong 1989; Ho, Liu, and Lam 1991). The problems here are twofold. First of all, fundamental population factors affect the current shortage of labor. Most important of all is the trend of decline in population growth. More interestingly, it is a vicious cycle in a failing process of restructuring the manufacturing sector. Manufacturers are eager to keep wages low to maintain their competitiveness, and whenever possible, they move their production to places with abundant supplies of low wage labor. These practices tend to discourage young workers from joining the manufacturing sector and, in turn, create further problems for labor recruitment (on problems related to the recruitment of female manufacturing workers, see Ng, Chan, and Wong 1989, 70–72). Third, another critical factor contributing to rising production costs is soaring prices in the property market. Between 1981 and 1990, rentals for private multistory factories have more than doubled, while prices have also made a remarkable increase of 66.6 percent (Hong Kong 1991c, 60, table 4.4). The high costs of factory premises are obviously unfavorable factors for industrial development, especially for those industries contending with others in cost sensitive, cutthroat competition.

In a survey conducted by the government on the manufacturing environment, 1,589 manufacturers were asked to indicate whether they perceived any of a given list of eighteen factors as constraints on the growth of their industries. Almost 90 percent of the respondents perceived high labor costs as a constraint, and 37.4 percent perceived it as a serious constraint. Other labor problems, such as labor shortage and labor turnover, were also high on the list of constraints, with 24.5 percent and 24.4 percent of the respondents regarding them respectively as serious constraints on growth. High costs of factory premises was also perceived as a serious constraint by 37.4 percent of the responding firms, making it the second most widely perceived constraint on industrial growth (Hong Kong 1992a: 287).

The government had in fact anticipated these problems encountered by the manufacturing industries. As early as the mid-1970s, there was an official attempt to deal with increasing protectionism and to recognize, in the words of the governor in his address to the Legislative Council in 1977, the "urgency to the long-term desirability of broadening our industrial base." (Hong Kong 1979, 1). Accordingly, an advisory committee was appointed by the governor to consider "the principal factors which have contributed to Hong Kong's economic growth over the past 15 years . . . the factors which have been influential in attracting or deterring the establishment of new activities in the manufacturing and other sectors of the economy . . . [and] comparative practices in comparable economies which have successfully encouraged the establishment of new industries" (2).

This official exercise of reviewing the matter of industrial diversification did not have much impact on the subsequent industrial development. Indeed, when the Report of the Advisory Committee on Diversification was finally made public in late 1979, it "was out of date as soon as it was published because of the new role for Hong Kong as a result of China's opening up in 1977" (Chen and Li 1991, 41). Two developments in the late 1970s to a large degree delayed the urgency of restructuring and rendered the report irrelevant for the early 1980s. First, China's open-door policy brought about the revival of entrepot trade and opened new opportunities for local manufacturing. Second, and equally important, the influx of legal and illegal migrants from mainland China since the mid-1970s had again, like previous waves of migration from the other side of the border, brought Hong Kong a new pool of low-wage labor for manufacturing production (Greenwood 1990; Skeldon 1986).[1] More important, it had the unintended effect of perpetuating the strategy of developing labor-intensive industries. Consequently, in the 1980s, Hong Kong's manufacturing industries continued to carry out export-oriented and labor-intensive production much the same as in the previous decades.

We have argued elsewhere that Hong Kong's manufacturing industries in general, and electronics and garment industries in particular, continued to rely on the labor-intensive methods of production to survive and compete in the world market in the 1980s (Lui and Chiu 1993; 1994). Garment manufacturers continue to produce high-quality fashion clothing as subcontractors for international brand-name fashion houses. This is done, however, without significant modernization and automation of the production process. The strength of the industry is in its experience and skills, as well as its reputation in the world market for manufacturing good quality clothing items. "The large number of small and medium-sized factories contribute to the strength of the clothing industry as providers of a variety of fashion products, and respond quickly to constant shifts in market demands under an efficient subcontracting network" (Hong Kong 1992a, 40). The electronics industry, on the other hand, has thrived by producing for niche markets (for example, fax machines, video games, application of specific integrated circuits, and talking toys). It has largely stayed away from mass market products (such as standardized microchips), which require large initial outlay and a high technological content. Also, it has not significantly upgraded the technology and capital intensity of its production process. Instead, relocation of the labor-intensive assembly lines to China became a common strategy from the mid-1980s onward. If it is almost "business as usual" amid marginal adjustments in the 1980s, what is the picture for the 1990s and indeed for the near future? Findings from the East-West restructuring survey give much needed up-to-date information about restructuring of the manufacturing industries in the 1990s.

East-West Survey on Industrial Restructuring

The survey on the garment and electronics industries was carried out from June to September 1992. The sampling frame was provided by the Hong Kong Census and Statistics Department. It consisted of a randomly selected 20 percent of all establishments of the chosen industries and gave an updated record of their addresses (as of December 1991). Manufacturing establishments of all sizes were included in this address list. Since not all the activities of the manufacturing establishments in the sampling frame were relevant to our research (for instance, tailors were also included as garment manufacturers), we carried out a screening exercise, eliminating inappropriate firms from the sample. Manufacturing establishments were selected by stratified random sampling according to establishment size. In other words, samples of different size categories were chosen in proportion to the size distribution of manufacturing establishments of the two industries. Altogether, 211 establishments were selected for interview. A letter explaining the background of the survey was sent to the owner or manager of the selected establishments. This was followed by a face-to-face interview with the owner or appointed managerial staff involving the completion of the questionnaire. Sixty-nine garment and fifty electronics establishments successfully completed the questionnaire. Quite a large number of the samples had closed their business, relocated, or stopped production, and the response rate was in the range of 67.6–73.5 percent.[2]

Comparing our sample with the industry population (table 4.2), the distribution of our sample was found to be skewed toward the larger size categories. While electronics firms hiring one to nine employees accounted for some 42 percent of the industry population, they accounted for only 24.5 percent of the sample. In garments, our survey also undersampled the smallest size category by about 10 percent. This is not surprising, since the response rate of the smallest firms is likely to be lower than that of other size categories. Small firms tend to be most unstable, so many might be listed in our sampling frame only to have closed down before the survey began. We also compared the sectoral distribution of the population with the sample within each industry and found that our sample consisted of a representative assortment of firms from each branch of the electronics and garment industries.

As pointed out earlier, Hong Kong's manufacturing is connected to the global economy primarily through the international network of commercial subcontracting and not, as in the case of Singapore, through foreign direct investments. This has its effect on the industrial structure of Hong Kong (see Chu 1988, King and Man 1979, Sit, Wong, and Kiang 1979, Sit and Wong 1989, and Ho 1992 for a description of the characteristics of local industrial establishments). First, Hong Kong's manufacturing establishments are predominantly small, local enterprises. Second, these small establishments are export oriented and rely heavily on the international and local subcontracting

Table 4.2 Distribution of Firms in Population and Sample, by Number of Employees and Industry Sector (percentage)

| | Garments | | Electronics | |
	Population[a]	Sample	Population[b]	Sample
Nc	10,024	69	1,660	50
Number of employees				
1–9	41.5	24.5	54.0	44.9
10–19	17.2	28.6	15.7	17.4
20–49	13.6	24.5	18.7	24.6
50–99	10.0	14.3	6.0	4.3
100+	17.6	8.2	5.6	8.7
Sectoral distribution[d]				
382	—	—	14.0	6.0
383	—	—	10.8	12.0
384	—	—	22.4	30.0
385	—	—	13.9	6.0
3868	—	—	3.1	0.0
3873	—	—	6.7	8.0
3893	—	—	28.9	40.0
3201	72.2	60.9	—	—
3202	7.7	2.9	—	—
3209	0.9	2.9	—	—
3221	1.5	4.3	—	—
3229	2.9	1.4	—	—
3275	0.3	1.4	—	—
3276	14.4	24.6	—	—
3277	0.0	1.4	—	—

Source: East-West Center Survey on Enterprise Strategy.

[a] Employees of firms in wearing apparel (HSIC 320 and 322) only. Size distribution of knitwear firms is not available.

[b] Employees of firms in HSIC 382, 383, 384, and 385 only (see note c below). Size distribution of firms in HSIC 3868, 3873, and 3893 is not available.

[c] The total number of establishments here (N) is not comparable to that in table 4.1, since the two sets of figures are quoted from different sources.

[d] Sectoral distribution is classified according to the Hong Kong Standard Industrial Classification (HSIC). 3201: outer garments; 3202: undergarments and night garments; 3209: other garments; 3221: gloves; 3229: other wearing apparel; 3275: hosiery; 3276: knit outwear; 3277: knit underwear; 382: office, accounting, and computing machinery; 383: radio, television, and communication equipment; 384: electronics parts and components; 385: electrical appliances and housewares and electronic toys; 3868: electronic industrial apparatus; 3873: other electronic products; 3893: electronic watches and clocks.

Table 4.3 Characteristics of Ownership and Sources of Orders of Garment and Electronics Industries (percentage of firms)

	Garments	Electronics
Locally owned	94.2	82.0
Owner-managed	92.8	74.0
Production for export: 50% or more	57.8	62.0
Order from overseas directly: 50% or more	10.4	42.0
Order from local import and export houses: 50% or more	47.9	28.0
Order from local factories: 50% or more	23.3	24.0
Order from own overseas outlets	2.8	8.0

Source: East-West Center Survey on Enterprise Strategy.

networks for survival. They receive their orders mainly from overseas buyers, local import and export houses, and local larger industrial establishments. In short, they are mainly original equipment manufacturing (OEM) producers and subcontractors for international sourcing agents and local factories.

Table 4.3 gives a brief description of the characteristics of our surveyed garment and electronics establishments. It is not surprising that in terms of the ownership of capital, reliance on exports, and the connection with international and local subcontracting, our samples were consistent with the general depiction of Hong Kong's manufacturing stated above. Only two points are worth further elaboration. First, compared with garment establishments, electronics establishments are more likely to be owned by foreign capitals (for a more detailed discussion, see Lui and Chiu 1994). Indeed, electronics is the local industry that has attracted the larger share of foreign direct investments. Second, the garment industry is relatively more reliant on import and export houses as a source of order, and receives fewer orders directly from overseas, than the electronics industry. It is quite clear that both the garment and electronics industries are obtaining their orders through the subcontracting network. Only a small fraction of our samples (8 percent and 2.8 percent of electronics and garments respectively) have their own outlets overseas. In short, in Hong Kong we are looking at how small, local industrial establishments cope with industrial restructuring in the changing business environment. Their limited resources and the subordinate position in the subcontracting network are pertinent to our understanding of their restructuring strategies.

Restructuring Strategies of Electronics and Garment Firms

As noted earlier, in the face of the changing business environment and rising production costs, Hong Kong's manufacturing industries find it increasingly difficult to maintain their labor-intensive production. However, despite enormous pressures on local manufacturing establishments to trade up (either by technological upgrading or moving to the upper end of the product markets), there are few signs suggesting that Hong Kong's manufacturing has undergone significant reorganization. The paradox is this: on the one hand, Hong Kong's manufacturing industries continue to fare reasonably well in the world economy (for instance, Hong Kong was the world's leading clothing exporter in 1989; see Dicken 1992, 241–42); on the other, their continuing growth is driven not so much by increases in the sophistication of production as by their quick response to changing demands of the world market.

Before we examine the institutional context that structures the restructuring of Hong Kong's labor-intensive industries, it is helpful to look at how local corporations respond to the changing business environment, focusing on the restructuring strategies of local corporations in garment and electronics production. Table 4.4 gives a summary of the production strategies of our respondents. It is evident that there are significant differences between the two industries in their restructuring strategies. Our data suggest that there is an industry effect on local corporations' response to industrial restructuring.

Compared with electronics, the garment industry is less likely to share in technological sophistication, is more restricted to Hong Kong–based production, and has a tendency to rely on various forms of informal work to enhance its production flexibility. The fact that the garment industry has made little effort to upgrade technology is not surprising. First, the industry itself has made little progress in applying new technology to the assembly process (Mody and Wheeler 1990, 38). Most of the technologically sophisticated and automated processes (such as computer-aided design linked to marking and cutting) are found in the preassembly and postassembly stages. In terms of computerization and automation, Hong Kong is no exception. Computer-aided pattern grading and marker making are commonplace. But "only limited automation of sewing operations has so far taken place" (Hong Kong 1992a, 39; also see Hong Kong 1992b, 19). Second, the appli-

Table 4.4 Production Strategies of Garment and Electronics Industries (percentage of firms)

Strategy	Garments (N = 69)	Electronics (N = 50)
Organization of production		
Capacity subcontracting	46.4	22.0
Outwork	47.8	10.0
Internal contracting	43.5	0.0
Employment of flexible workforce		
Temporary worker	40.6	26.0
Foreign worker	2.9	2.0
Part-time worker	17.4	22.0
Technological development		
New technology	21.7	48.0
R&D activities	4.3	46.0
Relocation		
Overseas production	30.4	52.0
Still running own factory production in Hong Kong	78.3	62.0

Source: East-West Center Survey on Enterprise Strategy.

cation of linked automation to garment-making processes makes it difficult to match the needs of volatile markets. In a case reported in the Report on Industrial Automation Study commissioned by the Industry Department (Hong Kong 1992b, 19), the garment manufacturer has an integrated computerized system of pattern grading, marker planning, and cutting. However, in order to realize the advantage of the automated system, production has to be based on large orders and the cutting of fabrics not requiring any pattern matching. Those producing fashion garments and working for small orders will not find such automation attractive (also see Bailey 1993, 38–39). Third, very often the restructuring of garment production involves shopfloor reorganization rather than technological sophistication. For instance, the so-called modular production system, that is, the formation of self-contained work units of five to twenty persons for the assembly of an entire garment, is essentially a new form of workplace organization, which helps reduce in-process inventories, improve productivity by "between 10% and 40%" and reduce "throughput time to one or two days" (Hong Kong 1992a, 39; also see Bailey 1993, 41-42). It does not involve the application of new technology. In short, technological upgrading is not an important strategy for the restructuring of the garment-making process. And this is especially so to most Hong Kong garment producers, because they are primarily small manufacturers producing for a volatile market of fashion garments.

Although Hong Kong's garment manufacturers are losing their cost advantages, garment production is still locally based. Our survey findings show that only 30.4 percent of our respondents have offshore production and 78.3 percent still have their factories located in Hong Kong (table 4.4). The study of industrial investment in the Pearl River Delta by the Federation of Hong Kong Industries (Federation of Hong Kong Industries 1992) also reveals that garment manufacturers are among the least likely investors in the region (26.2 percent, well below the average figure of the survey, 40.7 percent). There are two major reasons why garment manufacturing remains Hong Kong based. First, whereas larger firms with retail outlets in Hong Kong and other Asian cities can rely on their relocated plants in mainland China for production (see, for example, Giordano Holdings Ltd. 1991), other manufacturers produce primarily for domestic niche markets. In other words, for those small fashion producers manufacturing for the local market, there are few incentives for relocation. Second, the reason many garment manufacturers decide not to relocate offshore has to do with quota restrictions and the origin rules in force in Hong Kong. For those products exported to restrained markets, a "special outward processing arrangement is administrated by the Hong Kong Government Trade Department to ensure that goods manufactured in Hong Kong but partly processed in China only qualify for Hong Kong origin status if they fully meet Hong Kong's origin rules" (Hong Kong 1990, 40). As a result of such institutional restrictions, unless goods produced are targeted for local consumption or unrestrained markets, garment manufacturers have to continue their production in Hong Kong.

Given the institutional restrictions on relocation and the structural constraints on technological upgrading, garment manufacturers find themselves increasingly locked into a system of flexible production for volatile export markets. Except for the few manufacturers who possess the required quotas, obtain adequate orders for mass production, are capable of developing retail outlets in the domestic and East Asian markets, and therefore are able to turn to offshore production or adopt full-scale automation to enhance their competitiveness in large-scale production, most local manufacturers have to make every effort to increase their production flexibility in order to keep pace with rapid changes in styles and tastes at the end of fashion and garment retailing. The survival of garment making in Hong Kong hinges upon its success in fighting a battle on two fronts. On the one hand, it depends on local manufacturers' abilities to maintain their ties with the commercial subcontracting network of global capitalism. That Hong Kong's garment industry had its origin in strong commercial ties is an advantage (Birnbaum 1993; Chu 1988; also see Kurt Salmon Associates 1992, 72). This shapes local manufacturers' sensitivity to the needs of importing markets, especially at the level of retailing. As a result of economic restructuring in advanced industrial societies, production has been increasingly conditioned by the needs of the retailing market (Harvey 1989; Murray 1989). This is especially true for fashions and garments (Ward 1991). In this new world of consumption, the ability to handle such a volatile market is the basic requirement for success.

On the other hand, to respond quickly to changes in the consumption sphere, Hong Kong's garment manufacturers have to obtain a high level of flexibility in production. The extensive use of various forms of informal work by local garment manufacturers (see table 4.4) has to be understood in the light of such changes in the markets for garment products. Almost half the garment manufacturer respondents have used capacity subcontracting, outwork, and internal contracting. Such practices of flexible production, of course, can be seen as a game of risk shifting—whereas larger establishments are likely to farm out part of their production to subcontractors, small establishments, relying heavily on such subcontracting activities to maintain their production, in their turn shift part of the burden of risk to internal contractors and female outworkers. The interesting point to note is that the long history of export-oriented, small workshop production has given rise to a network of interdependent producers permeated with notions of personal connections and trust (compare S. L. Wong 1990). The existence of such a network makes various forms of subcontracting activities transaction-cost-efficient (compare Levy 1990). This constitutes an industrial structure that fits in well with the need to develop flexible labor-intensive production able to respond to rapid market changes.

Electronics establishments adopt a different strategy to cope with changes in the business environment. The leading restructuring strategy of the industry is relocation of production to mainland China, particularly the region of the Pearl River Delta (Hong Kong 1991b, IV-28). Among our surveyed electronics establishments, 52 percent of them have carried out offshore production. More interesting is that 38 percent of respondents do not have any production facilities in Hong

Kong and simply have all the manufacturing activities carried out in their plants in mainland China (table 4.4). The study on industrial investments in the Pearl River Delta conducted by the Federation of Hong Kong industries also confirms this trend of relocation. Almost 70 percent (69.4 percent) of the electronics establishments covered by the study have investment in the region (Federation of Hong Kong Industries 1992, 63). And it is suggested that:

> such a significant extent of investment can be explained by the labor-intensive nature of the industry. In Hong Kong, electronics products are turned out through many component-assembling processes which are mostly done manually. Since full scale automation is still uncommon, a large number of workers, particularly young workers, are needed. Faced with a severe shortage of labour in Hong Kong, which is complicated by the reluctance of the younger generation to enter the industrial workforce, the electronics industry has a strong incentive to take advantage of the abundant supply of labor across the border.

The same study reports that, on average, relocated establishments employ 905 persons. However, in terms of investment, electronics firms in the Pearl River Delta tend to concentrate in two clusters. At one end are small and medium firms with capital of less than $HK5 million (39.2 percent). And at the other are larger firms with capital of more than $HK20 million (20.8 percent). These findings suggest that the strategy of going offshore is by no means confined to larger firms. Given the geographical proximity between Hong Kong and the Pearl River Delta, many small and medium firms can make use of the abundant supply of labor there to reduce production cost.

Our survey findings also show that there is no significant association between the employment size of local establishments and that of offshore plants. In other words, those running larger establishments in Hong Kong will not necessarily have proportionately larger plants across the border. Although our survey data does not allow us go into a sophisticated statistical analysis of the strategic moves behind relocation, the answers solicited from our open-ended questions enable us to discern, at least tentatively, three possible strategic considerations of relocation. First is a strategy aimed at reducing assembly processes in Hong Kong, reorganizing the local plant into an R&D section, and sending the more labor-intensive processes offshore. Among our respondents in the electronics industry, there is a significant association ($X^2 = 6.93570$, df = 1, p < .01) between investment overseas and conducting internal R&D. This suggests that it is more likely that those manufacturers who have started offshore production carry out R&D in their Hong Kong establishments.

More sophisticated processes are retained in their Hong Kong premises, and assembly is carried out in their offshore plants. However, it is important to note that only about one third (34 percent) of our respondents are estimated to have adopted this restructuring strategy. The extent to which Hong Kong electronics manufacturers have adopted such a restructuring strategy should not be overestimated. Indeed, in terms of technological sophistication, Hong Kong's electronics industry falls behind its East Asian competitors. As pointed out in the review of industrial automation by the Industry Department (Hong Kong 1992b, 37), "on the whole, the industry only invests in hard automation equipment if forced to by their buyers, instead of continually seeking out opportunities to add extra value for, and hence extract extra value from, their customers." Most of the electronics manufacturers are OEM producers. Their R&D activities are more related to product modifications than to core technology development. In this regard, the progress of technological upgrading achieved in the electronics industry has to be interpreted with caution (see table 4.4; also Lui and Chiu 1994).

The second discernible strategy is similar to the first, except that the local establishment concentrates on trading instead of R&D. In our survey of electronics establishments, 38 percent of the sampled establishments do not have their own factory production in Hong Kong. And among these establishments, 50 percent rely solely on their offshore plants for production, one third carry out the production in relocated plants and subcontract out to local or offshore factories, and the rest have all their production finished by subcontractors. While some of these establishments have retained the product development process in their local plants, many have more or less changed into trading firms. In some cases, these firms assume the role of sourcing agent for transnational corporations. Given their business contacts with local subcontractors and manufacturers based in mainland China, they can be commercial agents in facilitating international subcontracting.

Last but not least is the strategy of expanding production capacity by relocation. This is a strategy adopted by many medium firms that see the advantages of the abundant supplies of cheap labor and cheap land across the border and try to make profits by expanding the scale of production rather than moving toward technological sophistication

(Hong Kong 1991b, IV-61). For the electronics industry as a whole, this strategy has the danger of further hindering the upgrading of production technology and thus may reduce the competitiveness of the industry in the long run. However, for individual manufacturers, this strategy allows them to continue labor-intensive production and make lucrative profits through significant increases in sales volume.

In brief, the relocation of electronics production is in full swing (also see Leung 1993). As expressed by some local producers, relocation is "the only means for the electronics manufacturers to survive. In order to stay cost competitive, they have to move to PRC" (Hong Kong, IV-28). In light of this change in production, it is not difficult to understand why various forms of informal work (like capacity subcontracting and outworking) are insignificant to local electronics manufacturers. When electronics firms look for production strategies to reduce costs and enhance flexibility, they turn to setting up their own plants in the Pearl River Delta or finding subcontractors across the border. The Hong Kong-based production strategy is losing its attractiveness.

Institutional Context of Restructuring

The restructuring strategies sketched above must be comprehended within a broader institutional context in Hong Kong. Firm and sectoral characteristics interact with Hong Kong's particular institutional configuration of state policy, industrial relations, and financial system to produce various corporate responses to the changing environment. On other occasions (Lui and Chiu 1992; 1993; 1994) we have argued for a perspective on restructuring that emphasizes the institutional "embeddedness" of firm behaviors. Pure market signals do not dictate firm responses. By and large, the East Asian newly industrializing economies studied in this volume have faced the same set of pressures from the mid-1980s onward. Yet the responses of the manufacturers in different localities are by no means identical. Each of the East Asian NIEs follows a distinctive trajectory of economic development, which necessarily conditions the pattern of industrial restructuring in the 1990s.

The above discussion of the industrial restructuring process has concentrated on the performances of local small factories in garment and electronics production. It appears that local small manufacturers have almost been left on their own to cope with problems arising from increasing protectionism, rising production costs, and changes in global capitalism. In fact, it is exactly our contention that this represents the institutional setting of Hong Kong's industrial economy—Hong Kong is an example of unorganized late industrialization. More precisely, we contend that local small manufacturers have been given neither assistance nor incentive to follow a different course of industrial restructuring.

In recent discussions of late industrialization, the state is often portrayed as the major agent of socioeconomic transformation (Amsden 1990; Gerschenkron 1966). For instance, Amsden (1990) argues that late industrialization is based on borrowed technology, which presumably requires large doses of investments, a high level of technological sophistication, and a long period of learning. That is why the state must come into the picture, since state intervention is required to help individual firms finance their investments in technology, promote technological upgrading, and bear the initial costs or losses of adopting foreign technologies. The case of Hong Kong casts doubt on the functionalist logic of the statist interpretation of late industrialization. From our earlier discussion of local manufacturers' responses to the changing economic environment, it is clear that state intervention remains tangential to the structuring of corporate strategies.

Concerning the role of the colonial state in economic development, few observers of the Hong Kong economy would have failed to recognize the relatively limited role assumed by the colonial state in economic development under the rubric of "positive noninterventionism." Nor would they have failed to notice the positive aspects of entrepreneurship and competition in fostering rapid growth. However, contrary to the picture portrayed by Friedman and Friedman (1980, 54–55), the colonial state is far from being passive in the facilitation of economic growth (Schiffer 1991). A notable example is the massive public housing program established in the 1950s. By now, state provision of public housing has been widely recognized as one of the most crucial factors contributing to the success of local industries (Castells, Goh, and Kwok 1988, chapter 2). In functional terms, the public housing program (the population living in public and aided housing in 1991, not including those in home ownership estates, was 36.5 percent of the total population) helps tackle the problem concerning the reproduction of labor power. This question is particularly pertinent, as Hong Kong's industries are mainly labor-intensive and their competitiveness depends heavily on the supply of cheap labor. In this connection, the public housing program has the effect of subsidizing the wage of the low-wage population—working-class families are able to survive on low wages received from their employers, and the latter are indirectly assisted in continuing their pursuit of low-wage, labor-intensive manufacturing. So, the assumption that the colonial state stays aloof from various aspects of social and economic affairs is basically inaccurate. In short, what we mean by positive noninterventionism is not the picture of laissez-faire conjured up in neoclassical economics texts. In the words of Youngson (1982, 132), "Hong Kong and laissez-faire have only an occasional acquaintance." Also, it is important to note that it is one thing to argue that the Hong Kong government has not attempted any direct intervention in the structuring of local manufacturing, it is quite another to generalize from this that it practices the laissez-faire philosophy in every domain of economic activities. In fact, the government assumes an important role in the regulation of matters concerning finance and banking, and at points of crisis, it comes to the rescue (Jao 1988, 53–54). Put differently, it is more accurate to describe the practice of the colonial state as selective intervention than as wholesale noninterventionism.

Nonetheless, we should not go to the other extreme and put the Hong Kong colonial state in the family of capitalist developmental states (compare Johnson 1982). Elsewhere, we have analyzed the role of the colonial state in Hong Kong's industrialization (Chiu and Lui 1993; Lui and Chiu 1992). Local industrialists have not been able to secure strategic linkages with the colonial state, and the latter, therefore, has a tendency to stay aloof from managing industrial development (Lui and Chiu 1992; also compare Henderson 1991, 174). The government-industry relationship is actually well captured by the notion of positive noninterventionism (Haddon-Cave 1984). Whereas various state policies in the provision of medical care and housing have the effect of lowering the cost of labor power reproduction (compare Schiffer 1991), the colonial state keeps clear of playing any interventionist or directive role in the development of industries. Compared with other NIEs in the region (for a brief summary of current research, see Onis 1991), Hong Kong falls far short of being a capitalist developmental state. Not only has it not formulated any strategic industrial policy, it also intentionally refuses to provide any long-term national rationality of industrial development or direction for the operation of the market economy. The aforementioned public housing program, as an example of the intervention of the colonial state in the economy, illustrates both the strength and weakness of positive noninterventionism. Whereas the provision of public housing helped to make low-wage, labor-intensive manufacturing a viable strategy for industrialization in the 1960s and 1970s, this form of indirect intervention does not propel local industries onto the track of industrial upgrading.

Under the noninterventionist banner, the emphasis of government policy on industrial development continues to be indirect involvement. These indirect involvements are mainly infrastructural and institutional supports (see Wong 1991 on the Hong Kong government's industrial policy). As regards infrastructural supports, the colonial state has long been active in financing education and building communication and transportation networks. However, in terms of human resources development, there is no industry-specific manpower training. Generally speaking, coordination between manpower training and industrial development is simply nonexistent. Concerning institutional supports, government expenditure is spent mainly on financing the work of the Industry Department and subventing activities of various industry-related bodies like the Hong Kong Productivity Council and the Hong Kong Design Innovation Company. On the whole, the government maintains its detachment from subsidizing any one industry and from directly assisting any particular industrial activity in terms of R&D and other matters related to technological development. Essentially, the colonial state stays aloof from the operations of industrial production. In the garment and electronics industries, for example, local manufacturers find themselves very much on their own in meeting the challenges of industrial restructuring (particularly in the area of technological innovation and upgrading), with minimum support from the government. Short-term economic calculations are, therefore, brought to the forefront in such a noninterventionist, and also politically uncertain (given the 1997 question concerning the future political conditions of Hong Kong after its decolonization), business environment.[3]

The scanty support given by the colonial state to industrial development and the arms-length relationship between the state and industry can be illustrated by our respondents' answers to questions concerning the public support system. When asked whether they thought support toward their business from a number of public bodies was adequate, manufacturers on the whole gave low ratings to the public support system of industrial development. Only the Trade Development Council was rated by more than half the respondents as adequate in its support. More than half of all responding firms regarded support from the Productivity Council, the Industry Department, the Labour De-

Table 4.5 Industrialists' Evaluation of Support from the Public Sector
(percentage of firms)

	Supportive	*Neutral*	*Unsupportive*
Trade Development Council			
Garments	44.1	13.2	42.6
Electronics	63.0	10.9	26.1
Average	51.8	12.3	30.6
Productivity Council			
Garments	11.9	23.9	64.2
Electronics	34.8	21.7	43.5
Average	21.2	23.0	55.8
Industry Department			
Garments	16.7	12.1	71.2
Electronics	15.6	28.9	55.6
Average	16.2	18.9	64.9
Vocational Training Council			
Garments	25.5	19.1	55.3
Electronics	25.5	19.1	55.3
Average	18.3	17.4	64.3
Labor Department			
Garments	10.4	25.4	64.2
Electronics	27.1	29.2	43.8
Average	17.4	27.0	55.7
Infrastructural provisions			
Garments	44.6	12.3	43.1
Electronics	53.3	17.8	28.9
Average	48.2	14.5	37.3

Source: East-West Center Survey on Enterprise Strategy.
Note: Due to rounding, some totals in the tables may be slightly more or slightly less than 100 percent.

partment, and the Vocational Training Council as inadequate. Evaluations of infrastructural facilities were mixed, with slightly less than half of all respondents claiming they were adequate. As can be seen in table 4.5, electronics firms were less critical of public supports than were garment-making firms. In every aspect of the public support system, negative ratings were more common among respondents from the garment industry.

The relatively more positive ratings given to the Trade Development Council and infrastructural facilities also reflect the colonial state's mode of involvement in industrial development. As argued above, the colonial state has refrained from pursuing a sectoral industrial policy that gives priority to manufacturing in the allocation of resources. It offers ample support and incentives to private capital accumulation in general while refraining from interfering with the flow and distribution of resources and capital across different sectors. Infrastructural provisions certainly serve this purpose well.[4] Furthermore, the state is also constrained by a limited resource base in exercizing interventions in the marketplace. On the one hand, as a colonial state, the home government expects industry to be self-sufficient without subsidies from the sovereign state. In recent years, the Chinese government has also had a close eye on Hong Kong's fiscal policy. The balanced-budget policy is actually written down in the Basic Law, the miniconstitution of the future administrative region of Hong Kong. Under these external constraints, the colonial state must be prudent in public spending. On the other hand, apart from land sales and taxation, the state does not possess any other means (e.g., financial system, foreign aid and loans, and public enterprises) of acquiring resources to implement interventionist strategies. Consequently, the state's support of industrial development is necessarily limited in scale and cannot involve a major increase in public spending or subsidies. Hence, the various public bodies (the Productivity Council, the Industry Department, and the Vocational Training Council) geared toward assisting industrial development are either limited in their scale of operation or operating on a self-financing basis. Most of them have served as mediums disseminating information to the private sector, with the Trade Development Council being most successful in such undertakings.

In short, state assistance to manufacturing appears to local industrialists as too little in scale and too limited in scope. Local manufacturers' reliance on restructuring strategies like relocation, flexible production, and concentration in small market niches amid the continuation of a labor-intensive mode of production is obviously attributable to this state-industry relationship. An even more illuminating finding from the survey is that when asked what kind of measures they would desire the state to carry out, about 40 percent and 46 percent of the respondents in electronics and garment making respectively replied "none." Some went on to explain their answer by adding that there was not much that the government could do. Four garment and two electronics firms responded that they hoped the government would establish an industrial loan scheme to help them weather the process of restructuring. A minority of seven electronics firms (none in the garment industry) hoped the government would put more efforts into technological development. Apart from these isolated cases, our findings clearly suggest that industrialists do not believe the state can assist their restructuring to any great extent.

A second component of the institutional context of industrial restructuring in Hong Kong is the financial system. It has been argued that the banking system has been the pillar of the development of manufacturing industries in East Asia (Wade 1985). Under the state's selective credit policy, banks in Japan, Korea, and Taiwan channeled large amounts of funds to the industrial sector. Even Singapore has an industrial bank responsible for the provision of long-term capital. Yet Hong Kong does not have the active partnership between finance and industry that other East Asian countries have. Indeed, Hong Kong's situation appears to be closer to that of Britain, characterized by an institutional separation of finance and industry (Ingham 1984). There is no industrial bank in Hong Kong. As shown in Lui and Chiu (1994), the share of loans and advances to the manufacturing industries accounted for less than 20 percent of the total in the 1960s and declined further in the 1970s and 1980s. The meager share of bank loans given to Hong Kong manufacturing industries is not commensurate with the contributions these industries make to the national product and is far below corresponding figures in the other East Asian NIEs (manufacturing accounted for some 22.8 percent of the gross domestic product in 1981; see Hong Kong 1982).

The inadequacy of support from the banking sector is most noticeable in medium and small manufacturing firms. Only larger firms with substantial collateral manage to solicit assistance from the banks; smaller firms are often denied financial assistance. As a study conducted in the early 1960s observed, "the degree of self-financing in Hong Kong industry is indeed abnormally high; a number of substantial firms rely exclusively on their own resources" (EIU 1962, 16). The same study also pointed out that even for the larger firms, long-term capital investment tended to be self-financed and most bank loans were directed to the financing of short–term working capital. Later studies also revealed the same pattern of the institutional separation of the small-scale manufacturing sector from the financial sector.[5] This institutional feature discourages restructuring strategies that require heavy capital investment and encourages capital-saving strategies, especially among the smaller firms.[6]

We are not, however, arguing that the banking system is altogether irrelevant to industrial enterprises. In terms of general banking services, Hong Kong's banking sector is one of the most advanced in Asia. Both the range and quality of banking services in Hong Kong are impressive. Industrialists in general hold positive views of the banking sector.[7] It is in the area of lending, especially long-term lending for capital investment, local manufacturers find the banking sector most unforthcoming. Again, our survey findings testify to the same relationship between manufacturing firms and the banking sector. Only three electronic firms and five of the garment makers were founded with 50 percent or more of the capital loaned from banks and finance companies. More than 80 percent of the electronics firms and all garment-making firms in the sample were founded with the entrepreneurs' own capital. Since then, more than 50 percent of the electronics manufacturers successfully borrowed money from banks. Garment firms had less luck, with only about one-third of the firms borrowing from the banks. More revealing is the fact that less than half of all responding garment firms had ever attempted to solicit finance from the banks. Forty-four percent of the electronics firms in the sample responded that they had never borrowed from banks.

We also asked respondents to evaluate the adequacy of banks' assistance to different aspects of their operation: working capital, trade credit, and fixed capital. Given that most firms had no previous experience in soliciting banking assistance in some of the three areas, a "no answer" response was rather common in the results. As shown in table 4.6, among those who had an opinion about these banking services, respondents were most satisfied with banks' assistance in providing trade credits. This is not surprising, given the origin of Hong Kong's banking sector in financing entrepot trades. The self-liquidating and short-term nature of trade credits also minimizes the risk borne by the banks. The evaluation of banks' assistance to the lending of working capital was mixed. The majority of the firms, however, regarded the banking sector's assistance to the lending of fixed capital as inadequate. On the whole, electronics firms had more positive ratings of the banking sector than garment-making firms. In all three areas, the proportion of electronics firms regarding banking assistance as adequate outweighed the proportion evaluating the banks negatively. The majority of garment-making firms in our sample, on the other hand, regarded banks' assistance as inadequate in the lending of both working capital and fixed capital. The size factor is evident here. As shown earlier, electronics firms, are larger on average than garment-making firms, in our

Table 4.6   Industrialists' Evaluation of Support from the Banking Sector
(percentage of firms)

	No Comment	Adequate	Neutral	Inadequate
Working capital				
Garments	22.2	20.6	20.6	36.5
Electronics	8.3	43.8	22.9	25.0
All	16.2	30.6	21.6	31.5
Trade credits				
Garments	28.6	27.0	15.9	28.6
Electronics	14.6	50.0	18.8	16.7
All	22.5	36.9	17.1	23.4
Fixed capital				
Garments	34.9	12.7	11.1	41.3
Electronics	18.8	35.4	25.0	20.8
All	27.9	22.5	17.1	32.4

Source: East-West Center Survey on Enterprise Strategy.

sample as well as in the population as a whole. Typically, smaller firms
in the sample felt more left out in the banking sector's services to the
manufacturing industries. Hence, while larger firms enjoyed international standard banking services, small-scale firms found few channels
to obtain funding for restructuring and upgrading. The lack of long-
term funding may explain to a large extent why industrial automation
has progressed so slowly in Hong Kong.

Although firms have not received much direct assistance from either
the state or the banking sector, they are given a free hand in restructuring their production by their employees and the trade unions (on recent development of unionism, see Levin and Chiu 1993). While private firms are not required by the state to bear any social responsibility
that limits their options, they are also not constrained by a strong labor movement in making decisions on restructuring production. Hong
Kong's union movement is numerically weak, with less than 20 percent
of all employees belonging to unions. Union membership in the manufacturing sector is even lower—less than 10 percent. Unions are also
organizationally fragmented into three "federations" of different political persuasions.[8] The shop-floor organization of unions is particularly weak; unions have very limited power in mobilizing collective actions such as strikes. At the community level, the political clout of the
union movement is equally limited. Consequently, in devising various

strategies of restructuring, industrial firms are almost completely free of resistance or interference from unions. Hence, they are rather flexible in their production strategies. In particular, unions are unable to resist the relocation of production to China. There is no need to negotiate with workers for the schedule of relocation, and employers do not have to honor or be bound by union contracts. Not surprisingly, then, most respondents (74 percent in garment making and 71.4 percent in electronics) reported "cooperative" labor relations within their firms. The overwhelming majority (over 95 percent) of the respondents also regarded unions as having negligible influence on the management of their enterprises.

Conclusion

This chapter emphasizes the particular blend of corporate responses to the changes in world and domestic market conditions. In contrast with other East Asian NIEs, Hong Kong's garment and electronics firms have not sought to upgrade the technological and capital content of their production process. Instead, their manufacturing operations remain labor-intensive and technologically unsophisticated. There are also significant sectoral divergences in firms' restructuring strategies. Electronics firms have come to link up more closely with the South China region and have established an extensive production base in the area. Garment making, while constrained by quota rules to relocate, has relied more heavily on flexible production methods and market intelligence to survive international competitions.

These patterns of restructuring are related to a broader institutional context of state policy, the financial system, and industrial relations. The state's intervention and assistance in industrial restructuring was too little, too late. The Hong Kong state serves as a conduit for disseminating information rather than as an engine of structural transformation for industries. The banking sector's traditional arms-length approach to manufacturing industries also narrows the range of restructuring options available to the firms. Most firms are simply too small to be able to tap financial resources from bankers. Finally, organized labor is too weak in Hong Kong to play a significant role in the firms' decision-making process.

We characterize the Hong Kong model of industrialization as unorganized late industrialization. Compared with other late industrializers, Hong Kong's developmental experiences appear to have been far

more unorganized, or decentralized: individual Schumpeterian entrepreneurs operated under unfettered market forces to find new niches
and seek profits. Merchant capital, which could be traced to the entrepot period, played an important part in Hong Kong's industrialization
by linking the international subcontracting network and domestic
manufacturers. The arms-length approach of the state and the banking
sector to manufacturing, as well as the weak labor movement, contributed to this model of unorganized late industrialization. Hence, the
restructuring strategies of recent years must be viewed in this context.

The immediate future of the manufacturing industries appears uncertain. The further growth of the South China region is expected to
spur further the profits of local manufacturers, both by providing a
cheap and abundant supply of labor for export production and increasingly by opening up the domestic markets to products of Hong
Kong-owned firms in China. The future of the garment industry in
Hong Kong will hinge on the continual existence of the international
trade regime and its quota system, which will tie at least part of the export-oriented garment production to Hong Kong. Hong Kong's manufacturing firms (especially those in electronics) have increasingly become a servicing and backup station to the vast manufacturing
establishment in China. How long these servicing and backup functions will remain in Hong Kong before they are also relocated to China
is a major question for the coming years. Finally, Hong Kong's manufacturers are increasingly acting more like merchants, but how successfully these merchant-manufacturers will compete in the coming
decade, and indeed in the twenty-first century, is an important issue
that deserves further research.

Notes

1. Census statistics suggest that in 1976–81, 58.0 percent of the population
growth could be attributed to net immigration. As regards the composition of
this incoming population, there was a predominance of males (60.7 percent),
and a large proportion of the immigrants were in the age group 15–34 (59.9
percent). It is also noted that the unemployment rate of 3.4 percent for the immigrants is significantly lower than the 4.0 percent recorded for the local pop-

ulation, possibly because the immigrants were more willing than local workers to take up jobs requiring lower levels of skill. A large proportion of the economically active migrants (73.9 percent) are found in production and related occupations, which provide the doorways for their participation in the local labor market. See Hong Kong 1982, 76–77.

2. A brief statement on response follows:

	Garment	Electronics
Addresses issued	129	82
Out of scope (closed, moved, stopped production,		
changed business, etc.)	27	14
Total in-scope addresses	102	68
Reasons for nonresponse		
Refusal	26	12
Noncontact	7	6
Successful cases	69	50
Response rate (%)	67.6	73.5

3. Political future and stability have been ranked as the most important investment factors in a survey of 1,832 manufacturing establishments carried out by the Industry Department in 1989 (Hong Kong 1990, 222–34).

4. The provision of industrial land, while aparently a piece of selective assistance to the manufacturing sector, is actually a far cry from an active industrial policy. As Ho (1989) and Chiu (1992) have pointed out, the colonial state's provision of industrial land has operated on a self-financing basis. Through the public auction system, industrial land users are made to pay the existing market price for industrial lots. The colonial state has actually been able to reap a hefty profit from industrial land sales. In industrial land development, the state has not substituted a public rationality for the market mechanism.

5. Several studies can be cited to support this argument. The Department of Commerce and Industry, in a 1968 survey of about 200 manufacturing establishments employing fewer than 100 workers, found out that merely eight establishments in the sample looked to commercial banks for their initial capital and only two establishments obtained money from commercial banks to buy new equipment (see Goodstadt 1969). A sample survey of 415 small manufacturing establishments conducted in 1978 also reported that 88.2 percent of the sample drew their start-up capital from the proprietors' own savings, and another 7.5 percent borrowed from the proprietors' relatives or friends (Sit, Wong, and Kiang 1979).

6. It must be noted that the larger firms have an additional option of floating capital in Hong Kong's well-developed capital market by issuing shares. In recent years, a number of larger electronics and garment firms have taken advantage of this channel to raise capital for expansion.

7. For example, in an official survey of 1,589 manufacturing establishments, 72.5 percent of the respondents regarded banking and financial facilities as a favorable investment factor in Hong Kong. See Hong Kong 1992a, 286.

8. Trade unions are divided into three groups according to their relationship to the two Chinese political regimes. The Federation of Trade Unions, affiliated with the Chinese Communist regime, is the largest group. The Trade Union Congress is a small faction related to the Nationalist government. The third force is constituted by 'independent' union not affiliated with either the Communist or the Nationalist regime. Many of these independent unions are affiliates of the Confederation of Trade Unions.

FIVE

Singapore: Maneuvering in the Middle League

K. C. Ho

With the increasing globalization of production caused by multinational corporate activity, advancements in communication and transportation, and increasing pressures of international market integration, the Asian NIEs are undergoing considerable structural transformation. To maintain international competitiveness, firms need to adjust their production organization first, as nation states need to reconfigure their macroeconomic and investment policies to suit changing external economic situations. These pressures, and the accompanying adjustments, have often been referred to as industrial or economic restructuring (e.g. Beauregard 1989).

The small city-state and open economy of Singapore, which experienced continuous economic growth over the 1970s and 1980s and which faces increasing international competition in the 1990s, faces perhaps a greater challenge than any other Asian newly industrialized economy in attempting to maintain competitiveness in the world economy. With the maturing of the economy and the city-state's ascendance into the middle league of world economies in the 1980s, attendant problems, such as increasing costs, labor and land shortages, and rising currency exchange rates, have made the old ways of doing things virtually obsolete. Firms are responding to these changed conditions by adjusting location, introducing technology, and changing their use of labor. There is also a search on for new state strategies to maintain Singapore's competitiveness in the world economy. As a host of previously less-developed nations have become the sites of low-cost production for multinational corporations, Singapore needs to adopt new competitive strategies involving very different technology, labor, regions, and industry sectors.

Singapore in the World Economy

The British developed and maintained Singapore as a port city. Manufacturing was never encouraged. Authorities believed that such activities were for industrial nations and that Singapore should concentrate on doing what it did best (i.e., commerce) and not dissipate its energies venturing into untried domains. This bias was reflected in a tariff structure that discouraged manufacturing (Dixon 1991). The local manufacturing that developed was mainly of a secondary, supportive character—food processing and beverages for the domestic market and processing of primary commodities from the region (e.g., wood products).

The industrialization effort began in the early 1960s with self-government, but the unstable regional political climate (the Indonesian policy of confrontation with Singapore and Malaysia in the 1960s, the separation of Singapore from Malaysia in 1965) and local political uncertainties (the contest of political parties for control of the state apparatus) dampened the efforts of industrial promotion. After the mid 1960s, many of the problems were on their way to being resolved. By controlling the militant trade and student unions and creating new organizations that assumed direct control of the development process, the Singapore government had acquired what Gamer (1972, 35) called the "political and administrative capacity to plan." In state-society relations, the government's early programs on housing, education, and health had also provided the crucial popular support necessary for state intervention, particularly in the massive land acquisition efforts necessary for conversion to industrial and commercial uses.

The 1966–67 period marked the beginnings of a new phase in relations between Singapore, Malaysia, and Indonesia. After replacing Sukarno, Suharto reversed many of the economic and foreign policies adopted by the earlier regime, including bringing an end to the confrontation Sukarno had engineered. The Singapore-Malaysia separation had been completed, and the countries had come to realize a relationship anchored on historic, economic, and sociocultural ties (Wilairat 1975). Toward the end of 1967, ASEAN, a loose regional grouping comprised of Indonesia, Malaysia, the Philippines, Thailand, and Singapore, was formed to promote regional stability and economic development.

The events and experience of the early 1960s decisively shaped the direction of Singapore's industrial strategy. Notions of an import substitution strategy based on a common market with Malaysia fizzled out after the separation. With diplomatic relations just restored, the memories of the recent past were too fresh for the three countries to work out a plan for regional economic cooperation (Ho and So 1993). With little indigenous manufacturing to nurture, and cut off from the economic hinterlands of Malaysia and Indonesia, Singapore in the late 1960s refined its industrial strategy by positioning itself as an export production site for multinational corporations.

Singapore's industrialization program coincided with the movement of production away from the First World. This globalization of production was triggered by rising wages in industrialized countries and facilitated by the erosion of international regulatory arrangements that supported post-war production and trade (Froebel, Heinrichs, and Kreye 1980; Rich and Linge 1991).

While labor costs in Singapore may be cheap compared to wages in the industrialized countries, it is important to note that on both cost and supply, Singapore was not as attractive to multinationals as Taiwan and South Korea (Hughes 1969). Various tax incentives offered by the state were appreciated by companies but were not crucial attractions (Linbert 1969). Linbert, who interviewed American firms that had production operations in Singapore, pointed out that the strategic location and good infrastructure were chief attractions, because this enabled the export-oriented companies to ship supplies in and goods out efficiently and at low cost. Thus, the colonial legacy of the entrepot economy provided important spillover effects for the push toward manufacturing. Another attraction was the relative ease in getting production facilities operational. Managers interviewed by Linbert cited the Economic Development Board, one of the several organizations set up by the new government, for the crucial service it provided in coordinating with various government agencies to obtain land, utilities, and labor.

A combination of local, regional, and global changes put Singapore into the global manufacturing circuit as multinational companies started investing and producing in Singapore. Mirza (1986) estimated that in 1975, 48.6 percent of the foreign direct investment in Asia ended up in Singapore. Different industries were to play important roles at different periods in Singapore's thirty-year industrialization effort. The textile and garment, petroleum, and transport equipment industries were all significant industries from the mid-1960s to the mid-1970s (Lee 1973). From the early 1970s, the electronics industry began to develop with the involvement of American, European, and Japanese multinational corporations. This industry continues to dominate the manufacturing sector, contributing 37.7 percent of the value of total manufacturing output in 1991. In the mid-1980s, multinational pharmaceutical companies also started to make their presence felt (Chia 1989; Ho 1993).

Thus, the post-war pattern of manufacturing largely for domestic and regional markets was significantly altered by the introduction of new export-oriented industries in the 1970s and 1980s. As a proportion of gross domestic product, manufacturing contributed 11.4 percent in 1961, expanded to 20.4 percent in 1970, and stayed at 29.1 percent in 1980 and 1990 (Singapore 1992). The rapid and sustained growth of industrial activities, which were largely accounted for by foreign capital investment, transformed the economy and created a new set of pressures for manufacturers.

The manufacturing sector began to dominate as the entrepot activities declined. As Singapore became a production platform for multinational corporations, manufacturing for export grew, and the volatility of an entrepot economy was reinforced now by the new export-based economy, which had become entwined with the economies of Singapore's major investors. Thus, with economic downturns at the center of the global economy, the multinational corporations have responded by decreasing output and cutting labor. In the electronics industry, for example, the downturn of 1974–75 resulted in the retrenchment of about 15,000 workers (Lim 1978). In the 1981–82 and 1985–1986 periods, output fell by 7.5 percent and 5.4 percent respectively, and the industry shed between 10,000 and 13,000 workers (Ho 1993).

The rapid growth of the manufacturing sector in the 1970s quickly soaked up the surplus labor that had built up in the 1960s. The unemployment rate fell steadily from 6 percent in 1970 to under 4 percent in 1977, and by the late 1970s Singapore had achieved full employment. In the 1980s, labor and related issues (job-hopping, foreign workers, shift work, part-time work, extending the retirement age, wage costs, productivity, etc.) became major concerns for both companies and the government. Job-hopping in the manufacturing sector is a particularly serious concern. For example, one survey covering seventeen out of eighteen firms operating in the southeastern Bedok New Town found that these firms recruited 7,898 workers over a ten-month period. During the same period, these firms lost 7,060 workers. This works out to a loss of seven out of eight workers hired over the ten-month period (*Business Times* 1989a).

Labor shortages have also led to an increasing reliance on foreign workers. Foreign workers contributed to a third of the growth in the workforce between 1975 and 1979. Between 1980 and 1984, more than half the workforce increase was accounted for by foreign workers (Singapore 1986b). In 1980, there were 79,275 foreign workers carrying valid employment passes (Singapore 1981). This rose to an estimated 150,000 in 1985 and then doubled within five years, to about 300,000 in 1990 (*Business Times* 1991b). Given the chronic labor shortage in Singapore in the 1980s, it is not surprising that the nation's labor costs were among the highest in the region. According to a U.S. Bureau of Statistics survey, the average hourly labor cost for production workers in the late 1980s was US$2.67 for Singapore, slightly lower than the US$2.71 for Taiwanese workers but higher than the US$2.46 for South Korea and US$2.43 for Hong Kong (*Business Times* 1989b).

An active land-use planning effort (especially in urban renewal, public housing, and land reclamation) in Singapore has allowed for reasonable supplies of land for various uses and has kept price inflation in check. The effectiveness of such intervention, however, depends heavily on the type of land use. The promotion of industrialization by the government has resulted in the systematic conversion of land to industrial use. In fact, there was a 359 percent increase in industrial land and a 40 percent increase in warehouse land between 1967 and 1982 (Singapore 1983). However, because the demand for industrial land is tied to the health of the economy, economic volatility is also reflected in the rental rates applied to industrial land. The Property Consultative Committee Report pointed out that "fluctuations in rental rates of factories have been relatively violent. Rental rates rose as fast as they sank." In 1985, rental rates were about equal to those of 1980, after peaking at about twice the 1980 rate in 1982. The same kind of fluctuations occurred in rental rates for office space (Singapore 1986a). Despite extensive land reclamation (which has added 5 percent to the main island's land area between 1967 and 1982), land-use conversion, and increasing land-use density, the inherent small size of the island means that there is less land available for new development of any kind. Hence, land cost inflation is inevitable.

The growing size of Singapore's foreign reserves and the need to maintain a strong dollar in order to develop the financial sector has also meant high export prices for Singapore manufacturers. The Economic Development Board's quarterly survey on business expectations (Singapore 1992) reveals that while more industries were beginning to feel the impact of the strong dollar in 1990, compared to the early 1980s, the appreciating dollar was more likely to affect the export orders of textile, garment, and footwear and food, beverage, and tobacco industries. For example, taking the average of the four quarterly surveys, 19.8 percent of companies in textiles, garments, and footwear and 14.3 percent of companies in food, beverages, and tobacco felt that the strong Singapore dollar was the most important factor limiting export orders in 1990, compared with the average of 7.5 percent for all industries (Singapore 1990). There have been suggestions that the strong dollar contributed in a significant way to the 1985–86 recession (e.g., Bryant 1989).

The emergence of new growth centers of production (e.g., the ASEAN 4 and China in the Asia-Pacific region) and newly emerging development areas (like Vietnam) has brought about increased competition among manufacturers of commodity product and among governments offering sites for production. State economic planners have come to realize that the presence of these low-cost competitors means that Singapore cannot compete on cost structure alone. Moreover, the tight supply of domestic land and labor shortages have created a zero-sum situation where the promotion of one area (industry or sector) may imply the withdrawal or restriction of resources from another (Singapore 1991a). Indeed, the high-wage policy initiated in the late 1970s has had the intended effect of redistributing workers from labor-intensive and low-value-added industries to more productive industries (see Rodan 1989, chapter 5).

This, then is the environment of the 1990s. Manufacturers in Singapore must constantly adjust to this rapidly changing global environment or face serious problems in the near future. More important, the increasingly tight labor market has restricted the opportunities for foreign and local capital alike to use Singapore as a low-cost production site; inevitably, these circumstances demand that new enterprise strategies be found and implemented. For the state, as the cushion of low-cost production is steadily deflated, the pressure to find new ways of sustaining the pace of manufacturing builds. Any strategies have to take into account the attendant problems of Singapore's transformation into a mature economy.

Objectives of the Enterprise Survey

While a number of data sources provide indicators of economic changes, these statistics are generally aggregate in nature. There have been few efforts to understand how firms are adjusting to the economic environment of the 1990s. Therefore, our enterprise survey (based on the East-West Center project) was initiated in an attempt to systematically study changes in the business environment and the responses of firms. The survey focused on four broad areas, all of which are crucial components of industrial restructuring:

> *The environment of firms:* What is the business environment as perceived by firms? Are their markets stable? How has sales volume changed over the past two years? What about the cost situation?
> *Location strategies:* Are firms exploring new plant locations as cheaper production sites? If so, where are the companies headed?
> *Technology strategies:* Does new technology have a crucial role to play in helping firms adjust? If so, is this role primarily geared toward production (e.g., product development, increasing output) or cost saving (e.g., reducing requirements for labor and land)?
> *Labor strategies:* How are firms using their workforce? Are overtime employment, subcontracting, and the use of foreign labor being adopted to cope with the tight labor situation?

The garment industry and the electronics industry were selected for study. These two industries were chosen because they are both major employers of labor. In 1991, for example, the electronics industry accounted for 34.4 percent of the manufacturing workforce, making it the largest employer in the manufacturing sector. The textile and garment industries, taken together, employed 7.2 percent of the workers in manufacturing (Singapore 1992). Although the number of workers in garments has declined slightly over the years, this industry is still the fourth largest employer in the manufacturing sector. Obviously, both industries have significant impacts upon the economy. Moreover, these industries were thought to provide a good contrast in enterprise strategy because of differences in

- local (garment) versus foreign (electronics) capital;
- domestic (garment) versus export (electronics) markets;
- low-stable (garment) versus high-evolving (electronics) technology; and
- a small (garment) versus a large (electronics) workforce.

A sampling frame for firms was compiled from the garment and electronics manufacturers' directories and membership listings from the two industry associations and from listings supplied by the Singapore Trade Development Board. The aim was to obtain a random sample from each industry. Of the 110 firms that responded, 51 were from the garment industry and 59 from the electronics industry. In terms of ownership characteristics, garment firms tended to be local (70.6 percent) or joint ventures with foreign firms (23.5 percent). Electronics firms, on the other hand, tended to be foreign owned (61 percent). Only 25.4 percent of the electronics firms surveyed were local, and 13.6 percent were joint ventures between local and foreign capital.

The greater participation of foreign capital in the electronics industry invariably results in larger operations. This is reflected in both the sales and the characteristics of the workforce. The average sales for 1991 in garments was about $9.9 million, while the average sales for electronics was $147.8 million. The average size of the workforce in the electronics subsample was about 6.6 times (652 versus 98) the size of the garment subsample.

In comparing the occupational structures of firms in the two industries, one difference was the number of professional and technical workers employed by the electronics firms. Although the ratio of workers employed by the electronics subsample in comparison to the garment subsample is 6.6 (i.e., the mean of the workforce in the electronics subsample divided by the mean of the garment subsample), the ratio for professional and technical workers is many times higher, at 37.1. This indicates the much higher level of technology required by electronics firms compared to garment firms. The ratio for the category that includes apprentices, security, and other workers not included in the above categories also stands out. The ratio for this category was

10.9, showing that electronics firms have more apprentices (indicating the need for a learning process) as well as other types of workers (reflecting the greater diversity of workers to support larger operations). The ratios for the other categories (managerial, administrative, clerical, sales, service, and operators) vary between 7 and 8, much closer to the ratio of 6.6 for the total sampled workforce.

Business Environment Confronting Singapore Firms

Firm size and participation of foreign capital affect the way goods make their way into markets. The survey data indicated that garment firms depend on intermediaries much more than electronics firms do. For instance, 23.7 percent of garment orders originated from local import-export companies, compared with only 12.3 percent of electronics orders. Another 17.1 percent of garment orders go to wholesale-retail establishments, compared to only 5.7 percent for electronics. The presence of multinational corporations in the electronics industry means that global and regional production chains link various subsidiaries in different countries, where the output of one subsidiary is the input of another (Henderson 1989; Ho 1991). In the sample, 18.9 percent of the orders in the electronics subsample were in the form of supplying back to overseas outlets, compared with only 1.3 percent for garment firms.

Orders from local factories provide an indication of the extent of the local subcontracting network and the state of development of the industry. This is particularly important for the electronics industry. Given the higher technology required for the manufacture of electronic products and components, a pool of local electronics subcontractors takes time to develop. The existence of a local network of electronics suppliers, therefore, indicates the maturity of the industry and provides an added incentive for multinational corporations to remain in Singapore. From the sample, 18.9 percent of the orders in the electronic subsample went to local factories, compared with 10.5 percent for the garment subsample. On the other hand, 38.7 percent of electronics firms orders and 39.5 percent of garment firms orders are direct.

The local orientation of garment manufacturers is also seen in the fact that 18.8 percent of the garment firms did not export any of their products, while all electronics firms surveyed exported a portion of their products. For those that exported their products, the export destinations show an interesting contrast between the two industries. Electronics firms tend to supply back to their own subsidiaries and parent companies. This can be seen in the good coverage in the major markets (Japan, 12.8 percent; North America, 20.1 percent; and Europe, 21.8 percent). Their Singapore location also allows electronics firms to cover the Asian NIEs (Taiwan, Korea, and Hong Kong combined making up 14.5 percent of exports) and Southeast Asia (17.9 percent). The exports going to Southeast Asia are particularly significant because they indicate a flourishing trade that is the result of the growing importance of Southeast Asia as a region for electronics manufacture (Henderson 1989). Garment firms export mainly to the North American (34.6 percent) and European market (35.9 percent).

The perception of business conditions by firms in the two industries is presented in table 5.1. While firms in both industries were inclined to define their markets as fairly stable ("stable" or "average") responses at the two extremes reflect differences between the two industries. Garment firms were more likely than electronics firms to characterize their markets as unstable (8.2 percent as oppose to only 3.5 percent), and more electronics firms were likely to say that their market is very stable (22.8 percent compared to 12.2 percent). The outlook of the two industries over the previous two years was very different. When asked if business over the previous two years had changed, 64.9 percent of the firms in the electronics subsample mentioned that sales had increased. Only 30.6 percent of the garment manufacturers gave the same response. A significant percentage (36.7 percent) of garment firms actually reported that sales had decreased over the past two years.

The key reasons for increases in sales were improved product quality (27.3 percent), increase in demand (20 percent), flexible pricing strategies (19.3 percent), and finding product niches (15.3 percent). For companies in both industries that mentioned experiencing declines in sales, decreases in demand (23 percent), high wage costs (22 percent), greater competition (21 percent), and high export prices because of the strong Singapore dollar (13 percent) were cited as the major problems.

Are the days of Singapore as a low-cost producer over? The answer is clear: only a small minority of firms (4 percent) attributed increasing business to low wages, while a large number of firms (23 percent) blamed business decline on higher wages.

Table 5.2 provides a gauge of the extent of labor turnover and labor cost changes, two indicators of a tight labor market. About 22 percent of the firms in both industries experience chronic labor turnover

Table 5.1 Business Characteristics, by Type of Industry (percentage of firms)

Characteristic	Garments	Electronics	Combined
Stability of market (N = 106)	49	57	106
Very stable	12.2	22.8	17.9
Stable	44.9	45.6	45.3
Average	34.7	28.1	31.1
Unstable	8.2	3.5	5.7
Total cases	49	57	
Change in sales in last two years (N = 106)			
Increased	30.6	64.9	49.1
Decreased	36.7	24.6	30.2
Remained the same	32.7	10.5	20.8
Total cases	49	57	
Reasons for business increase (N = 150)			
Product quality	34.1	24.8	27.3
Increase in demand	14.6	22.0	20.0
Flexible pricing	24.4	17.4	19.3
Niche market	14.6	15.6	15.3
Low materials costs	4.9	6.4	6.0
Low wage costs	0.0	5.5	4.0
Other	7.3	8.3	8.0
Total responses[a]	41	109	
Reasons for business decrease (N = 100)			
High wage costs	22.4	23.8	23.0
Decrease in demand	22.4	21.4	22.0
Greater competition	20.7	21.4	21.0
High prices due to local $	12.1	14.3	13.0
High materials costs	10.3	11.9	11.0
Labor disputes	5.2	0.0	3.0
Product quality	1.7	2.4	2.0
Other	5.2	4.8	5.0
Total responses[a]	58	42	

Source: East-West Center Survey on Enterprise Strategy.

[a] Multiresponse question; total may exceed number of cases.

of 30 percent or more. The electronics industry appears more able than the garment manufacturers to keep older, more-skilled workers. The turnover of skilled workers is much lower in electronics than in garments (9.3 percent versus 24.4 percent). The table also shows that it is younger workers are more mobile in electronics than in garments (78 percent versus 55.8 percent). The ability of the electronics industry to keep skilled labor could very well be due to higher wage increases.

Table 5.2   Labor Force Characteristics, by Type of Industry (percentage of firms)

Characteristic	Garments	Electronics	Combined
Labor turnover (N = 108)			
0–9%	38.8	47.5	43.5
10–29%	42.9	27.1	34.3
30–49%	8.2	13.6	11.1
50–69%	8.2	8.5	8.3
70% and more	2.0	3.4	2.8
Total cases	49	59	
Turnover by skills(N = 96)			
Skilled[a]	21.4	9.3	14.6
Unskilled	45.2	61.1	54.2
Both	33.3	29.6	31.3
Total cases	42	54	
Turnover by Age (N = 93)			
Young[b]	55.8	78.0	67.7
Old	7.0	4.0	5.4
Both	37.2	18.0	26.9
Total cases	43	50	
Nature of wage changes (N = 108)			
Steep increases	24.5	39.0	32.4
Moderate increases	69.4	59.3	63.9
Decreases	4.1	0.0	1.9
Remained the same	2.0	1.7	1.9
Total	49	59	

Source: East-West Center Survey on Enterprise Strategy.

[a] More than three years of experience.

[b] Less than twenty-five years of age.

Thirty-nine percent of the firms in the electronics subsample mentioned experiencing steep wage increases, compared to only 24.5 percent of firms in the garments subsample.

Firms in both industries share a number of similarities, particularly in terms of their experience of labor turnover and wage increases. These represent the pressures faced by companies operating in Singapore, triggers of firm restructuring in the sense that they force firms to act. Failure to do so reduces the competitiveness of the products. But the differences are also worth noting. The labor-intensive and low-value-added garment firms are less able than electronics firms to maintain older, more-skilled workers. The electronics industry, on the other hand, has much higher participation by foreign capital, is totally export oriented, and, from the reports of many firms, faces an expanding market for its products.

These different situations reflect the very different organization of the two industries and the particular niche that Singapore firms occupy within these industries. Garments is a basic industry, with a large share in the industrial structure of developing countries (Choi, Chung, and Marian 1985). With labor cost comprising about 60 percent of the total cost, the high labor intensity and stable technology of garments imply that this is often the ideal industry to begin the export-oriented phase of manufacturing for countries entering into the global marketplace.

In the 1970s, garment exports from East Asia, particularly Hong Kong, Korea, and Taiwan, were growing rapidly, penetrating both Europe (Froebel, Heinrichs, and Kreye 1980) and the United States (Ghadar, Davidson, and Feigenoff 1987). By the 1980s, China, India, Indonesia, and the Philippines rapidly increased their garment exports to the United States. Hong's (1987) analysis shows convincingly how rapidly industrializing countries in Southeast Asia have been able to compete effectively in the low-cost, labor-intensive industries. Within this particular type of industry environment, Singaporean firms are therefore feeling the growing competition from below in terms of costs, unable to match the competition from developed countries in terms of quality and design and without the advantage of being close to major consumer markets.

The electronic industry, on the other hand, has a very different organization. Unlike the garment industry, the technology is still rapidly changing, and with the exception of Korea, the industry is still very much in the control of multinational corporations from the United States, Japan, and Europe. There is also considerable evidence that a regional clustering is occurring in Southeast and East Asia, not only for semiconductors but also in consumer electronics (UNCTC 1987; Henderson 1989). This can be seen in the overseas investment characteristics in table 5.3.

Thus, the business environment of firms and an understanding of firm strategy must take into account two logics. The locational logic (production in Singapore) provides both opportunities, in terms of access to infrastructure, certain types of labor, and other benefits, and costs, which act as pressure points for firm restructuring. Henderson

Table 5.3   Foreign Direct Investment Characteristics, by Type of Industry
(percentage of firms)

Characteristic	Garments	Electronics	Combined
Investment in factories overseas in last five years (*N* = 108)			
No	67.3	57.6	62.0
Yes	32.7	42.4	38.0
Total cases	49	59	
Reasons for overseas investment (*N* = 120)			
Lower wage costs	30.2	28.4	29.2
Fewer labor problems	26.4	20.9	23.3
Cheaper, available land	18.9	20.9	23.3
Currency advantages	17.0	10.4	13.3
Easier market access	3.8	16.4	10.8
Cheaper production	3.8	3.0	3.3
Total responses[a]	53	67	
Location of new plants and factories (*N* = 62)			
Malaysia	48.0	35.1	40.3
Indonesia	20.0	10.8	14.5
Asian NIEs	12.0	8.1	9.7
N. America	0.0	10.8	6.5
European community	4.0	8.1	6.5
China	0.0	10.8	6.5
Philippines	0.0	8.1	4.8
Thailand	0.0	5.4	3.2
Brunei	4.0	0.0	1.6
Other SEA countries	0.0	2.7	1.6
Japan	0.0	0.0	0.0
Other countries	12.0	0.0	4.8
Total responses[a]	25	37	

Source: East-West Center Survey on Enterprise Strategy.

[a] Multiresponse item; total may exceed number of cases.

(1989) shows that the location element is embedded in a wider industry logic, where the organization and evolution of the industry defines
for individual firms the nature of supply linkages and the boundaries
for markets. This interplay of the two logics can be seen in the various
firm strategies adopted.

Location Strategies and Overseas Direct Investment

Historically, the movement of multinational corporations to Singapore in the middle to late 1960s, was part of the big wave of foreign investment to Third World countries. This movement of capital was, in part, a response to cost problems facing producers in First World countries (Froebel, Heinrichs, and Kreye 1980; Massey 1984; Dicken 1992). Confronted with increasing costs at home, the movement of production to cheaper production sites has been one important option for manufacturing capital. In the 1990s, with two decades of development and rising costs in the Asian NIEs, the stage is set for a further elaboration of the international division of labor in manufacturing, as capital moves from the Asian NIEs to other cheaper production locations. From the survey sample, 42.4 percent of the electronics subsample and 32.7 percent of the garment sample have set up factories in other countries in the last five years (see table 5.3). The smaller size, the lower involvement of foreign capital, and a local market orientation continue to keep garment manufacturers from investing overseas.

Problems associated with labor (lower wage costs [29.2 percent] and fewer labor problems [23.3 percent]) were cited as the main reasons for investing in plants and factories overseas (table 5.3). The cheapness and availability of land in foreign countries was mentioned as another major reason by 20.0 percent of the firms. Garment firms felt that the exchange rates of other countries also provided an incentive (17 percent). Electronics firms have also started locating plants overseas in anticipation of access to markets (16.4 percent). As a firm strategy, market access is particularly significant because these firms are driven not only by cost (which tends to be reactive) but also by demand or, more important, the anticipation of demand.

Examination of the location of overseas production sites shows interesting differences between the electronics and garment industries. Of the two, the electronics industry has a broader range of production sites. Investments in Malaysia, Indonesia, and the Asian NIEs reflect the growing importance of the region for electronics manufacture and partly explain the tendency for a regional division of labor to develop. One consequence is the emphasis on regional sourcing for components producers (Salih, Young, and Rasiah 1988). A small number of suppliers (10.8 percent) have already moved into China. Of the major markets for electronics, only North America and Europe have investments from firms in Singapore. With respect to the flow of investments between Japan and Singapore, it is only one-way: there are no Singapore electronics investments in Japan. The pattern of investment in offshore sites of garments is strongly regional, being concentrated particularly in Malaysia (48 percent), Indonesia (20 percent), and the Asian NIEs (12 percent).

Malaysia, Singapore's immediate neighbor, is the most popular locational choice for both industries, with 51.9 percent garment firms and 35.1 percent electronics firms investing in the country. Investment figures from the Malaysian Industrial Development Authority indicate that by 1989, Singapore had become the second biggest investor, after Japan, in textiles and textile products, accounting for 28.6 percent of total investments in this industry; in electronics and electronic products, Singapore investments accounted for 9.4 percent of total investments in Malaysia's electronics industry (Kamil, Pangestu, and Fredericks 1991). A recent case study of Singapore firms expanding their operations into Johor (the Malaysian state closest to Singapore) reveals a clear division of labor in firm operations. Managerial-professional, engineering-technical, and clerical-sales-advertising workers account for 27.1 percent of the workforce in Singapore-based operations but only 5.2 percent of operations in Johor. Clearly, 93.1 percent of the workforce of Singaporean firms in Johor are production workers (Tham 1992). Thus, the data suggest that production operations are moving to Malaysia, with service, technical, and management functions remaining in Singapore.

Technology Strategies

New technology in production has been given different roles by the popular and academic literature in management and the social sciences. When associated with the popular phrase "flexible production" (a term that describes a production situation incorporating automation, highly skilled labor, and a particular form of work organization), technology is seen to provide a competitive edge by increasing variation to suit consumer taste and by producing and delivering "just in time" (see, e.g., "Brace for Japan's hot new strategy"; Sayer and Walker 1992, 162–90). In the Singapore context, the state-sponsored push for increased automation in the late 1980s can be seen as an attempt to reduce labor requirements and to use labor more efficiently (see, e.g., *Straits Times*, 1988a; 1988b; 1988c). The survey data show that, as is

Table 5.4   Technology Investment Characteristics, by Type of Industry
(percentage of firms)

Characteristic	Garments	Electronics	Combined
Introduce new technology (N = 109)			
No	47.1	25.9	35.8
Yes	52.9	74.1	64.2
Total cases	51	58	
Reasons for technology[a] (N = 195)			
Increase output	25.0	21.8	23.1
Improve product quality	23.7	19.3	21.0
Cut labor costs	22.4	16.0	18.5
Produce new products	5.3	20.2	14.4
Reduce skilled labor	9.2	5.0	6.7
Cut material and energy costs	7.9	5.0	6.2
Reduce wage costs	2.6	5.0	4.1
Reduce supervisory costs	2.6	0.8	1.5
Save space	1.3	1.7	1.5
Other	0.0	5.0	3.1
Total responses[b]	76	119	
Type of technology invested in[a] (N = 150)			
Production technology	40.0	33.7	36.0
Design technology	16.4	25.3	22.0
Quality-control technology	21.8	21.1	21.3
Office technology	14.5	8.4	10.7
Inventory control technology	7.3	9.5	8.7
Other technology	0.0	2.1	1.3
Total responses[b]	55	95	

Source: East-West Center Survey on Enterprise Strategy.

[a] Only those firms that have invested in new technology.

[b] Multiresponse item; total may exceed number of cases.

the case for overseas investment, electronics firms are more able and willing than garment firms to introduce new technology. Approximately 74 percent of the firms in the electronics subsample indicated that they had introduced new technology in the past two years, compared to 52.9 percent of garment firms (see table 5.4).

While reducing labor costs is significant, other cost-cutting reasons (including reduced need for skilled labor [6.7 percent], wages [4.1 percent], supervisory costs [1.5 percent], and saving space [1.5 percent]) elicited low responses from both industries. Production considerations seem to provide the major incentive for the introduction of new technology in manufacturing. Major reasons cited include increasing output (23.1 percent), improving products (21.0 percent), and producing new products (14.4 percent). In terms of industry differences, it should be noted that the electronics industry is particularly driven by the need to develop and manufacture new products in decisions to introduce new technology (20.2 percent compared to 5.3 percent for garment firms). Thus, investments for electronics are mainly directed at production technology (33.7 percent), design technology (25.3 percent), and quality-control technologies (21.1 percent). While overseas investment is clearly a strategy to overcome some of the cost constraints of producing at home, the introduction of new technology seems to be driven more by production and demand than by cost.

Labor Utilization Strategies: Contracting, Overtime, and Foreign Labor

The most immediate way of adapting to a tight labor market is not by substituting labor with technology but in the labor utilization strategies adopted by firms in the two industries. One way of coping is to contract out less essential work processes, a strategy adopted by 72.5 percent of the firms surveyed (see table 5.5). The quality of work is guaranteed by a contract, and labor problems are transferred from the contracting firm to the contractor. The advantages of such a strategy can be seen from the responses summarized in table 5.5. Some 25.7 percent of the firms surveyed mentioned the labor shortage in Singapore as a reason for contracting out work. In a situation where product demand is volatile, contracting out work is an advantage, because output can be increased or decreased through contracts instead of by changes in the size and composition of the company's workforce. This advantage is cited by 18.6 percent of the firms as a reason for contracting out work. There is also a significant proportion (15.8 percent) who used contractors specialized in work not centrally related to the company's production (plant maintenance, security, transport, etc.). For garment firms in particular, subcontracting is an important way of adapting to the problem of labor shortage.

About 86.4 percent of the firms interviewed mentioned relying upon employees working overtime to cope with labor shortage. For 45.9 percent of the firms that used the overtime option, this was an essential mechanism for meeting production deadlines. Another 25.3 percent of

Table 5.5   Labor Utilization Stretegies Characteristics, by Type of Industry
(percentage of firms)

Characteristic	Garments	Electronics	Combined
Does company contract work? (N = 102)			
No	34.0	21.8	27.5
Yes	66.0	78.2	72.5
Total cases	47	55	
Reasons for contracting out (N = 183)			
Labor shortage	33.8	19.4	25.7
Fluctuating demand	18.8	18.4	18.6
Specialized skills	8.8	21.4	15.8
Lower admin. costs	10.0	12.6	11.5
Lower wage costs	7.5	13.6	10.9
No fringe benefits	15.0	2.9	8.2
Lower training costs	2.5	3.9	3.3
Other	3.8	7.8	6.0
Total responses[a]	80	103	
Does company use overtime work? (N = 110)			
No	15.7	11.9	13.6
Yes	84.3	88.1	86.4
Total cases	51	59	
Reasons for over time work (N = 146)			
Meet deadline	48.5	43.8	45.9
Inadequate labor supply	34.8	17.5	25.3
Increase in demand	13.6	32.5	24.0
Other reasons	3.0	6.3	4.8
Total responses[a]	66	80	
Does company use foreign workers? (N = 109)			
Yes	80.0	81.4	80.7
No	20.0	18.6	19.3
Total Cases	50	59	
Reasons for using foreign workers? (N = 87)			
Labor shortage	46.5	54.5	50.6
Work unpopular shifts	46.5	31.8	39.1
Lower wages and fewer benefits	7.0	9.1	8.0
More suited for job	0.0	2.3	1.1
Other	0.0	2.3	1.1
Total cases	43	44	

Source: East-West Center Survey on Enterprise Strategy.

[a] Multiresponse item; total may exceed number of cases.

the sampled firms said that the use of overtime was a way of coping with the shortage of labor. The use of overtime to meet production deadlines may also be a reflection of the labor shortage, the result of having a smaller pool of workers. The frequent dependence on overtime to cope with production deadlines is a reflection of this situation. In contrast, a production situation that has some slack in terms of labor utilization can afford to use this surplus to meet deadlines without resorting to overtime. Some firms have reacted to this situation by "hoarding" labor during a downturn. By keeping surplus labor even when production volumes do not justify the numbers, they have sufficient workers to keep pace with production when the upturn begins.

An equally high proportion of firms (80.7 percent) used foreign workers to supplement the local workforce. The current labor shortage was mentioned as a major factor causing this (50.6 percent). Another 39.1 percent of firms mentioned the willingness of such workers to work unpopular shifts and assignments as a reason for hiring foreign workers. Hiring foreign workers is not without its attendant problems, but, interestingly, the problems mentioned by firms have not so much to do with the workers themselves (e.g., attitudes of workers) but with the cost (e.g., levy and housing) and institutional restrictions (e.g., approvals and quotas).

Considering the data presented in the five tables, two factors are consistently considered important in determining various firm strategies. Labor costs and labor shortages have pushed wage rates up and have affected business adversely. Labor-related issues have also been a major factor encouraging foreign direct investment, particularly in Malaysia and Indonesia. Faced with the tight domestic labor market, companies have also been forced to supplement their workforces with foreign labor and to rely on overtime work.

Of the two industries, garment firms, as labor-intensive and lower-value-added manufacturers facing increasing competition from low-wage countries, have had more difficulties adjusting to the problem of higher costs. As these firms tend to be much smaller operations and are mostly fully locally owned, they are more likely to remain in Singapore in spite of higher costs. Their small scale and the nature of garment production also constrain the use of technology as an option. Of the three types of strategies, garment firms are most likely to vary the use of labor as a response to industrial restructuring. These firms contract out work as a way of keeping various costs (e.g., employee benefits) down and as a way to cope with the labor shortage. The use of overtime and foreign workers are also important means to deal with the labor problem.

In the 1960s, when there was high unemployment in Singapore, the garment industry played an important role as an employment generator. Since the late 1970s, it has been a victim of high labor costs, the result of the government's high-wage policy designed to replace low-end with high-value-added manufacturing. The state's industry-specific policies—the encouragement of electronics and other capital- and skill-intensive industries and the lack of support for others, including garments—can be seen in table 5.6. At the same time, garment manufacturers have faced increased competition from overseas, as the industry has relatively low entry costs. The garment industry is also under international regulation through the Multifibre Arrangement (MFA), which sets limits on exports from various countries to the major markets (Choi, Chung, and Marian 1985). Such arrangements tend to increase the participation of countries in the global economy but restrict the relative export contribution of individual countries. At the firm level, the presence of the MFA means that expansion or increase in profits can only occur by moving to less restrictive categories in the MFA or into new export markets. Such restrictions are particularly inhibiting for the Singaporean firm, since experimentation with new product lines may be difficult to realize because of the small domestic market and forays into new markets seem limited to neighboring countries (see table 5.3), given the inherent costs associated with discovering tastes and forming marketing and sales linkages.

The electronics industry in Singapore tells a different story. The industry is continuing to enjoy a growing demand, a demand that is being driven by incremental innovations in technology and design. Thus, it is not surprising that electronics firms in Singapore perceive a robust demand for their products (see table 5.1) and are likely to invest in production technologies that expand output and create new products (see table 5.4). The greater spread of overseas investment in Southeast Asia is also a sign of the concentration of the electronics industry in the region. Since the mid-1970s, the electronics industry has grown rapidly in Malaysia to become the largest offshore semiconductor production facility in the world. By 1983, the Philippines had overtaken Singapore in terms of semiconductor exports to the United States. Singapore may still be a major center for consumer and industrial electronics, but many multinational corporations have diversified production operations into Malaysia as part of the restructuring process. Investments in

Table 5.6   Industrialists' Evaluation of Support from the Public Sector by Type of
Industry (percentage of firms)

Characteristic[a]	Garments	Electronics	Combined
Access to loans			
Supportive	47.6	64.3	57.1
Unsupportive	52.4	35.7	42.9
Infrastructure provision			
Supportive	69.2	93.0	84.1
Unsupportive	30.8	7.0	15.9
Access to markets			
Supportive	62.5	62.5	62.5
Unsupportive	37.5	37.5	37.5
Information sharing and consultation			
Supportive	68.4	82.8	77.1
Unsupportive	31.6	17.2	22.9
R&D support			
Supportive	29.4	67.6	54.9
Unsupportive	70.6	32.4	45.1
Business regulations			
Supportive	23.1	61.5	42.3
Unsupportive	76.9	38.5	57.7
Industrial relations			
Supportive	60.0	90.0	80.0
Unsupportive	40.0	10.0	20.0
Regulating labor			
Supportive	6.7	19.4	13.6
Unsupportive	93.3	80.6	86.4
Upgrading worker skills			
Supportive	72.7	93.0	86.2
Unsupportive	27.3	7.0	13.8
Regulating land			
Supportive	6.7	19.4	13.6
Unsupportive	93.3	80.6	86.4
Most urgent attention needed on			
Access to loans	9.3	9.3	9.3
Infrastructure	2.3	1.9	2.1
Market access	9.3	13.0	11.3
Info sharing/consultancy	2.3	0.0	1.0
R&D support	2.3	1.9	2.1
Business laws	16.3	3.7	9.3
Regulating labor	55.8	61.1	58.8
Skills upgrading	0.0	1.9	1.0
Regulating land	2.3	7.4	5.2
Total cases (N)	43	54	97

Source: East-West Center Survey on Enterprise Strategy.

[a] Companies that mentioned "neutral" are excluded.

television, radio cassette recorders, and computer components production have also been strong in Thailand (UNCTC 1987).

The clustering of the industry within Southeast Asia shows a clear division of labor based on the logics of cost and sophistication (capital and skill intensity), with Singapore at the apex, Malaysia in the middle, and Thailand, the Philippines, and Indonesia at the low-cost, labor-intensive end. One result of this clustering is the increasing regional sourcing of components, away from the United States and Japan (Salih, Young, and Rasiah 1988). Electronic multinationals have started centering their purchasing arms in Singapore, and the entrepot trading in electronic components has been increasing (Ho 1991; Singapore 1994). Thus, the interindustry differences in firm responses have to be understood within the logic of a particular industry's organization and Singapore's position within this organization.

State Policy and Restructuring

Any examination of enterprise strategy has to take into account the efforts of the state to improve local and overseas business environments. Table 5.6 is a record of how firms in the sample survey perceived the effectiveness of the government in various policy domains. The public sector is generally seen to be supportive of business in infrastructure (84.1 percent), the upgrading of worker skills (86.2 percent), the sharing of information (77.1 percent), and industrial relations (80 percent). As anticipated, firms' frustration over rising labor and land costs is made obvious by their perception that the public sector is unsupportive of business in attempts to regulate labor (86.4 percent) and land (76.5 percent). Businesses also expressed dissatisfaction with public sector support in business regulations (57.2 percent), research and development support (45.1 percent), and access to markets (37.5 percent). There is a corresponding broad consensus on labor as the most urgent issue that the state needs to tackle.

More garment firms than electronics firms believe that the public sector is generally unsupportive in the ten policy areas listed in table 5.6. In an interesting way, the sentiments expressed in the survey illustrate the tensions described earlier in this chapter. The different opinions expressed by representatives of the two industries may be traced back to a belief that Singapore is experiencing a zero-sum situation, where resource allocation can benefit one sector only at the expense of others. The high-wage policy that was to redistribute labor to high-value-added industries had severe affects on the garment industry, because it is labor-intensive and produces relatively low-value-added products. At the same time, its labor intensity and its low-value-added nature makes this an ideal industry for new economies emerging in the global marketplace. Thus, while the garment industry faces domestic difficulties in securing labor, it is also experiencing increasing competition from lower-cost producers in these countries. This can be seen from the industry's responses given in table 5.1.

The frustration of manufacturers over labor and land costs may belie the government's role in managing an environment conducive for business. In Won Bae Kim's analysis (chapter 9, this volume) of management opinions of government support over a range of issues (including infrastructural provision, access to loans, information and consultation, and regulation and laws) among the Asian NIEs, Singapore is the Asian NIE with the highest satisfaction scores regarding government support. In the case of labor, for example, the government has made various attempts—increasing female labor-force participation, encouraging part-time employment, extending the retirement age of workers—to increase the domestic labor supply. Of these attempts, the targeting of women workers seems to have been most effective. The female labor force participation rate increased from 29.5 percent in 1970 to 44.3 percent in 1980, growing to 48.4 percent in 1990; even so, this has been offset by a slight decline in the male participation rate. As a result, the overall labor-force participation between 1980 and 1990 hovered at around 63 percent (Singapore 1991b).

Faced with a slow-growing domestic labor force, firms have expressed a greater willingness to supplement their workforce by using foreign labor rather than part-time labor or older workers. Managers argue that foreign workers are less likely to job-hop, because work permits limit their mobility. Moreover, firms claim that foreign workers are preferred because of their positive work attitudes (including willingness to work extra hours and night shifts), higher education levels, and relative youth. Electronics companies, for instance, find it difficult to use older workers to assemble miniature components, which is an essential part of the production process (*Straits Times* 1989a).

Alarmed by the rapid growth in the number of foreign workers in the late 1970s and early 1980s, the government considered phasing out the dependence on unskilled foreign workers by 1990 (Pang and Lim 1982). The concern was that the presence of a large foreign-worker population might cause social and political problems (Singapore

1986b). Given the inherent inflexibility of part-time and older workers and the pressure from manufacturers to use foreign labor as a means of keeping costs down, the government's original position in the late 1970s and early 1980s of viewing the use of foreign workers as a temporary stopgap measure has changed to one that allows for a carefully controlled intake. In 1989, the labor minister, while continuing to caution against an overreliance of foreign workers, mentioned, as government policy, the use of foreign workers as a buffer to even out swings of the business cycle (*Straits Times* 1989b). Most significant, the 1991 Strategic Economic Plan advocated the use of foreign workers as a strategy to overcome labor imbalances (Singapore 1991b). Accordingly, the government has developed more indirect foreign-worker policies by using the foreign-worker levy and quotas to constrain the growth in numbers. The size of the levy and quota differs between skilled and unskilled workers and also varies for different industries.

The state-initiated push toward greater factory automation was conceived as a way of escaping the problem of overdependence on foreign labor. Specially targeted at smaller firms and those relying on foreign labor, the automation effort is supported by a number of low-interest loans and leasing and consultancy schemes. A 1989–90 survey commissioned by the Singapore Industrial Automation Association (SIAA), covering 995 companies from a broad spectrum of industries, revealed that, with the exception of standard production machines (e.g., power presses, machines tools, injection molding machines), the use of other types of automated equipment (e.g., computer numerical control machinery, industrial robots, programmable process-control equipment) remained very low. The survey found that between 70 and 98 percent of the companies surveyed had no intention of obtaining these types of automated equipment (SIAA 1990). Some of the reasons companies gave for refraining from undertaking automation projects remained consistent for the two surveys commissioned in 1987–88 and 1989–90. The most important reason for not undertaking automation was the high cost of automation investment and the uncertain returns for such expenditures. This reason seems well founded. One conservative estimate indicated that at $100,000 per robot installation and a savings of one worker at $1,000 per month working on two shifts, the payback period was slightly over four years (*Straits Times* 1987). Of course, many robotic installations cost more than $100,000.

Thus, while the automation push is designed to resolve the problems of the tight labor market, it seems that automation effort and the labor situation in Singapore are linked in contradictory ways. On the one hand, while wage levels in Singapore are rising, these new levels are still not high enough to shorten the period of return on automation investments so that companies are willing to invest. And at the same time, the shortage of trained personnel in Singapore acts as a key impediment to automation efforts.

The examination of state action with respect to labor costs reveals that it was not the lack of state effort, but resource exhaustion, stemming from Singapore's small size and maturing economy, that kept production costs climbing. In this sense, by the mid-1980s the government had done all it could do to keep domestic business conditions from becoming even more adverse. A logical move for the state to maintain competitiveness was to take some of the pressure off resources by encouraging a regional division of labor, where labor-intensive and low-value-added activities were encouraged to shift to lower-wage and land-rich neighboring countries, while maintaining control (i.e., management operations) and keeping services (e.g., sales, training, advertising) and higher-end production activities at home. This is what happened in the late 1980s with the triangle-of-growth concept involving Singapore's immediate neighbors, Malaysia and Indonesia.

The growth triangle cooperative arrangements between the three sovereign nations is important because it marked a shift in state action—from maintaining a domestic business environment conducive to capital investment to active regional cooperation between states. Significantly, on the Singapore side, a major part of the arrangement involves utilizing the expertise of various government-linked companies (GLCs) in financing, building, and managing infrastructural provisions like new towns (e.g., the Chee Tat estate project in southern Johor, Malaysia [*Business Times* 1991a]) and industrial parks (e.g., the Batam Industrial Park [*Business Times* 1991c]).

Such strategies necessitate some rethinking about the role notionally assigned to the state in the industrial growth and restructuring literatures. The concept of the developmental state was formulated to capture a notion of a state that actively intervenes in order to initiate and sustain development. As argued by Johnson (1987), Rodan (1989) and Wade (1990b), the developmental state does not just take a background role as regulator and provider of public goods but actively intervenes to circumvent various problems in the developmental process instead of relying on market adjustments. The developmental state can also be a corporatist arrangement where the state acts as a broker to foster cooperative relations between capital and labor.

Singapore's role in the growth triangle arrangement adds a new element to this conceptualization. By investing directly overseas, the state is acting in a new role as entrepreneur. Several related developments in the late 1980s and in 1990 reinforce this idea of Singapore as an entrepreneurial state. In 1989, Temasek Holdings, the state's investment arm, entered into a partnership with a local company, Yeo Hiap Seng, to purchase an American food company, Chun King (*Business Times* 1992a). In the same year, Singapore Airlines, Singapore's biggest GLC, invested about US$180 million in the United States' Delta Airlines (*Business Times* 1991d). More recently, spurred by its success in the growth triangle projects, the government announced its intention to develop an industrial estate in Fujian, China, about ten times the size of the one it developed in Batam, Indonesia (*Business Times* 1992c).

These examples illustrate an emerging policy agenda of the 1990s. While the emphasis of managing the state's financial resources continues to be on portfolio assets (shares, bonds, and debentures) in order to ensure a high rate of return to Singapore's foreign reserves, attention is now focused on the use of direct investments overseas to maintain Singapore's competitiveness (*Straits Times* 1991b). The Economic Development Board (EDB) describes this policy in terms of strategic investments, defined as those which increase business opportunities for Singapore (Singapore 1992). Between late 1988 and 1991, about S$2 billion of international direct investment was made. The *Business Times* (1991d) estimated that 70 percent could have come from the Singapore government and GLCs. The direct participation of the state in business ventures abroad is intended to have a demonstrative effect on local firms. The EDB has extended the Local Enterprise Finance Scheme to provide low-interest loans of up to S$5 million to help local companies buy equipment and industrial facilities outside Singapore (*Business Times* 1992b). A related program allows for tax exemptions on income received from overseas ventures, while any capital losses incurred can be fully written off for tax purposes (*Straits Times* 1991c).

This notion of a Singapore entrepreneurial state (as suggested by the Singapore government's involvement) goes beyond Eisinger's (1988) and Amsden's (1989) illustration of the concept. Eisinger's discussion centered on how, at the subnational level, local and state governments in the United States have been engaged in limited, sporadic, and experimental efforts at boosting local employment and revenue by implementing policies designed to encourage small local businesses, to establish overseas markets, and to fund research and development activities. The difference lies not in the range and scale of activities but, more important, in the active involvement of the government in foreign direct investment through government-linked companies. The activity of the Singapore government is thus entrepreneurial in the sense that it is a closer approximation to the function that Eisinger (1988, 9) attributes to the entrepreneurial state: "to identify, evaluate, anticipate, and even help to develop and create . . . markets for private producers to exploit, aided if necessary by government as subsidizer or coinvestor."

Amsden (1989) expands on the Schumpeterian notion to capture the entrepreneurial function of planning assumed by the state in Korea. This includes the perception of new opportunities, control over resources, supervision, and coordination. While both Korea and Singapore assume this role, the difference lies in the direct nature of Singapore state involvement in the economy via GLCs. With the divestment of state-owned enterprises under a South Korean–American agreement in 1954 (Cheng 1990), the Korean state has exerted control indirectly through the national banking system, restriction of entry to new industries, price controls, and regulation (Amsden 1989). More important, the Singapore state assumes the entrepreneurial role in its readiness to deploy state planning agencies as frontline troops in seeking new investment opportunities abroad, as indicated by involvements in China, Malaysia and Indonesia.

These initiatives in expanding the external economy have important implications for firm strategy. While firms in Singapore have historically a strong working relationship with the state (see table 5.6), it is becoming increasingly clear that Singaporean state initiatives overseas will foster an even tighter coupling between state and firm strategy. The examples of state sponsorship of overseas ventures provided here not only involve large sums of money but necessitate close working arrangements, information sharing, and accountability of enterprise to the state. Enterprises that are beneficiaries of such schemes realize crucial advantages in financial backing. Firms (smaller ones in particular) may also enjoy a number of public goods provided by earlier state initiatives overseas—the cooperation of local officials, access to factory sites and amenities (especially when the Singaporean government is involved in infrastructural projects), information sharing regarding local production conditions—strategic relationships and market intelligence that are vital elements in establishing production and sales sites overseas. The nature of the corporatist arrangement between state and local capital and the mutual learning process that results can also be appreciated by the fact that overseas investment missions typically involve a team of high-level government officials and corporate managers.

Future Prospects

One hundred and forty-five years after Mundy's description, Singapore still performs a role similar to "a shop opened in a crowded thoroughfare" (quoted in Turnbull 1972, 162). As the city-state has changed from an entrepot to a production center and now increasingly to a regional financial and operations center, the strategies of firms operating in Singapore have also changed accordingly. Some of these changes in firm activities have been in response to state policies crafted to achieve desired structural transformation of the economy. For the state, development policy has increasingly shifted outward to regional and international investments as a way of overcoming the constraints of limited resources and a maturing economy.

As this role of the entrepreneurial state deepens and the volume of direct international investments increases, several issues have emerged. At the organizational level, an important question is whether GLC managers can cope with the new demands of managing overseas investment projects—a function very different from portfolio management (Krause 1989). Indeed, the finance minister recently acknowledged that the main constraints on acquiring and participating in the running of overseas companies are knowledge and personnel to oversee these direct investments (*Straits Times* 1991a).

Another issue is whether foreign direct investment will have the desired benefits to the wider population of Singapore. Will local labor and subcontractors linked to existing production operations of multinational corporations benefit from this exercise? This question is tied to a number of other issues, one of which is whether a technical and sectoral division of labor can be effectively created out of this process. Investments closer to Singapore, like the ones within the growth triangle region, will provide the proximity necessary to ensure this division will benefit local labor and capital. The investments further away may not necessarily maintain this division. A related question is whether these types of investment outflows eventually return to Singapore. A crucial distinction is between GLCs and private capital. The GLCs, because of their direct links to the state, can be effective instruments that will ensure that strategic investments will enhance the growth of the domestic economy.

Such successes of the entrepreneurial state at the economic front will have to be balanced by more diplomatic actions on the political front. The experience of the growth triangle arrangement between Singapore, Malaysia, and Indonesia has shown that it is difficult to maintain the perception that all parties benefit equally by maximizing the comparative advantages of individual countries, when the economic logic creates a division of labor that spreads economic activities unevenly among the three countries. While the political leadership of the three countries remains committed to the cooperative arrangement, concerns have been raised about the possibility of Johor (the Malaysian state participating in the triangle) and Riau (the chain of Indonesian islands involved) becoming the hinterland and industrial backyard of Singapore and developing closer relations with Singapore than with their respective countries (Kamil, Pangestu, and Fredericks 1991; Pangestu, 1991). This problem may not necessarily evaporate as investment moves further offshore, since the political issues accompanying foreign direct investment are obviously magnified when the state is involved. This is the case even with indirect state involvement, as, for example, where the government-linked corporations are operated as profit-making ventures.

If these difficult issues are managed and kept from being divisive, then Singaporean firms, in addition to technology and labor strategies, will find greater latitude to maneuver in planning their locational choices as the entrepreneurial state reduces the uncertainties of doing business abroad.

Seoul, Korea: City and Suburbs

Sam Ock Park

Seoul has been the capital city of Korea for six hundred years, and accordingly the Seoul metropolitan area has developed as a national core. During the last three decades, the Seoul metropolitan area has experienced dynamic industrial changes and has developed as the primary industrial core of Korea. Industrial changes within this area have been so dramatic that a comparison between the city of Seoul and its suburbs, Kyonggi and Inchon, provides a distinctive story of Korean industrial restructuring. There are considerable differences in the pattern and process of industrial restructuring and adjustments within the Seoul metropolitan area, differences that have been explored with the examination of firm strategies in the process of industrial restructuring.

After a quarter century of continuous growth, Korean industry is now confronted with several problems in regard to international competitiveness and industrial restructuring. Firm strategy has become more important in the process of industrial restructuring since the late 1980s. During the period of rapid industrialization in the 1960s, 1970s, and early 1980s, the role of the state was critical for industrial change and spatial restructuring in Korea (Markusen and Park 1993; Park 1991; Song 1990). The role of the state is still very important in industrial restructuring, with the government managing industrial changes and promoting both sectoral and spatial industrial policy in Korea. However, the government in its role as entrepreneur was not omnipotent when the competitive advantages associated with low wages became vulnerable to several external and internal factors. These factors include severe competition in the international market with the rise of lower-cost economies of Southeast Asia and China, price and exchange rate fluctuations, increasing wages, and labor shortages in production.

Firm strategies aimed at controlling labor, reorganizing the production system, changing locations of production facilities, and developing technology have become relatively more important and independent in Korea since the late 1980s. In the late 1980s, rapid increases in wages, serious labor disputes, currency revaluation, high financial costs, a decline in the rate increase in labor-productivity, and a shortage of production workers were the major triggers of industrial restructuring in the Seoul metropolitan area (Park 1994). Confronted with the erosion of competitive advantages in the labor-intensive industries in Korea, firms have responded dynamically in the restructuring process according to firm size, industry type, and local characteristics. This dynamic restructuring process embraces or combines technological changes, organizational transformation, and changes in the local labor market. Because of these dynamics, industries and industrial landscapes do not evolve according to fixed developmental trajectories; rather, they go through a dynamic process of change, transformation, and reorganization (Florida and Kenney 1992).

This chapter investigates dynamic firm strategy in the process of industrial restructuring in the city of Seoul and its suburbs. Information was gathered from questionnaire surveys. For convenience, the Inchon and Kyonggi region, which surrounds the city of Seoul, is regarded as the suburban area of Seoul. Because structural changes and major triggers of industrial restructuring in the Seoul metropolitan area have been examined in previous studies (Park 1993a; 1994), firm strategies on labor, production organization, location, and technology are the major concerns here. A unique story of city and suburbs is described through the examination of the effects of firm size, industry type, and local characteristics on dynamic firm strategies.

Firm Size, Industry Type, and Region in Firm's Competitive Strategy

Firm size, industry type, and local characteristics are significant variables affecting the dynamic process of industrial restructuring. Sometimes these factors may not be mutually exclusive and, rather, are interrelated to each other in firm strategies on labor, business organization, location, and technology in the process of industrial restructuring.

Firm size has been regarded as one of the most significant variables in industrial location. Furthermore, firm size is an important variable in determining the significance of sunk costs (Clark and Wrigley, forthcoming). Small firms may be more dependent on the external labor market and external economies with low fixed and sunk costs, while large management-controlled corporations may be more dependent on economies of scale and scope and less flexible in short-term adjustment because of relatively high fixed and sunk costs. Small firms seem to be more able to respond to changes in design and fashion, whereas large firms with higher sunk costs might be slow and long-term oriented in their competitive strategy. Gereffi and Korzeniewicz (1990), for example, emphasize the size of firms in the consequences for the capture and consolidation of market niches in the footwear industry. With differences in fixed and sunk costs, externalities and flexibilities in operation, firm strategies on technology, labor, location, and production organization are assumed to be different according to the size of firm. In this chapter, firms with more than 300 employees are regarded as large firms. There is no generally accepted definition of large firms according to the size of employment, but, in Korea, firms with fewer than 300 employees are officially regarded as small and medium in size. Firms with fewer than 60 employees are regarded as small in this chapter.

Industry type is also an important variable affecting various firm strategies in the process of industrial restructuring. Industry type is frequently related to the ratio of labor to capital. Firms' competitive strategies in the labor-intensive industries can be different from those of capital-intensive industries. Labor-intensive industries are more sensitive to changes in labor costs and labor supply and are vulnerable in their competitive advantages in an environment of rapidly rising labor costs and labor shortages. Capital-intensive industries may have difficulties in responding immediately to external changes due to their high fixed and sunk costs.

The garment and electronics industries are both regarded as labor-intensive industries. However, the electronics industry is not a typical labor-intensive industry like the garment industry—it lies somewhere between typical labor-intensive and capital-intensive industries. The garment industry has the lowest values in both acquisition of fixed assets per employee and cumulative acquisition of fixed assets per employee in Korea, revealing that the industry is a typical labor-intensive industry. However, the values for the electronics industry are similar to the averages of the total manufacturing sector. Values of acquisition of fixed assets per employee (in million won) were 0.7, 5.0, and 4.9 for the garment industry, the electronics industry, and total manufacturing respectively in 1989. Values of cumulative acquisition of fixed assets per employee (in million won) were 3.8, 15.8, and 19.1 for garment, electronics, and total manufacturing industries respectively in 1989. Even though the electronics industry is midway between labor-intensive and capital-intensive industries, the differences in the capital-to-labor ratio between the garment and electronics industries will result in different competitive strategies with regard to labor, production organization, location, and technology.

Local characteristics can also be a significant variable affecting firm strategy in the process of industrial restructuring; regions can be a part of the competitive strategy of firms. Clark (1993a, 20–21) identifies three ways in which regions have strategic value for firms: (1) as sites of flexible adjustment and in situ restructuring with respect to potential new competition; (2) as sites of experimentation and innovation; and (3) by virtue of their capacity to link management and finance efficiently. In addition, in a given industry, firm strategy in restructuring can be different by regions because regions have different institutional and social environments, which determine the social relation of production (W. B. Kim 1993b, 42). As a consequence, firms' strategies interact with local characteristics and accordingly are differentiated by geography.

Seoul has been the center of national political power, education, finance, and management for a long time. In the early industrialization stage, Seoul was also a center of manufacturing in Korea. Because of the dominance of Seoul in relation to these functions, the Korean population has become overwhelmingly concentrated in this city in the last three decades. Various government policies have focused directly on the control of population growth in the city, while industrial dispersal policies implemented since the 1970s have also been related to the control of Seoul's population growth. Restrictions on industrial location in Seoul have resulted in the rapid industrial growth of the suburbs and in the shift of industrial dominance from the city to the suburbs. The decentralization of production functions, especially branch plants, also resulted in a spatial division of labor within the Seoul metropolitan area. For example, more than 85 percent of corporate headquarters with spatially separated manufacturing plants are concentrated in Seoul (Park 1985). Because of these special regional characteristics of Seoul, there may exist significant differences in firm's competitive strategy with regard to labor, production organization, location, and technology between firms located in Seoul and those in the suburban areas of Inchon and Kyonggi.

Structural Transformation of Industries

In the early industrialization phase of the 1960s, the city of Seoul was the center of industrial growth in Korea. Since the beginning of the 1970s, the rate of industrial growth in Seoul, however, has continually been lower than the national average, while that of the suburbs has been much higher than the national average. In 1975, Seoul's proportion of the national total employed in the manufacturing sector was about 34 percent. This figure decreased to 22 percent in 1990, whereas the share of Inchon and Kyonggi increased from 17 percent in 1975 to 29 percent in 1990. The relative industrial decline in Seoul and the growth in the suburbs are related to government's sectoral and locational policies.

Since the end of the 1960s, decentralization of industries from Seoul has been strategically promoted because of the overconcentration of population in the city. Several industrial parks were established in the suburbs of Seoul in the early 1970s, to which many plants were relocated. The government also established several local industrial estates in the provincial areas, but the dispersal effect from Seoul to provincial areas was almost negligible in the early 1970s. Heavy and chemical industrial promotion policy in the 1970s resulted in rapid industrial growth in the southeastern coastal region, with the establishment of large industrial complexes. High-tech industrial policy in the 1980s further promoted industrial decentralization from Seoul to its suburbs. Because of legal restrictions on industrial location or expansion in Seoul, most high-tech firms established branch plants in the suburbs or relocated plants to the suburbs while retaining headquarters in Seoul (Park 1987). Most high-tech firms wanted to stay in the Seoul metropolitan area, where high-tech engineers and managers could commute from Seoul. Most high-tech laborers and managers did not want to leave Seoul because of the disruptions such a move would cause to their children's education and the cultural and social attractiveness of the city.

During the spatial restructuring process resulting from sectoral and locational policies, contrasting industrial structures have evolved between Seoul and its suburbs. The dominant industry type of the nation and suburbs of Seoul shifted from labor-intensive industries to assembly industries (which include technology-intensive industries). Based on factor analysis and cluster analysis of structural variables of the Korean industries, twenty-eight industries of Korean Standard Industrial Classification (KSIC) three-digit level were classified as five industry types (for details, see Park (1993b)). In Inchon and Kyonggi, the proportion of the labor-intensive industries decreased continuously from 38.5 percent in 1975 to 17.8 percent in 1990, while the proportion of assembly industries increased continuously from 29.7 percent in 1975 to 59.1 percent in 1990 (table 6.1). The Inchon and Kyonggi region has a greater concentration of assembly industries than the national average which was 45.2 percent in 1990. While the trend of industrial transformation of the suburbs is consistent with that of the whole nation, the case of Seoul is a different story.

The development of technology-intensive industries in Seoul began in the early 1970s. In 1975, the proportion of assembly industries was 32.6 percent, and the proportion of electrical machinery industries (SIC 383) was 15.6 percent, both considerably greater than the figures for the suburbs (see table 6.1). The proportion of assembly and technology-intensive industries in Seoul has not changed much since that time, and accordingly its share of those industries is currently much less than that of the suburbs. The proportion of labor-intensive industries has not decreased much (it is still about 35 percent), indicating that Seoul has a relatively high proportion of such industries.

The industrial structure of Seoul has remained relatively stable during the last two decades and seems to be unique compared to its suburbs and other areas of the nation. The unique characteristics of Seoul's industrial structure are more obvious in the dominant industry among the twenty-eight industries at the three-digit level of the KSIC. In 1975, the garment industry was the dominant industry in Seoul. Since the late 1970s, however, the garment industry has taken over as the city's dominant industry, with the proportion of that industry located in Seoul currently more than 20 percent. Inchon and Kyonggi were homes of large proportions of the garment industry in 1975, but since the end of the 1970s, the region has been infiltrated by the electrical machinery and electronics industry.

Even though the proportion of the electrical and electronics ma-

Table 6.1   Industrial Structure of Seoul and Its Suburbs, by Type of Industry
(percentage)

Industry	Seoul				Inchon and Kyonggi			
	1975	*1980*	*1985*	*1990*	*1975*	*1980*	*1985*	*1990*
N[a]	334	541	602	685	168	443	597	906
Resource								
Food	6.5	6.2	5.9	5.5	5.4	4.8	5.8	4.8
Wood products	0.8	0.7	0.7	0.4	5.7	4.7	2.6	2.2
Paper	1.9	1.8	1.7	1.4	4.2	3.2	2.8	2.5
Petroleum coal products	0.8	0.6	0.4	0.6	0.2	0.2	0.2	0.2
Nonmetal products	1.5	1.7	2.0	1.4	2.9	3.3	3.3	2.6
Nonferrous products	0.2	1.1	0.2	0.5	0.9	0.7	0.7	0.8
Total	11.7	12.1	10.9	9.8	19.3	16.9	15.4	13.1
Assembly								
Leather	2.1	1.9	1.6	2.1	2.7	1.8	1.8	2.0
Furniture	0.4	0.6	0.4	0.3	0.9	1.8	3.1	3.0
Plastic	1.6	2.7	3.1	3.4	1.1	2.2	4.1	4.6
Fabrication metal	5.3	6.0	5.4	5.5	5.1	7.0	9.9	8.8
Machinery	3.7	4.3	5.0	7.2	4.6	5.4	5.9	9.1
Electrical and electronics	15.6	14.9	14.1	15.5	11.8	17.2	19.0	22.3
Transportation equipment	2.2	2.5	2.5	2.5	2.7	3.2	3.5	7.8
Professional goods	1.7	1.8	1.4	1.4	0.8	2.1	1.7	1.4
Total	32.6	34.7	33.5	37.9	29.7	40.7	49.1	59.1
Labor-intensive								
Textiles	17.7	11.1	10.0	8.0	22.0	13.6	9.9	7.6
Apparel	11.3	16.6	20.9	20.7	10.2	7.4	6.7	3.4
Footwear	—	1.5	1.2	1.0	—	1.4	1.5	1.0
Rubber	1.9	1.5	0.7	1.0	1.0	0.9	0.8	0.9
Other industries	7.4	4.8	6.0	4.2	5.3	5.5	5.6	4.9
Total	38.3	35.5	38.8	34.9	38.5	28.8	24.4	17.8
Capital-intensive								
Industrial chemicals	1.0	1.2	0.9	1.1	1.5	1.2	1.9	1.5
Petroleum refining	0.4	0.3	0.4	0.6	0.4	0.3	0.2	0.1
Iron and steel	1.7	0.8	1.2	0.8	3.2	2.3	1.1	1.3
Total	3.1	2.3	2.5	2.4	5.1	3.8	3.2	2.8
Special								
Beverages	1.7	1.8	0.7	0.4	0.4	0.9	0.5	0.7
Tobacco	0.0	0.0	0.0	0.0	0.0	0.0	0.0	0.1
Printing	5.0	6.8	7.3	9.5	0.4	0.8	0.8	0.9
Other chemicals	6.4	5.8	5.6	4.3	3.8	4.8	3.9	3.8
Pottery	0.1	0.3	0.2	0.1	1.0	1.7	0.7	0.4
Glass	1.2	0.9	0.5	0.7	1.9	1.4	1.9	1.4
Total	14.4	15.6	14.3	15.0	7.5	9.6	7.8	7.2

Source: Korea (1976, 1981, 1986, and 1991).

[a] N is the number of workers employed in manufacturing, in thousands.

chinery industry with respect to total manufacturing in Seoul has not changed greatly, Seoul's share of the national electrical machinery and electronics industry decreased from 50 percent in the mid-1970s to 22 percent in 1990. Before the mid-1970s, Seoul was the center of the electrical machinery and electronics industry in Korea. However, this is no longer the case. Instead, Seoul has become the center of the Korean garment industry. Seoul's share of the national garment industry has increased continuously and is now approximately 58 percent. The Inchon and Kyonggi region has emerged as the center of the electrical machinery and electronics industry in Korea since the early 1980s, with more than 42 percent of the national electrical machinery and electronics industry located in the region.

Primary Findings of the Survey

The questionnaire surveys were conducted in August and December of 1992. The major contents of each survey were questions related to technology, labor costs, labor supply and turnover, subcontracting, investment decisions, and future plans. The surveys were implemented by direct visits to individual firms, using the predesigned survey format common to all the studies reported in this volume (and reproduced in the appendix). In the first survey (conducted in August 1992), 205 Seoul-based garment and electronics firms were selected by stratified random sampling from the Korea Business Directory (Korea 1992). Of the 205 selected firms, only 120 responded to the survey (about 50 firms could not be contacted, and some firms refused to respond). Because of the insufficient number of responses, a second survey was conducted in December 1992. In the second survey, 250 sample firms were selected in the same way; of these, 137 firms responded. All 257 responding firms were analyzed in this study. Of the 257 responding firms, 68 could not be categorized as either garment or electronics industries, because their major products were more typical of the machinery or other industrial sectors.

The distribution of the responding firms by size, industry type, and region in the year of establishment is shown in table 6.2. In general, more than half the large firms were established before 1969, whereas more than a half the small firms were established after 1986, revealing a significant correlation between the size and age of firms. Firms in the garment industry are, in general, slightly older than firms in the electronics industries. Even though there are no significant differences in

Table 6.2   Year of Establishment by Region, Number of Employees, and Type
of Industry (percentage of firms)

| | | Year of Establishment | | | |
| | | Cumulative | | | After |
	N^a	to 1969	1970–1979	1980–1985	1986
Number of Employees					
Seoul					
<60	53	7.5	17.0	26.4	49.1
60–299	70	17.1	28.6	34.3	20.0
300+	34	58.8	29.4	5.9	5.9
Inchon and Kyonggi					
<60	42	2.4	19.0	21.4	57.1
60–299	39	10.3	30.8	43.6	15.4
300+	11	45.5	54.5	0.0	0.0
Industry					
Seoul					
Garments	49	28.6	16.3	24.5	30.6
Electronics	77	13.0	29.9	26.0	31.2
Inchon and Kyonggi					
Garments	16	12.5	37.5	31.3	18.8
Electronics	47	8.5	27.7	23.4	40.4

Source: East-West Center Survey on Enterprise Strategy.
[a] N is the number of responding firms in each category.

the overall pattern of the year of establishment by region, there are
more younger garment firms in Seoul than in Inchon and Kyonggi,
while, on the other hand, there are more recently established electronics firms in Inchon and Kyonggi than in Seoul. This difference between
Seoul and its suburbs supports findings from the industrial transformations, in which Seoul has become the center of the Korean garment
industry, while its suburbs have emerged as the center of the electronics industry.

Most of the employees of the sampled firms are full-time workers.
In June 1992, 94.2 percent of workers were full-time, while 5.8 percent were part-time or temporary workers. Compared to the 1987 figures, however, the proportion of part-time and temporary workers had
increased considerably. In 1987, only 3.6 percent of workers were part-
time or temporary workers. The proportion of full-time workers in
Seoul (93.1 percent) is less than that of its suburbs (96.0 percent) because Seoul has a greater proportion of part-time workers compared

to the suburbs. Seoul has more employees working in higher-level occupations than the suburbs, as is to be expected. The share of higher-
level occupations (such as managerial-administrative, professional-
technical, and clerical-sales) in Seoul is 52 percent, while in the suburbs
the proportion is around 38 percent. The differences between Seoul
and its suburbs are more prominent in the garment industry and with
small firms than in the electronics industry and with large firms. Overall, since 1987, higher-level occupations have increased as a proportion
of the total workforce, whereas lower-level occupations such as unskilled workers have decreased.

About 67 percent of the firms export some proportion of their products, and about 22 percent of firms export more than three quarters of
their production. There are, however, considerable differences in the
proportion of firm exports by region, size of firms, and industry type.
Overall, the proportion of the firms that do not export at all is higher
in Seoul (36 percent) than in the suburbs (27 percent). More than 60
percent of the small firms in Seoul are producing only for domestic
markets. In general, smaller firms are more oriented to the domestic
market, and medium and large firms more export-oriented. Firms in
the garment industry are more export-oriented than firms in the electronics industry. Overall, Japan, the United States, and Southeast Asia
are the major export markets for Korean firms. Small firms are more
dependent on the Japanese market, whereas large firms are more dependent on the U.S. market. In addition, firms in the garment industry
are more dependent on Japanese and U.S. markets, while firms in the
electronics industry have more diversified export markets.

From 1990 to 1992, more than one-quarter of the firms experienced
a decrease in business. Nevertheless, two-thirds of the firms experienced business increases during the same period. According to the survey responses, the most important factor responsible for decrease in
business is high wages and salaries. Higher costs of raw materials and
inputs and stiffer competition are also regarded as important factors
contributing to business decrease by more than one third of the surveyed firms. The most important factors responsible for business increase are increase in demand and product quality. In addition, specialization in niche markets is also regarded as a significant cause of
business increase.

Firm Strategy in Industrial Restructuring

Firms confronted with major external and internal threats may adopt various strategies in order to remake competitive advantages. The various firms' competitive strategies can be related to labor, production organization, location, and technology. These strategies are not mutually exclusive. For example, technical change prompts and necessitates changes in production organization, on the one hand, and has resulted in changes in labor demand, on the other (Chapman and Walker 1991). Bearing in mind the interactions among labor, production organization, location, and technology, firm strategies with regard to the four major topics are analysed in this section.

Firm Strategy on Labor

In order to understand differences in labor strategy by firm size, industry type, and region, changes in the distribution of employees by occupation need to be examined. In general, 1992 figures show that firms in Seoul, small firms, and firms in the electronics industry have a higher proportion of managerial-administrative and professional-technical employees than firms in Inchon and Kyonggi, large firms, and firms in the apparel industry, respectively. The differences in distribution in 1987 were even greater, but the differences by firm size and region have been reduced during the last five years. Firms located in Inchon and Kyonggi have increased their proportion of managerial-administrative and professional-technical employees during the last five years. The ratio of skilled operatives, unskilled workers and apprentices to total workforce decreased in most cases during the last five years. The differences in the distribution of occupation by firm size, industry type, and region may reflect differences in labor strategy attributable to those three variables.

Small firms seem to be more dependent on flexible labor and the external labor market. Even though the overall ratio of part-time and temporary workers to total employees was only 3.6 percent in 1987, this ratio had increased to 5.8 percent in 1992. Generally, small firms have a greater proportion of part-time and temporary workers. It is clear that there is a relationship between region and firm size. For example, small firms in Seoul have a much higher proportion of part-time or temporary workers (8.1 percent) than small firms in the suburbs (4.8 percent). Large firms in Inchon and Kyonggi have a considerably higher proportion of part-time and temporary workers, but this can be attributed to one large firm that has an exceptionally high proportion of part-time and temporary workers.

The most important retention strategy of small firms is provision of higher wages and benefits. Training and retraining is relatively insignificant as a retention strategy for small firms, whereas it is the most important retention strategy for large firms (table 6.3). The use of part-time and temporary workers and the offering of higher wages and benefits as a retention strategy indicates that small firms generally employ one of two types of labor strategies: the use of flexible labor and the use of external labor. Small firms have more part-time and temporary workers because they are relatively flexible at quantitative adjustment. Furthermore, small firms tend to externalize skill formation, instead of internalizing it through training and retraining. In fact, small firms seek to become free riders on the social infrastructure of the large city, a strategy that can be regarded as a parasitic labor strategy (Peck 1992). This parasitic labor strategy can be related to the reduction of setup sunk costs. The extremely low level of unionization within small firms is also indicative of the flexible and external labor strategies of these firms. Large firms are, on the contrary, more dependent on internal labor markets with an emphasis on training and retraining of labor.

The effects of industry type on the labor strategy of firms are not as clear as the effects of firm size. The less significant differences may be the result of the fact that the electronics industry is not a typical capital-intensive industry and is rather similar to a labor-intensive industry (or at least midway between labor- and capital-intensive industries). However, firms in the garment industry have more part-time and temporary workers, because high wages and labor shortages are more problematic there than in the electronics industry. The effect of industry type seems to also interact with the effect of region in the labor strategy of firms: because firms in the garment industry are more dependent on flexible labor, they tend to concentrate in the city of Seoul. A recent study of the garment industry suggests that a considerable number of Seoul firms utilize housewives as part-time workers, most of whom are in their thirties and forties (Lee 1993). Such utilization of flexible labor in Seoul has surely contributed to the concentration of the garment industry in the city. This finding suggests that there is a distinctive interaction effect, in which firms in the garment industry consider local characteristics in choosing their labor strategy.

It is clear that firms interact with local labor markets in designing

Table 6.3 Retention Strategies, by Number of Employees and Type of Industry
(percentage of firms)

	Strategy					
Region	Higher Wages and Benefits	Training and Retraining	Improved Working Conditions	Shorter Working Hours	Stock and Profit Sharing	Other
Number of Employees						
Seoul						
<60	45.2	16.1	22.6	3.2	9.7	3.2
60–299	30.2	20.9	34.9	4.7	7.0	2.3
300+	30.4	43.5	13.0	0.0	8.7	4.3
Inchon and Kyonggi						
<60	39.3	10.7	28.6	10.7	3.6	7.2
60–299	30.4	30.4	26.1	8.7	4.3	0.0
300+	28.6	57.1	14.3	0.0	0.0	0.0
Industry						
Seoul						
Garments	25.9	29.6	33.3	3.7	3.7	3.7
Electronics	46.8	19.1	21.3	0.0	10.6	2.1
Inchon and Kyonggi						
Garments	33.2	16.7	25.0	8.3	0.0	16.7
Electronics	36.0	32.0	20.0	12.0	0.0	0.0

Source: East-West Center Survey on Enterprise Strategy.

competitive strategies with regard to labor. In general, firms located in
Seoul are more dependent on flexible labor strategies than those in Inchon and Kyonggi. A relatively high proportion of part-time and temporary workers in Seoul and a relatively low level of unionization compared with that in Inchon and Kyonggi support the firms' flexible labor
strategy in Seoul. Overall, the survey results regarding labor strategy
suggest that the different local characteristics and industrial structures
between Seoul and its suburbs (as examined in the previous section of
this chapter) interact with the effects of firm size and industry type and
then impact on firms' competitive labor strategies.

Firm Strategy on Production Organization

Enhancement of flexibility in the production system can be one of
firms' competitive strategies under the increased levels of business un-

certainty and fragmentation of consumer markets (Scott 1989). Enhanced flexibility can be achieved through either the introduction of process innovation or vertical disintegration in the production system. Because the enhancement of flexibility through the introduction of process innovation or flexible production lines needs considerable capital investments, most firms introduce it into only a part of their production processes.

The most significant firm strategy on production organization for the surveyed firms seems to be subcontracting. Subcontracting is not only an organizational strategy of firms but also can be regarded as a firm's labor strategy. Subcontracting is more than simply a means of procuring goods and service functions from other organizations. Subcontracting is a firm's strategy that "involves consideration of relative costs and prices, the risks associated with production within and without the company, and the mechanisms available to ensure compliance with contracts and deter defection from the chain-of-links system" (Clark 1993c, 26–27). On the other hand, subcontracting can be used as a strategy by firms to extend control over labor. By embracing subcontracting, firms can move jobs and functions from large, unionized plants to small, nonunionized workshops (Holmes 1986).

About one-third of the firms surveyed responded that they operated mainly by subcontracting from other firms. Small firms, firms in the garment industry, and firms in Seoul tend to depend more on subcontracting from other firms than do large firms, firms in the electronics industry, and firms in Kyonggi and Inchon respectively (table 6.4). However, in the electronics industry, firms located in Inchon and Kyonggi are slightly more dependent on subcontracting from other firms than those in Seoul.

The higher ratio of subcontracting firms in Inchon and Kyonggi in the electronics industry may be related to the considerable agglomeration of the electronics industry in the Inchon and Kyonggi region. At first, Seoul was the center of the electronics industry in Korea. But since the late 1970s, the restriction of new industrial location in Seoul and the government's industrial dispersal policy have contributed to the establishment of branch plants, the relocation of large plants, and the development of new plants in the suburbs. In the mid-1970s, many firms in Seoul established their branch plants in the suburban areas around the axes of Seoul-Inchon and of Seoul-Suwon (Park 1987). Since the mid-1980s, the Inchon-Kyonggi region has replaced Seoul as the center of the electronics industry. The development of the industry in In-

Table 6.4 Subcontracting and Contracting Out, by Region, Number of Employees, and Type of Industry (percentage of firms)

	Subcontract	*Contract Out*
Number of Employees		
Seoul		
<60	36.5	75.7
60–299	38.6	74.3
300+	26.5	78.8
Inchon and Kyonggi		
<60	33.3	47.6
60–299	20.5	73.7
300+	18.2	100.0
Industry		
Seoul		
Garments	55.1	83.7
Electronics	26.3	74.0
Inchon and Kyonggi		
Garments	43.8	60.0
Electronics	29.8	78.7

Source: East-West Center Survey on Enterprise Strategy.

chon and Kyonggi has also contributed to the agglomeration of many new plants, most of which operate mainly as subcontractors to large plants in the region. Therefore, it is natural that the Inchon-Kyonggi region has surpassed Seoul with respect to the ratio of firms operating mainly by subcontracting in the electronics industry.

Although more than 70 percent of the surveyed firms contract out work to other establishments, there is no consistent trend in the ratio of all firms in the region that contract out work to other establishments. However, some logical observations can be made. In the Inchon-Kyonggi region, the ratio of the number of firms contracting out work correlates with the size of firms, which is a quite reasonable expectation (table 6.4). In Seoul, however, there is no significant relationship between the ratio and the size of firms. In Seoul, even small firms show a high ratio of contracting out work: the ratio is much higher than that of the Inchon-Kyonggi region. The small firms in Seoul can save considerable sunk costs by becoming free riders on the social infrastructure of the city, but in situ expansions are not possible because of the lack of space, high land price, or restriction of expansion by law. In this environment, even the small firms can contract out work to other establishments without consideration of relocation to other regions offering adequate space for production.

A recent case study of Seoul's garment industry reveals a second tier of subcontracting activities and vertical disintegrations (Lee 1993). The higher ratio of firms contracting out work to other establishments and the relatively high ratio of the number of firms subcontracting from other establishments in the garment industry in Seoul seems to confirm this finding. That is, there exists a considerable industrial agglomeration with hierarchical subcontracting activities and vertical disintegration in the garment industry in Seoul. Activities contracted out are mainly those related to components and parts production. However, a significant proportion of large firms contract out maintenance (including security) work. Labor and cost-related factors are very important for contracting out work. More than half the firms regard labor shortages, lower administrative costs, and lower wage costs as the main reasons for contracting out work. According to the survey results, from firms that contract out work, about 3 percent and 89 percent of the small firms contract out maintenance work and components and parts production respectively, compared with about 22 percent and 71 percent respectively of the large firms. Specialized skills and fluctuating demand are also regarded by about 30 percent of the firms as main reasons for contracting out work. In general, cost-related factors are more important for large firms, whereas the labor shortage is regarded as more important for small firms. In this respect, firm strategy on production organization of small firms in Seoul is related to their labor strategy.

Firm Strategy on Location

Since the mid-1980s, several large industrial estates have been established in the western coastal region of Korea in an attempt to attract branch plants and new industrial investment in that region. However, there has been insufficient industrial investment in the area since that time. Instead of investing in the new industrial estates, many firms consider foreign direct investments because of the high wages and labor shortages in the Korean manufacturing sector. Therefore, foreign direct investments can be regarded as a firm strategy of location in the process of industrial restructuring.

The overseas investment in plants by Korean firms is a rather recent phenomena. Before 1989, overseas investments were made mainly by large firms. Small firms have begun to invest only in recent years. More

Table 6.5 Firms that Have Invested or Plan to Invest in Overseas Plants, by Region, Number of Employees, and Type of Industry (percentage)

	Have Invested	Plan to Invest[a]
Number of Employees		
Seoul		
<60	3.8	21.2
60–299	10.1	32.4
300+	36.4	50.0
Inchon and Kyonggi		
<60	0.0	30.0
60–299	5.3	27.8
300+	54.5	45.5
Industry		
Seoul		
Garments	25.0	55.3
Electronics	5.3	25.0
Inchon and Kyonggi		
Garments	12.5	37.5
Electronics	8.5	29.5

Source: East-West Center Survey on Enterprise Strategy.

[a] Ratio of the number of firms that have plans to invest in overseas plants to the number of firms that have not invested overseas.

than 56 percent of the overseas investments have been made since 1989. About 12 percent of firms have invested in overseas plants and factories during the last five years. Large firms and firms in the garment industry tend to have a higher ratio of direct overseas investments than small firms and firms in the electronics industry, which indicates that the variables of firm size and industry type are related to overseas investments (table 6.5). Overall, firms in Seoul have a higher ratio of direct overseas investments than those in the suburbs. However, there exist interaction effects among region, firm size, and industry type. On the one hand, in the case of small and medium firms, Seoul has a higher proportion of direct overseas investments than its suburbs, whereas Seoul has a lower proportion than its suburbs in the case of large firms. On the other hand, Seoul has a higher proportion of firms that have made direct overseas investments in the garment industry, whereas the Inchon-Kyonggi region has a higher proportion in the case of the electronics industry (table 6.5).

Most of the surveyed firms regarded lower wage costs and easier access to markets as the main reasons for investing overseas. Because lower wage costs is the most important reason for overseas investments, more than half the investments have been made in Southeast Asia. One of the significant findings that emerges from the survey is the fact that about one-third of the firms that have not invested in overseas plants and factories plan to do so within the next three years, which is a much higher proportion than those that have invested overseas in the last five years. The overall trend of overseas investment planning by firm size, industry type, and region is similar to that of overseas investments in the last five years. However, a considerable proportion of small and medium firms are planning to invest overseas (table 6.5).

The most significant reason for planning to invest overseas is lower wage costs. More than 90 percent of the surveyed firms regarded the lower wage costs as the main reason for planning overseas investments. Easier access to markets is the next most important reason. Cheaper component and parts production and cheaper or more available land are also regarded as the main reasons by about 21 percent and 16 percent of the firms respectively. Areas in which firms are planning to make investments have become more diversified. Southeast Asia (35 percent) is still regarded as the most attractive region for overseas investments, but China (30 percent) and Asian NIEs (23 percent) are also preferred by a considerable percentage of firms. Because direct overseas investment is closely related to high wages and labor shortages, it also can be regarded as a firm's labor strategy.

Technology Strategy of Firm

Introduction of new technology is regarded as one way of remaking competitive advantages by most of the surveyed firms. More than 62 percent of the firms have introduced new technology during the last two years. Most of the large firms (more than 90 percent) introduced new technology in the last two years, while only 56 percent of the small firms did so, which indicates that firm size is a factor affecting the introduction of new technology. Firms in the electronics industry are more enthusiastic about the introduction of new technology than those in the garment industry. Firms in Seoul tend to introduce new technology more often than those in the suburbs, but the effect of the region on the introduction of new technology is not clearly sorted out, because the effects of firm site and industry type interact with the effect of the region.

About 70 percent of the new technology introduced in the last two years has been production technologies. New technologies of quality control and design share 14 percent and 11 percent respectively of total new technology introduced. The main purposes of introducing new technology are to improve product quality, to increase output, and to produce new products. Productivity and quality of products are considered central issues in the introduction of new technology by most of the firms, whereas reducing various costs are not regarded as main purposes. More than two-thirds of the responding firms regarded improvement of product quality and the increase in output as the main purposes of the introduction of new technology, whereas only about 10 percent of the firms regarded cost-related factors as the main purposes. Industry type seems to be a significant variable affecting the technology strategy of firms. The type of new technology introduced differs according to industry type. For example, the introduction of production technology is more popular in the electronics industry than in the garment industry, whereas the introduction of design technology is more significant in the garment industry than in the electronics industry (table 6.6). The introduction of new technology ensuring quality control has been more emphasized in the electronics industry. Such quality-control technology has also been introduced by more small firms in Seoul.

Imported technology is introduced more by firms in the garment industry than by those in the electronics industry. On the other hand, in-house-developed technology is introduced more by firms in the electronics industry (table 6.7). This difference in the source of technology introduced by the type of industry suggests that technology development is a more important strategy for firms in the electronics industry. The fact that the average ratio of R&D expenditure to total sales was higher in the electronics industry (3.7 percent in 1991) than in the garment industry (2.1 percent in 1991) also indicates the importance of the technology development strategy for the electronics industry.

The effect of firm size on the introduction of new technology is significant, as mentioned before. However, for those firms that introduced new technology, technology strategy was not significantly different by firm size. Only the sources of the new technology introduced are different by firm size. That is, large firms tend to depend more on imported technology as the source of new technology introduced, whereas small firms depend more on in-house-developed technology (table 6.6). Continuous increase in the average ratio of R&D expendi-

Table 6.6   Type of Technology Introduced, 1990–1992, by Region, Number of Employees, and Type of Industry (percentage of firms)

	Production	Design	Office	Quality Control	Inventory Control and Others
Number of Employees					
Seoul					
<60	70.0	6.7	3.3	20.0	0.0
60–299	71.4	19.0	2.4	7.1	0.0
300+	70.0	16.7	0.0	6.7	6.6
Inchon and Kyonggi					
<60	68.2	4.5	9.1	18.2	0.0
60–299	69.2	7.7	3.8	19.2	0.0
300+	77.8	11.1	0.0	11.1	0.0
Industry					
Seoul					
Garments	53.6	35.7	3.6	7.1	0.0
Electronics	76.5	5.9	2.0	13.7	2.0
Inchon and Kyonggi					
Garments	63.6	27.3	0.0	9.1	0.0
Electronics	65.6	3.1	8.4	21.9	0.0

Source: East-West Center Survey on Enterprise Strategy.

Note: Numbers are ratios to total number of firms that introduced technology.

ture to total sales over the last five years is evidence of the technology development strategy of small firms. (Based on the results of the questionnaire survey, the average ratio of R&D expenditure to total sales of small firms in each year from 1987 to 1991 was 1.5, 1.6, 2.2, 3.1, and 3.6 percent respectively in Seoul; and 2.2, 2.4, 2.7, 3.2, and 3.6 percent respectively in the Inchon-Kyonggi region). However, the potential of technology development of small firms is not remarkable, because the absolute amount of R&D expenditure of small firms is relatively limited.

A slightly higher proportion of Seoul firms than Inchon and Kyonggi firms introduced design technology, although the reverse is true regarding the introduction of quality-control technology (table 6.6). The proportion of firms that referred to imported technology as the source of their new technology is slightly higher in Seoul than in Inchon and Kyonggi, while the reverse is true for in-house-developed technology. Plant automation has also been one of the competitive strategies used

Table 6.7 Source of Technology Introduced, 1990–1992, by Region, Number of Employees, and Type of Industry (percentage of firms)

	Imported	Developed Domestically	Developed In-house
Number of Employees			
Seoul			
<60	33.3	20.0	46.7
60–299	31.0	31.0	38.0
300+	73.3	13.3	13.3
Inchon and Kyonggi			
<60	22.7	31.8	45.3
60–299	46.2	26.9	26.9
300+	50.0	10.0	40.0
Industry			
Seoul			
Garments	51.9	29.6	18.5
Electronics	38.5	23.1	38.5
Inchon and Kyonggi			
Garments	36.4	36.4	27.3
Electronics	33.3	24.2	42.4

Source: East-West Center Survey on Enterprise Strategy.

Note: Numbers are percentages of total number of firms that introduced technology.

by firms in relation to process technology. The average ratio of automated process to total manufacturing process of surveyed firms was 42.8 percent, much higher than in 1987 (21.7 percent). In general, the average ratio of automation of small firms was lower than that of medium and large firms. This ratio was slightly lower in Seoul than in Inchon and Kyonggi. The average rate of automated process to total manufacturing process for small firms in 1992 was 25.9 percent in Seoul and 39.1 percent in its suburbs. The lower ratio of automation in the small firms of Seoul seems to be related to the utilization of flexible labor and organization strategies by Seoul firms.

Conclusion

This chapter examines firm strategies regarding labor, production organization, location, and technology in the process of industrial restructuring in Seoul and its suburbs. It is assumed that firms' competitive strategies vary according to size, industry type, and region. Even though the three variables are not always mutually exclusive and are sometimes interrelated in the process of industrial restructuring, the three variables do assist in explaining and understanding various firm's competitive strategies.

The size of firms is a very significant factor affecting the labor strategy of firms. Small firms tend to depend more on flexible and external labor in their competitive strategy. Small firms are more dependent on pools of part-time and temporary workers, making them more flexible in quantitative adjustment. These firms seek to become free riders on the social infrastructure of the large city in order to avoid setup sunk costs. This external labor strategy can be regarded as parasitic. The effects of industry type and region are somewhat blurred. This is due to the presence of an interaction effect between industry type and region, on the one hand, and the fact that the electronics industry is not a typical capital-intensive industry and rather is midway between labor and capital-intensive industries on the other. Firms in the garment industry depend more on flexible labor (because high wages and labor shortages are more problematic in the industry than in the electronics industry) and tend to concentrate in the city of Seoul. In general, firms in Seoul are more dependent on flexible labor strategies than those in the Inchon-Kyonggi region. In fact, it is clear that firms interact with local labor market characteristics in their labor strategies.

Subcontracting has been the most significant firm strategy regarding production organization in the process of industrial restructuring. In general, small firms, firms in Seoul, and firms in the garment industry are more dependent on performing subcontracting for other firms than large firms, firms in the suburbs, and firms in the electronics industry respectively. Considering both subcontracting and contracting-out activities, Seoul is the center of the Korean garment industry, while the Inchon-Kyonggi region is the center of the Korean electronics industry. Firms in the garment industry have agglomerated in Seoul with vertical disintegration and contracting out of parts and components production. This strategy on production organization of firms in the garment industry in Seoul is related to their labor strategy and their interaction with local characteristics. On the other hand, firms in the electronics industry in Inchon and Kyonggi (where government policy initiated the development of the electronics industry) are now agglomerated and promote vertical disintegration and subcontracting activities as competitive strategies. In general, labor and cost-related factors are the main reasons for contracting out work. Cost-related factors are more important for large firms, whereas labor shortages are considered more significant for small firms.

Overseas direct investment was regarded as a significant firm strategy on location in recent years. The ratio of Korean firms that have invested in overseas plants is low compared to that of Hong Kong or Singapore, as identified in the other chapters of this book. However, a greater proportion of firms have plans for direct overseas investments. Firm size and industry type are significant variables in direct overseas investments. Again, effects of firm size and industry type interact with the effect of region in the firm strategy on location.

Introduction of new technology is very important for most of the firms. The main purposes of introducing new technology are related to improving product quality and productivity as well as saving costs. Industry type is a significant variable in differentiating the technology strategy of firms. Production technology and in-house technology development is more important for firms in the electronics industry, whereas design technology and imported technology are more important for firms in the garment industry. In general, technology development strategy is more significant for firms in the electronics industry. Large firms and firms in Seoul are somewhat more dependent on imported technology than small firms and firms in the suburbs, whereas the reverse is true for in-house-developed technology. Small firms have continuously increased R&D expenditure as a proportion of their total sales during the last five years and are more dependent on in-house-developed technology than large firms are. However, caution is required in the interpretation of the technology strategy by firm size, because the ratio of small firms that introduced new technology in the last two years was much lower than that of large firms, and the actual amounts of R&D expenditure of small firms are quite limited.

Firm size, industry type, and region are significant variables effecting various firms' competitive strategies, even though interaction effects between variables sometimes blur the solid effects of each variable. Firm's competitive strategies on labor, technology, and production organization are not mutually exclusive but, rather, are interrelated. Firm strategy has become important since the late 1980s in Korea. However, firm strategy alone can not remake competitive advantages in Korea, because global competition inevitably becomes regulated competition (Yoffie 1993). With the current severe and dynamic global competition and uncertainty, it is essential that firm strategy and government policy in Korea be coordinated. Korea has been heavily dependent on international markets for its economic growth, and this dependence will continue in the future. In the 1970s and 1980s, Korea experienced significant economic and industrial growth, but many problems and difficulties hamper continued growth in the future. For example, during the last five years, Korea has been confronted with problems of high wages and labor shortages in the production sector, especially in the labor-intensive industries. Competitive advantages based on cheap and abundant labor are no longer applicable to Korean industry. Labor-related problems are likely to cause a slowdown in future economic growth (Song 1990). In addition, technology transfer from the developed economies will be more difficult and more expensive as the technology gap narrows.

Based on the analysis of commodity chains, Asian NIEs have been defined as semiperipheral in the global economy (Gereffi and Korzeniewicz 1990). Scott (1987), on the other hand, suggests that Asian NIEs are the core of Southeast Asia, where industry has become more highly developed and territorially differentiated. Can Asian NIEs continue to grow rapidly and join the ranks of non-Western advanced economies following Japan? The answer depends on how the Asian NIEs can overcome the problems and difficulties that have emerged in recent years.

Firms' competitive strategies on labor, production organization, location, and technology are surely important in regaining competitive advantages. Among them, firms' strategy on technology in the Asian NIEs seems to be most important in the long-term perspective, because strategies on subcontracting, labor, and foreign direct investments without accompanying technological progress can be regarded as only a short-term adjustment strategy and might be vulnerable in the long-term. Asian NIEs should concentrate on both technological development and technological diffusion in the Asian Pacific Rim areas. In order to join the ranks of non-Western advanced economies, Asian NIEs should, first of all, assume a core role in the Asian Pacific Rim areas. Interactions between firm strategy and government strategy are inevitable and become especially important in the strategies concerning technological developments.

The story of city and suburbs within the Seoul metropolitan area clearly suggests that local characteristics and history are crucial for industrial development and restructuring. National government should carefully evaluate the significance of regional characteristics and utilize them in their industrial strategy and regional industrial restructuring.

Business linkages at both the local and international levels should be supported in order to improve innovation potential and promote technological diffusion. Asian NIEs should also intensively participate in regionally based industrial development projects in the Asian Pacific Rim areas with technological transfer and direct investments. The Asian Pacific Rim is one of the world's most dynamic regions in terms of economic growth and in its history. The open-door policies of China and Russia and the establishment of diplomatic relations among the countries of the region have created and will continue to create many opportunities for Asian NIEs to develop and increase the industrialization of the region. The future of the Asian NIEs, accordingly, depends on utilization of these opportunities through economic cooperation and technological development within the Pacific Rim area.

SEVEN

Pusan, Korea: Second-City Blues

Jung Duk Lim

The rate of restructuring of an industry depends largely on the speed of transformation in output, production process, marketing, and management. Economic laws relating to the life cycle dynamics of competition prevail for every commodity, firm, and industry. This means either that every commodity, and perhaps its industry, must face a phase of economic decline sooner or later during its life in the market or that the industry must radically restructure to remain competitive. The life of a commodity, or an industry, could be prolonged, although not necessarily in the same place of production, by the comparative advantage of its home industry or location. In economics, the theory of comparative advantage is used to explain the competitive equilibrium of differential production between countries and the decreasing gap between regions in terms of their income and trade. The comparative advantage theory of interregional trade tries to prove the potential, mutual benefits of the international division of labor. In the case of the Korean footwear industry, however, economic theory is not necessarily of great benefit to specific regions.

In spite of its labor-intensive characteristics, the athletic footwear industry is still one of the major exporters in Korea. The footwear industry is the most important industry in Pusan in terms of employment and value added. The future income and employment of Pusan depends crucially upon the fate of this labor-intensive industry. The second largest city in Korea, with a population of approximately four million, Pusan is dominated by the footwear industry in many respects. The future of the Korean footwear industry holds important lessons for the restructuring of other labor-intensive industries as well as other regions in Korea and other developing countries.

The Korean footwear industry, especially athletic footwear manufacturing, is clearly part of the new international division of labor (Donaghu and Barff 1990). In the 1970s and through to the early 1980s, the international market for athletic shoes was controlled by oligopolistic, interfirm competition, wherein manufacturers had some leverage in product price setting. After the emergence of major brand-name companies, such as Nike and Reebok, during the 1980s, the production market became increasingly vulnerable to the pricing practices of these firms. Manufacturers in Korea now depend on a few buyers' orders, even though they arguably produce the world's best-quality athletic shoes. Under severe international price competition, and through the rapid changes in the domestic factor markets, the restructuring process of the footwear industry of Korea has had significant consequences for local income and employment.

Unless producers acquire parts of the marketing or distribution processes in the near future, the Korean footwear industry faces a significantly deteriorating situation. Foreign direct investment is not a practical solution in this case because of the characteristics of the original equipment manufacturing (OEM) system of production. Diversification of production sites throughout Southeast Asia may be beneficial to the major buyers, assuring the supply of inexpensive products. But such a solution would not be beneficial for Korean producers. The situation facing the Korean garment industry is similar. Restructuring by introducing flexible manufacturing systems in order to meet the demand for smaller quantities of higher-value-added products has been preferred as one way to solve the problems faced by these industries. The development of Korean brand-name products and increased specialization in the manufacture of parts have also been suggested as possible remedies. Support for the industry in the focus of maintaining regional growth and stability are also being considered. The success of this restructuring process depends, then, on some combination of industrial and regional policy. Other possible means and ways of restructuring are also discussed in this chapter.

The Pusan survey covered two industries—the footwear and textile-garment industries. However, the analysis in this chapter is mostly concerned with the footwear industry because it operates under many of the same pressures facing the textile-garment industry. As it is the city's dominant industry, the Pusan footwear industry also dominates the Korean footwear industry in every aspect.

The Rise and Fall of Pusan Footwear

Korean footwear manufacturers produce and export all kinds of footwear. Among their various products, athletic shoes (such as jogging and tennis shoes) are the major items, measured simply in terms of the volume of production. The focus of this analysis is mainly on the athletic shoe-industry. The term footwear is generally used to describe athletic shoes and sports shoes throughout this chapter.

The Korean footwear industry developed rapidly from the late 1960s. Footwear was a most suitable production item for Korea at that time, given that the industrialization process had only just begun and given the chronic shortages of capital and educated workers. About that time, the footwear industries of the United States and Japan began to rapidly lose their relative competitiveness, partly because of factors internal to those countries and partly because of the rise of new competitors. Korea and Taiwan were the only countries in Asia during the 1970s to supply inexpensive, high-quality athletic shoes (Gereffi and Korzeniewicz 1990). For the Korean manufacturers, foreign orders poured in, and those orders were backed up by low-interest bank loans during a period of domestic hyperinflation. Pusan attracted new footwear factories because it had the best port and port facilities in Korea, and thus the city came to locate over 80 percent of Korean footwear factories and footwear workers. Young female workers from surrounding rural areas were the principal source of labor; firms were able to keep wage levels low and quality of work high (Lim 1993a).

Production was entirely by the original equipment manufacturing (OEM) method. The OEM method suited Korean producers at the time, because to make a profit they had only to manufacture the desired high quantities of products to fill preassigned orders, paying no attention to marketing, advertising, and R&D. Donaghu and Barff (1990) associated this practice of specialized commodity production with the new international division of labor, which can be differentiated from the traditional international division of labor in that some international buyers now do not own any production facilities at home or abroad except their R&D functions. Buyers do not supply parts to their contractors, either. Instead, buyers import and supply products

Table 7.1 Export and Production Characteristics of Footwear Industry, Selected
Years, 1980–1993

	1980	1984	1988	1992	1993[a]
Number of lines[b]	530	653	716	437	406
Number of firms	73	138	280	255	246
Number of lines per firm	7.3	4.7	2.6	1.7	1.7
Number of employees (thousands)	92	115	92	92	8.5
Number of employees per firm	1.26	0.83	0.33	0.36	0.35
Production (million pairs)	298	376	573	366	77
Export amount ($US million)	904	1,398	3,801	3,184	619
Index change	100	155	420	352	—
Export quantity (million pairs)	202	279	451	250	48
Average unit price ($US)	4.47	5.01	8.43	12.47	12.90
Index change	100	112	189	285	289

Source: Korean Footwear Industry Association (1992, 1993).

[a] 1993 data for January, February, and March 1993.

[b] Includes footwear manufacturers only.

carrying their brand names to wholesalers or national retail chains. They intensively advertise their products, mainly in the U.S. market. The Nike and Reebok companies are good examples of this type of firm.

Nike, Reebok, and L.A. Gear have significantly influenced the major Korean footwear producers over the past decade. The rapid growth of these commodity producers, in general, was most profound in Pusan. The Korean footwear industry produced 298 million pairs of shoes in 1980; by 1988, production had increased to 573 million pairs (see table 7.1). During the same period, exports rose from 202 million pairs to 451 million pairs. As a big buyer, the total Reebok order from Korean producers increased from 1 million pairs in 1981 to 52 million pairs in 1988. Measured in terms of export value, Reebok increased the value of its Korean orders from US$4.4 million in 1981 to US$611.9 million in 1988.

From the peak of 1988, production and export volume has decreased dramatically. Production dropped to 366 million pairs and exports to 250 million pairs in 1992. The cause of this abrupt drop is explained by Lim (1994) and is consistent with other related studies in the literature. Donaghu and Barff (1990) show that Nike successfully maneuvered itself into a solid position within the new international division of labor by using international subcontracting and increasing its flexibility by networking across a broad range of suppliers. The success of Nike can be attributed to the fact that the company was relatively free of sunk costs and fixed costs (Clark and Wrigley, forthcoming). However, Nike's early success has become a great burden to manufacturers in Korea. To meet rising demand in the 1980s, Korean producers expanded their production lines at their own initiative (see table 7.1), expecting continuing orders from the major buyers and also expecting relatively favorable competitive conditions. The abrupt decrease in orders in the late 1980s was extremely damaging to Korean manufacturers, especially to the larger firms. It has caused the failure of a number of large firms and the loss of a great number of jobs for many employees (tables 7.1 and 7.2).

Since the Korean manufacturers have no control over marketing, the severance of bulk orders from major buyers has caused the closure of some very large firms. The Samhwa Company, employing more than 5,000 workers, was the major manufacturer of Nike products for over a decade (Donaghu and Barff 1990). The company was completely closed immediately after Nike announced the withdrawal of orders in the summer of 1992. Although there could be other reasons for the failure of Samhwa, nobody would deny that the order cut was the major precipitating cause of the company's failure.

Over the last twenty years, the market structure and nature of demand for footwear has changed fundamentally in the United States, the major consumer market of athletic shoes (Donaghu and Barff 1990). After the emergence of Nike, Reebok, and L.A. Gear as major brands in the early 1980s, the market for high-quality sports shoes became more oligopolistic in nature. On the supply side, until that time the market for the production of athletic shoes had been quite competitive (with respect to producers' relations with buyers)—Korea was perhaps the only country to produce high-quality products at an inexpensive price. Even though contracts were based on the OEM system, manufacturers were able to bargain for price adjustments to reflect changes in input costs. The buyers, having no alternative low-cost manufacturers available, were forced to accommodate producer's requests for price increases.

After the mid-1980s, the production market in Korea became an oligopsonistic market where there were, in effect, two or three major buyers and numerous sellers. In these circumstances, the buyers began to exert more control over price and quantity. The manufacturers, of

Table 7.2 Employment Structure in Footwear Industry, by Number of Firms and Firm Size, Total Number of Employees, Selected Year, 1982–1991

	1983		1984		1986		1988		1990		1991	
	Number of Firms	Number of Employees	Number of Firms	Number of Employees	Number of Firms	Number of Employees	Number of Firms	Number of Employees	Number of Firms	Number of Employees	Number of Firms	Number of Employeess
<10	8	66	13	100	39	284	39	314	35	291	75	567
11–20	16	244	21	340	54	837	64	1,005	70	1,122	106	1,618
21–50	43	1,325	93	3.486	128	4,790	230	8,551	350	9,354	314	11,271
51–100	42	3,225	69	5.053	95	6,814	144	10,467	75	13,025	147	10,279
101–200	31	4,486	38	5.415	57	8,515	98	14,395	98	14,602	63	9,158
201–300	19	5,125	17	4.048	24	5,894	24	6,057	30	7,599	33	8,057
301–500	14	5,465	24	9.513	23	9,586	27	10,984	25	10,365	20	7,661
501–1,000	18	12,918	14	9.860	23	15,521	30	21553	23	17,263	14	10,155
1,001–2,000	9	11,137	14	17.268	19	26,209	19	26,698	15	22,148	8	12,713
2,001–5,000	4	13,477	4	37.461	3	44,959	6	17,919	5	17,998	10	30,798
>5,000	6	59,886	6	59.728	6	49,888	6	46,019	6	50,940	1	9,916
Totals	210	117,693	313	129.495	471	138,419	687	163,961	732	164,707	791	107,977
Average	—	559	—	486	—	368	—	239	—	221	—	142

Source: Pusan Chamber of Commerce, Pusan Business Directory (1983–92).

Table 7.3   Foreign Direct Investment of Footwear Industry, by Country

Country	Number of Firms	Number of Lines
N	30	121
Indonesia	14	67
China	5	31
Thailand	2	6
Sri Lanka	1	3
Philippines	1	5
Bangladesh	1	2
U.S.	2	3
Chile	1	1
Jamaica	1	1
Dominica	1	2

Source: Korean Footwear Industry Association (1992, 6).

course, during this period attempted to control the situation. A few manufacturers created their own brands and carried out their own marketing programs. These efforts were not successful, largely because of the high cost of advertising in foreign markets and the threatening attitude of major buyers to potential competitors (their actual suppliers). As of late 1992, less than 5 percent of total footwear exports from Korea was from companies with their own brand names.

Given these conditions, foreign direct investment (FDI) has been seen as one way for producers to revitalize their relationships with major buyers. High labor costs and other production costs have been noted as reasons for local firms moving to places with lower factor costs. And Korean footwear firms have been active foreign investors. As of 1991, thirty production units in more than ten countries were created through FDI or through joint ventures (table 7.3). The results of these investments have been mixed. It could be argued that Korean FDI is a natural outcome of the industrial life cycle; Korean firms have merely copied the coping strategies of other firms in earlier-developed countries. In addition, FDI is both directly and indirectly encouraged by the major buyers (as argued by the Japanese; see chapter 3, this volume). Although we were not able to collect concrete evidence to back our argument, it appears from interviews that the major buyers of products were often insistent on Korean footwear firms shifting their production facilities offshore. Responding to the threat of social unrest and fast wage increases during the late 1980s, major buyers have strongly encouraged FDI by Korean manufacturers to secure a stable supply of manufactured goods from firms they know and trust. Under oligopsonistic market conditions, producers are forced to comply with buyers' requests (although producers sometimes attempt to subvert the buyers' power).

For the home units of Korean manufacturers, FDI creates another direct competitor unless they completely close their local production facilities. Orders are placed by buyers, and buyers always want a cheaper product (relative to its final sales price) regardless of the place of manufacture. Furthermore, Korean manufacturers who do move out or become subcontractors in foreign countries face an uncertain future, as buyers also encourage local entrepreneurs to emerge and compete with Korean firms. Donaghu and Barff (1990) incorrectly indicate that FDI by Korean and Taiwanese manufacturers forms a secondary core in the production hierarchy in producing and supplying high-quality products and parts. Since the investment is made by manufacturers, not buyers, the risk is assumed by the investors and is not shared with buyers. Technology transfer is welcomed, and sometimes urged by buyers, under the existing competitive environment as a means to lower costs for buyers and local manufacturers.

On the other hand, FDI by Korean manufacturers has been successful from the standpoint of major buyers. While the Korean economy was experiencing significant currency revaluation during the late 1980s, the countries where Korean firms focused their FDI have experienced currency devaluation. For example, the Indonesian currency was devalued 55 percent during the same period. The relative change in exchange rates alone became a significant factor in accelerating the decline in the competitiveness of Korean firms. For example, the Korean export price of athletic shoes rose by 50.0 percent between 1986 and 1988 but by only 15.3 percent between 1988 and 1990—this later period being one in which Korean manufacturers experienced the most rapid real wage increases and currency revaluation in the nation's history.

Labor-Intensive Industries of Pusan

With so many problems and unfavorable market conditions, the footwear industry is still one of the major manufacturing industries of Korea in terms of output, export, and employment. Most footwear factories are located in Pusan and its immediate vicinity. As noted, the footwear industry is Pusan's largest industry in terms of employment, output, and export (Lim 1994). The future of the footwear industry will no doubt have enormous influence, both directly and indirectly, on the economy of Pusan. The textile-garment industry was similarly an important industry in Pusan up to the early 1970s. Since then, the importance of the industry to the Pusan economy has been decreasing quickly, as has the position of the industry in the national economy. However, the textile-garment industry is still Pusan's second most important in terms of employment and the third most important in terms of value added. Since the garment industry experienced declining fortunes earlier than the footwear industry, it is not surprising that the former started restructuring sooner than the latter.

The survey of the footwear and textile-garment industries of Pusan was conducted in July 1992. The Directory of the Pusan Chamber of Commerce listed about 722 footwear-related firms and 783 garment-related firms in 1991. Among the listed firms, 128 firms were selected as the sample group for footwear and 120 firms for apparel, taking into account the firms' employment size and production characteristics. The survey questionnaire was sent by mail, after which an interviewer visited each firm. The survey found that 56 out of 128 firms in the footwear industry and 50 out of 120 firms in the garment industry had either gone out of business or had changed location without notice during the year. Of these firms, about 44 percent of footwear firms and 42 percent of garment firms in Pusan left the industry within the year. One of the two largest footwear firms, employing more than 5,000 workers, was closed immediately after the survey was completed. Some of the most important findings and characteristics of the survey can be categorized as follows.

Firm Characteristics

About 90 percent of the surveyed footwear firms were established after 1970, with about 75 percent established after 1980 (see table 7.4). In contrast, only about 42 percent of the surveyed garment firms were established after 1980. This difference reflects the relatively higher entrance and exit rates of footwear firms in and out of the industry and the volatility of the footwear market relative to the garment market. Most of the surveyed firms are independent, locally owned, and managed by their owners. About 33 percent of the surveyed footwear firms and 44 percent of textile-garment firms utilize a subcontracting system

Table 7.4 Characteristics of Surveyed Firms (percentage)

	Footwear	Garments/Apparel
Year established		
Before 1980	24.7	58.1
After 1980	75.3	41.9
Ownership		
Domestic	100.0	97.2
Foreign	0	1.4
Joint venture	0	1.4
Listing		
Listed	16.4	13.0
Unlisted	83.6	87.0
Firm type		
Independent	90.4	89.9
Branch/subsidiary of another Organization	9.6	10.1
Employment status		
Male full-time	24.5	31.6
Female full-time	61.6	63.1
Male part-time	2.8	0.7
Female part-time	8.7	2.9
Male temporary	0.8	0.7
Female temporary	1.6	1.0

Source: East-West Center Survey on Enterprise Strategy.

for the production of the total manufactured product. About one third of the surveyed footwear firms employed more than five hundred workers, and about 19 percent of the surveyed footwear firms produce and sell more than $5 million worth of goods annually. By contrast, about 7 percent of textile-garment firms sold more than $50 million worth of stock in 1991. The larger firms tend to be more export oriented in both industries.

The most distinctive characteristic of the labor-intensive industries is the high proportion of total costs contributed by labor costs (see table 7.5). Only a small portion of the surveyed firms in both industries responded by noting that their ratio of labor compensation to total costs is less than 20 percent. About 67 percent of footwear firms and 36 percent of textile-garment firms indicated that their labor compensation ratio is between 20 and 40 percent. In the case of the garment industry, small firms reported that over 50 percent and, in some

Table 7.5 Share of Labor Cost in Total Costs (number and percentage of firms)

Labor Cost Ratio	Footwear (N = 70)	% of Firms	Garments (N = 67)	% of Firms
0–10	3	4.1	2	2.9
11–20	9	12.3	14	20.2
21–30	28	38.4	16	23.2
31–40	21	28.8	9	13.1
41–50	4	5.5	1	1.4
51–70	2	2.7	15	21.8
71–90	2	2.7	10	14.5
90+	1	1.4	—	—

Source: East-West Center Survey on Enterprise Strategy.

Note: Three footwear firms (4.1%) and two garments firms (2.9%) did not provide data.

cases, even over 70 percent of total costs were made up of labor costs. These figures are significantly higher than the official statistics compiled by the Bank of Korea, where the ratio is around 34 percent including contracting out cost (Bank of Korea 1992). Regardless of accuracy, this high level of labor cost is a direct burden to firms in these labor-intensive industries.

Enterprise Size and Market

Most employees are hired on a full-time basis in both industries, and about two-thirds of full-time employees are female. The ratio of female to male workers is much higher among part-time employees in both industries (see table 7.4). In the footwear industry, over two-thirds of employees are skilled production workers, wherein females are three times more prevalent than their male counterparts. The ratio of skilled production workers to total employees in the textile-garment industry is about 50 percent, significantly lower than in the footwear industry. Apprentices make up a very small proportion of total employees in both industries. The ratio of female workers to total workers in both industries is over 65 percent, again indicating by gender the labor-intensive characteristic of the industries. (See chapter 9, this volume, for an international comparison.)

Footwear manufacturing is largely divided into two production processes: the manufacturing of parts and the assembly of those parts.

Parts producers may not export directly, but all assemblers try to export unless they are trapped in subcontract production. About 38 percent of surveyed firms did not export at all. About 43 percent of the firms exported more than 90 percent of their products. In 1991, 72 percent of footwear products from the region were exported. However, as noted, the proportion of exports has been declining in the past several years. About one half the surveyed firms export to the North American region. In the case of the textile-garment industry, about one third of the surveyed firms do not export at all, the large majority of which are very small firms. About 30 percent of surveyed textile-garment firms export more than 80 percent of their output. In short, production in the Pusan footwear industry is in general larger, more volatile, more export-oriented, has a greater output, and hires more female workers than the textile-garment industry. Both industries have to contend, however, with a high proportion of labor costs to their total cost structures.

Business Conditions and Plans

Only one-third of the surveyed footwear firms reported increased sales during the past two years. Less than one-third of textile-garment firms reported increased sales. About 58 percent of the footwear firms (including all the large firms) experienced decreased sales in 1991. During the past three years, most of the surveyed firms reported cost increases coupled with decreased sales. Increased wages and higher raw-material prices were cited as the main reasons for declining business. To footwear firms experiencing sales increase, increased demand coupled with the specialization of products were cited as favorable factors, whereas those textile-garment firms experiencing similar increases referred to their adjustment of prices as the reason for their good performance.

With regard to changes in the range of products, about one-half of the surveyed firms in both industries reported increasing their range of products. However, the increased range of products has not always led to a significant increase in employment (only 35 percent in footwear and 20 percent in textile-garment). More firms experienced unchanged employment despite increasing the range of products produced. New products tend to require more sophisticated technology rather than increased labor power. In this sense, technological change is endogenous to the industry, being driven by changes in demand, rather than being exogenous to the industry, the product of technical innovation unrelated to demand.

Sixteen out of seventy-three surveyed footwear firms invested overseas during the past five years; five out of sixty-nine apparel firms invested overseas during the same period. Cheaper labor costs was the single most important reason cited for overseas investment by these Korean labor-intensive firms. Most footwear firms have invested in the Southeast Asia region, excluding Singapore. China was considered the next favorable region for foreign direct investment. In the case of textile-garment firms, three firms had relocated to Southeast Asia, and the other two to South America. The average employment size of overseas plants was large: 1,391 persons for footwear firms and 563 persons for textile-garment firms. Many firms (twenty-six surveyed footwear firms and fourteen surveyed textile-garment firms) were considering investing overseas over the next three years. The most important reason cited for planned overseas investment was, again, cheaper labor costs. Parts production was the next most popular reason given for foreign investment. The most desired destination for overseas investment for footwear firms was Southeast Asia, followed by China, although for textile-garment firms the most attractive place to invest was China.

In summary, even though both labor-intensive industries have been suffering from high domestic production costs, their restructuring strategies have differed because of different industrial characteristics and stages of the product life cycle. Recent trends suggest that footwear firms are more likely to go abroad than textile-garment firms. As mentioned earlier, the textile-garment industry had experienced an earlier decline some years before the current crisis in footwear production.

Labor Market Conditions

As of July 1992, the average monthly wage for a production supervisor in the footwear industry was US$975, for skilled operatives, the average wage was US$710, and for unskilled workers it was US$544. The wage system in Korea is complicated, and it is not a unified system. Wages are divided into three parts: a basic monthly salary, various kinds of benefit compensation, and bonuses. Bonuses are given monthly, quarterly, or biannually, according to the local labor agreement and the ability of the firm to pay. Therefore, bonuses and added compensation may or may not be included in the official reported monthly wage. In the textile-garment industry, the average monthly wage for the same three categories of workers was US$967, US$693, and US$528 respectively. All surveyed firms reported that the wages of production workers have increased over the past three years, and the majority of firms (more than two-thirds) described the rate of increase as rapid. One of the most distinctive characteristics of both industries (although more pronounced in the footwear industry) is the very high rate of labor turnover. About 60 percent of footwear firms reported a labor turnover rate of between 10 and 49 percent in 1991. The turnover rate has been increasing over the past three years. The turnover rate is highest of among younger and unskilled female workers. Interestingly, the majority of movers transferred to other firms in the same industry.

Enterprise Strategies

Technology

During the past two years, one-third of the surveyed footwear firms introduced new technology. It is interesting to note that textile-garment firms introduced technology more actively than footwear firms. About 42 percent of textile-garment firms introduced new technology quite recently. The new technologies introduced in the footwear industry were mainly production related (46 percent) and design related (29 percent), whereas those introduced in the textile-garment industry were largely related to production. New technology was mainly developed domestically, but a certain portion was imported. The newly introduced technology mainly resulted in reduced employment or no change in employment. The new technology usually reduced the range of production tasks and operations, as might be expected. However, one-fourth to one-third of new technology required an increased range of labor tasks. One-half of the surveyed footwear firms reported that new technology reduced demand for labor, whereas about two-thirds of textile-garment firms reported increased demand for certain types of labor. New technology has the capacity to improve productivity, but it does not necessarily reduce the range of work or the complexity of tasks. The introduction of new technology seems inevitable under the severe international price competition now being experienced by both industries.

Contract, Part-Time, and Shift Work

Two-thirds of the surveyed firms in both industries indicated that they used a subcontracting system to meet shifts in demand. The rest of the firms are basically parts producers. Contracting out appears to be used mainly for parts production. Subcontract work is more frequently carried out by small and medium firms employing fewer than five hundred employees. Foreign subcontracting has also been used by seven of seventy-three surveyed footwear firms and in three of the sixty-nine textile-garment firms. The countries that have received most of this subcontract work are, again, Southeast Asian countries and China. The reasons cited for contracting out were many—labor shortages were most frequently cited reason, along with lower administrative costs, lower labor costs, and the need for specialized technology. The ratio of contracting-out costs to total costs is usually under 40 percent, with a ratio of under 20 percent being most common.

During the past two years, more than one-third of the surveyed firms hired temporary or casual workers. The footwear industry hired fewer temporary workers than the textile-garment industry. This lower rate reflects the local labor market conditions of the footwear industry, in which the inflow of full-time employees is very limited. Most temporary workers come from local areas. It appears that temporary and casual workers generally perform the unskilled work. The most common reason cited for hiring temporary workers was labor shortage. Because of the nature of the production process, firms prefer workers with experience in the industry, although labor market realities are such that firms must sometimes resort to temporary inexperienced workers. Because of the lower labor costs involved, a small number of firms have been hiring foreign workers. More firms (fourteen in footwear and twenty-one in textile-garment) hope to hire foreign workers in the future for the same reason. In the footwear industry, the average number of foreign workers hired by firms is twenty-four, of which the ratio of females to males is two to one. The average number of foreign workers per firm in the textile-garment industry is much smaller. All foreign workers appear to carry out unskilled work.

Redundancy, Retraining, and Retention

Most footwear firms plan to decrease or merely maintain their labor force over the next two years. Some firms, of course, plan to increase the number of their employees, but the number of these firms is relatively small. The same is true for textile-garment firms, although more firms in that industry plan to increase employment over the next two years. Reasons given for such plans can be divided into three categories: business fluctuations or an uncertain future; technological change (like automation and process restructuring); and anticipated increases in labor costs and other expenses. No responses referred to union activities in either industry.

About one-half of the footwear firms and more than two-thirds of the textile-garment firms have enacted labor retention plans. These plans have two common features: wage increases and better working conditions. Of the two factors, it seems that wage and fringe benefits are much more important than working conditions. A substantial proportion of firms in both industries have not implemented any training or retraining programs for current employees. The major reason cited for this situation is the labor-intensive nature of the industries—costs would be too high relative to expected returns. Among the firms conducting training programs, in-house programs were the most common, followed by outside programs and government subsidies for training expenses. However, it should be noted that only one company in each industry received government subsidies, and these were of very small amounts.

Labor Unions and Management Options

About 30 percent of the surveyed firms in both industries were unionized to some degree, and two-thirds of the surveyed firms were fully unionized. Almost all firms reported that labor-management relations were cooperative or neutral in impact on business decisions. That assessment is surprising, and a complete turnaround from the attitude that prevailed up until early 1990. The overall industrial situation and worsening economic climate faced by labor-intensive industries seems to have been the cause for changing attitudes. In effect, unions have only a mild influence on corporate strategy, although about one-third of the surveyed firms did indicate that unions had a stronger influence than this statement would lead us to believe. Local industry-wide efforts to improve production efficiency have not been very important. And these efforts have been less intense in the footwear industry, which is suffering from the most pronounced changes. Numerous examples of efforts at increasing productivity were given, including increased automation, increased quality of raw material inputs, and the development of research capacity. Textile-garment firms saw computer-aided design (CAD) and production management as important factors aiding increased productivity. On the other hand, footwear firms paid more attention to the Korean Footwear Research Institute, which was established in Pusan in 1987.

Most footwear firms rated the public sector's supportiveness as very poor or unfavorable in every area of concern, including access to bank loans, social overhead investment, and industrial and labor relations. The textile-garment industry was, in general, a little less critical of the public sector, although firms in both industries believed that government was passive or indifferent to their plight, providing little or no marketing assistance and R&D, especially over the past two years. Similarly, legal and local institutions were seen as unfavorable for business activity in the past or at present. Most footwear firms are more in need of financial assistance or loan arrangements than of other, more well known policy measures, such as industrial policy or labor policy. Many firms also asked for a more active industrial policy, whereas textile-garment firms emphasized the need, again, for financial and fiscal support. In both industries, in general, small and medium firms desired greater planning intervention into industry by government than the larger firms suggested appropriate.

In summary, both the footwear and textile industries are experiencing economic hardship, indicating a likely push toward fundamental restructuring. The textile-garment industry experienced an earlier setback and has thus adjusted more to global conditions than the footwear industry, which has been late in restructuring in many respects. Paradoxically, and following earlier Korean experience, most labor-intensive firms expect government to play a more substantial role in the process of restructuring, but most feel that current regulation is unfavorable to their business. Common efforts across industries to improve productivity or product quality were relatively underdeveloped, especially in the footwear industry. As mentioned several times, above, the footwear industry is the most important industry in Pusan in terms of employment, output, and export. The future of the industry will determine the direction and content of regional industrial restructuring in the second largest city of Korea.

Restructuring and Enterprise Strategy

The restructuring of the footwear industry in Korea provides a model for the future of labor-intensive industries in developing countries. Some basic factors, and the economic environment of the footwear industry, are discussed here, as well as further discussion of corporate restructuring strategies.

Economic Environment for the Footwear Industry

Changing labor market conditions in Korea are well understood simply by reference to rapid increases in wage rates and dramatic labor shortages for the manufacturing sector. The average nominal wage in Korean manufacturing increased by a factor of 2.7 from 1986 to 1992. Given these changes, any industry with low-value-added characteristics will quickly lose international competitiveness unless it has distinctive advantages in terms of unique products or marketing prowess. In this context, contemporary labor market conditions and production costs have drastically affected the competitiveness of Korean labor-intensive industries. Changes in foreign currency exchange rates is another factor to be considered (see chapter 3, this volume). As of 1986, the exchange rate of the Korean won against the U.S. dollar was 881 per dollar. By 1989, it had fallen slightly to 671, before rising again to 788 in 1992. The Korean won has been devaluating very slowly against the U.S. dollar since 1989, but its relative standing against other developing countries' currencies has significantly strengthened. The devaluing won exchange rate has been marginally helpful to the footwear industry, but its impact has been small and appears to have come too late, since it has also been negatively affected by competing countries' currency movements.

A third factor that should be considered is the separation of production from marketing. The OEM method is the dominant production system adhered to by Korean manufacturers, and it seems likely that this method will continue to be important over the near future. Korean manufacturers desperately need their own brand products to counter buyers' power. But it has proved to be too costly to penetrate the world market, where large firms and well-known brands dominate. Korean footwear is rapidly losing its world market share, even though world demand is not decreasing. In these circumstances, there are few strategic options, other than production cost reduction, to deal with changing market conditions.

Potential Competitiveness of the Footwear Industry since 1960

Korean industries have grown rapidly in output, scope, and structure; they now produce everything from airplanes to microchips. However, Korea's best-manufactured product in terms of quality and the application of technology is still footwear, of which it is recognized as the world's best producer. Despite price increases, Korean producers can still claim a competitive edge in terms of product quality, production time, parts, and delivery time (Lim 1994). They also produce high-quality raw materials for high-priced athletic shoes. These advantages should be important for the survival of the industry, if restructuring toward a viable path of accumulation takes place in the near future; life-cycle dynamics (destruction of the local industry) need not be an unavoidable result of competition. Buyers in the United States (Nike), the United Kingdom (Reebok), Germany (Adidas), and Japan (Asics) may have provided a clue for imagining a future for the Korean industry—that is, to retain essential skills at home but to manufacture elsewhere in the world. In this respect, changes in comparative advantage are not sufficient to understand local circumstances if factors other than labor costs are considered in analyzing international competitiveness. For instance, Japan's labor costs are the highest in the world, but the nation still manufactures and exports various kinds of products, including labor-intensive products. Japan's international competitiveness is still extremely high in most sectors.

Scale-Down Strategy

Through the 1970s and 1980s, the Korean footwear industry, in its attempts to meet the bulk orders placed by major foreign buyers, embarked on a policy of large-scale production. Essentially, the production technology used in the industry required production lines using about three hundred to four hundred workers. Larger scale in footwear production means introducing and setting up more production lines, a strategy that does not necessarily reap the benefits of economies of scale. In 1984, there were six Korean footwear firms employing more than five thousand workers; one even employed twenty-one thousand workers. This strategy of large-scale production can be contrasted with

Taiwan, where small and medium firms dominate. Whereas it was a competitive strategy for Korean firms in the past, because of fixed costs and transaction costs, large-scale production has proved to be a disadvantage in times of recession and reduced demand.

Not surprisingly, then, the restructuring process in the Korean footwear industry began with adjustments in firm size. In 1990, there were six large firms (employing more than five thousand workers), but in 1991 five of these either closed or reduced the size of their workforce. In 1992, another firm also reduced its workforce to under five thousand. By the end of 1993, five of these large firms either had closed or had gone out of business. As shown in table 7.2, the average firm size (the number of workers employed) in the industry has rapidly declined since 1990, whereas the total number of firms has increased. The average size of footwear firms was 559 employees in 1982, before falling to 142 in 1991. Restructuring has clearly worked against large firms in favor of firms with fewer than 100 employees. By implication, this means that parts production is more profitable or labor-saving than standard assembly-line production. Clearly, the exit of inefficient firms from the market is a form of restructuring. In 1990, 51 of 362 manufacturing firms in Pusan were closed. Of the 382 firms that closed in 1991, 119 were footwear firms, and in terms of employment, 26 percent of workers attached to closed firms that closed in 1990 worked in the footwear industry; that figure grew to 55 percent in 1991.

Increased Productivity

Since labor wages and costs benefits are rising in conjunction with the declining labor supply, and since cost transfers to buyers are impossible, increased labor productivity is also a vital strategy of restructuring. One way of increasing productivity is automation. It has been reported elsewhere that the automation rate was only 6.9 percent as of 1991 (Korea Footwear Association 1992). This slow rate of automation can be attributed to three factors: product differentiation, a shortage of sufficient highly developed skills for the production of athletic shoes; and the high cost of investment. With respect to product differentiation, it should be noted there are thirteen basic foot sizes and, if sex variation is taken into account, the basic size classification doubles to twenty-six. Since each brand-name product carries a different outfit, material, and color for product distinction, an average OEM production system has to deal with about two hundred sizes. This is a crucial factor in a firm's decision about the introduction of automation in the production of athletic shoes. Added to this is the fact that a new cutting and sewing machine using CAD techniques costs about US$130 thousand per unit. In practice, such an investment is a new cost to production, not a replacement investment, even though it saves labor and increases productivity. According to our survey, about 38 percent of footwear firms had plans to introduce automation technology.

So far, automation has not proved to be the only way of enhancing productivity. Introducing flexible manufacturing systems (FMSs) could be another way of increasing productivity. Automation is one obvious example of an FMS. Subcontracting or contracting out could be another form of FMS. One particular report (Suh 1993), suggested that an appropriate strategy would be to reduce the average number of employees per line from 421 in 1992 to 180 in 2000 through automation and technological improvement. But diversified orders from several buyers has required flexible manufacturing systems, although the burden of sunk costs (like iron molds) and the holding and supply of parts can be a barrier to industrial restructuring.

Research and development and investment in new technology is another way of increasing labor productivity. Still, about two-thirds of the surveyed firms have not introduced new production technology. This could be one reason for local industrial decline and, at the same time, the result of decline where local firms and financial institutions are reluctant to invest in new methods of production. The president of a local commercial bank told the author of this chapter that he would be cautious in lending money to footwear firms because of the apparent relatively high risk. He recognized the potential of Korean footwear manufacturing but worried about the uncertainty involved. Thus, the Korean Footwear Research Institute, which was established in 1987, has been plagued by a shortage of research funds. Because of their dependence upon the OEM system, Korean firms and the Korean government failed to appreciate the significance of alternative configurations of production and failed to appreciate the risks involved in their dependence.

Relocation Strategy

Foreign direct investment or joint ventures are a form of restructuring. Korean manufacturing firms began FDI in the mid-1980s. As noted above, most of the offshore facilities and new investment have gone to

Southeast Asia and China. For instance, since 1987 one of the largest firms in Pusan has transferred a substantial portion of its production capacity to Indonesia (eight production lines) and China (four production lines), leaving only four production lines in Pusan as of May 1993. The company is now planning to close local production lines sometime soon and will shift production to its overseas plants. Interestingly, the initial FDI decision by the firm was taken on the advice of a buyer; to reject the advice would have lost the company the production orders of that buyer. The problem with foreign investment for the footwear industry is the OEM method of production. Since buyers often place orders directly with overseas plants, local manufacturers often do not have control over their foreign subsidiaries. The competitiveness of foreign subsidiaries tends to expedite the decline of home factories, whereas, at the same time, foreign subsidiaries face competition from home plants as those plants lead technological innovation in production. The worst-case scenario is that buyers send orders directly to local overseas firms trained by Korean manufacturers, leaving Korean firms with empty order books. As those firms themselves face competition from other firms in even cheaper locations, technology transfer to new sites of production becomes a means of leap frogging from place to place. This is clearly a scenario envisioned by MITI (see chapter 3, this volume). The question here is whether the Korean government should help in mediating the process of industrial transformation.

The hiring of foreign workers in home factories is one variation on the FDI strategy. It is illegal in Korea to hire foreign workers without government approval. Foreign trainees are only allowed to stay for six to twelve months at a time. According to our survey results, very few firms employ foreign workers. However, this number might be underestimated because of the fear of legal problems involved in disclosing their hiring of foreign labor. As an indication of this possibility, many firms expressed interest in having foreign workers if legal barriers and union resistance were removed.

Own-brand Manufacturing and Marketing

Whereas the restructuring of the footwear industry has been directly related to production, marketing and design have the potential to deliver higher value added than enhanced productivity. The retail price of Nike or Reebok in the U.S. market is four or five times higher than the FOB price in Korea. Because Korean companies are absolutely dependent on the buyer's order, they have been unable to share in the profitable circumstances of the previous oligopsonistic market structure. Only a few large Korean footwear companies have tried to enter the U.S. market with their own brand names, and this occurred only after Nike and Reebok consolidated their production sources. Less than five percent of Korean footwear products are exported under manufacturers' brands at present.

If Korean footwear firms are to survive in the global marketplace in the foreseeable future (regardless of whether they wish to continue production at home), developing an own-brand name is essential. The problem is that such a strategy will take enormous financial resources, and the fight for market share will be with the world's big buyers, who operate efficiently within the international division of labor. Hence, some commentators believe that Korean manufacturers should (and can only) supply high-quality parts and manufacturing technology to countries at the periphery while producing low-volume high-priced shoes for a narrow market segment. Even so, the high-quality athletic-shoe market is not an institutionally or legally protected system. Nike and Reebok may be challenged by new entrants at any time. The financial losses recorded by IBM and Sony in 1992 were surprising, but real. Not all high-value-added products are profitable, just as not all mature industries are unprofitable. Consumers never stick to a specific brand or product permanently. Fashion is also affected by price.

Restructuring and Regional Labor Market

Obviously, one of the main reasons for industrial restructuring stems from conditions in the Korean labor market. Both labor shortages and rising real wages have greatly affected the labor-intensive industries and have made restructuring practically inevitable. The supply of younger workers has been drastically reduced, and the turnover rate is also high for younger age groups. Both elements are a product of intense competition for labor from other sectors of the economy able to pay higher wages for clerical work. Nevertheless, the footwear industry remains the most labor-intensive industry in Pusan and employs about one-third of all manufacturing industry workers. As employment declines in this sector, the whereabouts of those separated workers may be a useful clue in detecting the consequences of restructuring for the region. So, for example, the fact that many workers who leave their employment in the industry are not fully absorbed into the same industry is indicative of the ongoing structural transformation of the local and national economies.

The trend so far is that younger workers tend to leave the industry completely, while older workers usually attempt to find employment within the same industry. Similarly, the role of labor unions is quickly changing. During the period of labor unrest from 1987, the industry union was the main force behind wage increases and worker militancy. Unfortunately, this period of industrial unrest coincided with the onset of decline in the footwear industry. For a variety of reasons, the voice of the union can hardly be heard now in the region. In our survey, most firms responded by noting that labor unions act in a manner somewhere between cooperative and neutral. At best, a few unions have assumed the role of clearing committee, ensuring that failing firms pay out promised wage and pension benefits.

Intervention or Laissez-faire?

Industrial policies in Korea can be thought to have promoted government-led economic growth. In this respect, industrial policies of the government could be classified into two types: general growth promotion policies and industry-specific support policies. General policies have included expert promotion, special loans, and tax support for industrial growth—policies that cover all or some parts of industries quite indifferently. Industry-specific policies have been aimed at providing- intensive support in order to develop a specific industry, such as the microchip industry. However, the footwear industry is one industry that has not received any special support from the government. Even though footwear has been ranked among the ten major export products for many years, the Korean government has provided no special assistance to the industry. Only after the industry began to experience severe economic problems did the government consider support. The government could have predetermined that the footwear industry is in terminal decline and could have decided that silent transformation and restructuring would be more desirable than economic support. However, since the industry is so important to Pusan's economy, the complete failure of the industry would have been too great a political burden on the government. Thus, the government has finally decided to facilitate the industry's restructuring process.

The Korean government designated the footwear industry as an industry for rationalization (IFR) for three years, beginning March 1, 1992. The designated subsectors of the footwear industry for rationalization were athletic shoe, all-rubber shoe, and working shoe manufacturing. The designated parts manufacturers were those that produce soles and the uppers of leather shoes. These subsectors will be protected by the regulation of entry to the industry and of facility expansion. Financing will be provided for automation, modernization of equipment, and facilities and technology development. Marginal firms will be encouraged to leave the industry, with the aid of a rationalization fund or financing package (Lim 1994). For the firms to which the policy applies, a special fund has been established at local banks. The size of the fund is 200 billion won (US$250 million) for three years, and the interest rate for loans from the fund is 2–3 percent lower than that set for commercial loans. The fund is to be used for replacing old facilities with new or labor-saving technology. The old technology and equipment must be scrapped or exported. The government and the footwear industry association expect to reduce the numbers of production lines by 20 percent with this fund.

After one year of IFR status, the industry has not experienced the policy's desired effects. The number of production lines has been decreasing (table 7.1), but mainly through the failure of large firms. During the first year, only about 10 billion won in IFR fund loans was applied for, out of the 70 billion won allocated. The main reason for the sluggishness of the program appears to be a general shortage of physical assets by which to guarantee the payback of loans. Most firms in the industry do not have adequate land or buildings to offer as security. Another reason is that all firms urgently need an operating fund, instead of an investment fund, to meet the severe current production problems. That is, their most pressing problem is shortfall of expected revenue, given fixed costs and contractually agreed variable costs. In terms of Strong and Meyer's (1990) theory of corporate finance, most firms in the footwear and garment industries face a liquidity crisis; the volume of residual funds available in those firms for sustaining investment often falls short of their immediate needs, and there are few if any funds available for discretionary investment. Some firms have also complained of a shortage of automated machinery, domestically available for purchase. Automation technology for athletic-shoe manufacturing is really only available overseas.

In essence, the IFR policy seems to have been implemented too late. Restructuring is easier while market conditions are still strong and revenue predictable. Late intervention brings about a real dilemma. That is, the industry and the government agree together that something has to be done for the ailing industry. While the government has insisted that structural overhaul is needed in order to keep the level of assistance balanced with other industries and industrial policies, the industry and individual firms have asked for the immediate and simultaneous injection of revenue and income as life-saving medicine. For consistent industrial policy, the government is reluctant to help individual firms with such a policy program; but not to help will cost a substantial number of jobs and have a negative impact on the regional economy. Since 1986, eight industries have been designated as IFR eligible. Some of them were revitalized by the IFR policy, and some were not. The automobile industry could be considered a successful case. It remains to be seen if the footwear industry will be so successful.

The aggravated financial situation of existing firms in the industry is also a barrier to restructuring. The average debt ratio within the footwear industry is at least two times higher than the average of the entire manufacturing sector; the industry average of owned capital is one-half of the manufacturing average. Therefore, foreign investment strategies are very difficult for financially troubled firms, even with the cooperation of the IFR policy. Another limitation of the IFR policy is that there are no measures for international marketing or developing a common brand-name product. It is generally acknowledged in Korea that the industry itself is not able to carry out the development of a brand name for common marketing or distribution because of the problem of reconciling individual firm's interests with the industry or community interest. The IFR strategy may help in this regard, although there remains the problem of fairness—selective investment in particular firms as opposed to general policies available to all firms (but perhaps irrelevant to the most deserving firms).

Conclusion

Whether the country needs an industrial policy for sustained economic development or a specific industry and firm-based strategy in the global economy is now a vital issue for Korea. Korean footwear manufacturing firms have developed the best manufacturing skills in the world and can produce the best-quality parts in the world, as well. However, the labor-intensive characteristics of the industry, the rising labor cost of production at home, and the rising real productivity of competing foreign producers have all contributed to the decline of the industry's international competitiveness. The industry produces 95 percent of its product by the OEM method, where producers have no control over buyers' orders. The production market is such that a few buyers dominate the production market. And as the major buyers have begun to move overseas in an attempt to take advantage of cheaper labor costs, it seems too late for Korean firms to escape from the OEM system and to establish an own-brand-name system. Footwear is Pusan's single most important industry; the future of the city depends on the path of industrial restructuring chosen by the individual firms. This is the given situation of the footwear industry in Korea.

Is it best to follow the path apparently preordained by the industrial life-cycle theory? to follow the theory of comparative advantage? or to pursue a strong government industrial development policy? Or is it best to leave the future of the industry and the region in the hands of individual corporations?

Gordon Clark (1993b) develops a model of the globalized small firm, one having characteristics consistent with, but exploitive of, the new international division of labor. This model is useful to consider, because it allows us to see with greater clarity the current predicament of labor-intensive industries in Korea. The major buyers of Korean-made athletic footwear possess many of the same characteristics of Clark's "CORPORATION X," including the significance of transaction costs, the low portion of labor costs in final retail price, the high value added of design and marketing, and the international reputation of brand names. One difference from Clark's model, however, is that the major buyers of footwear products are very big, relative to the Korean manufacturing market, and use their R&D functions at their headquarters to protect patents along with the brand image in large consumer markets like the U.S. Clark's CORPORATION X maintains close relations with agents and producers, forming business alliances and linkages to sustain the flow of products onto the market. In this case, the dependency relation between CORPORATION X and other firms is mutual, whereas in the case of Korean footwear firms the relationship is more often unilateral because of the competitive power of buyers in the global new international division of labor.

The production technology of the footwear industry resembles that of the electronics and automobile industries. In assembling an athletic shoe, about a hundred different parts are needed. For the assembly and sewing operations of the production process, labor costs are crucial factors in the fight to remain competitive. Korean firms should be able to maintain a competitive edge in parts production for a long time. In the Korean electronics industry, the most important parts are still supplied by Japanese manufacturers. For example, the motor head of the VCR is supplied by the Japanese, even though Korea is producing the world's best products. Likewise, holding on to control of the production of footwear parts and their supply to manufacturers all over the world could be a way of ensuring a role for Korean firms in the industry. However, to do so depends on a high rate of technical innovation and investment at a time of severe financial crisis.

Other options would be to mimic what Nike and Reebok have done in the past or, perhaps, to copy the structure and activities of CORPORATION X. Both may be viable alternatives. Both imply, though, that the only way out is to establish a marketing company rather than a production company with those facilities at home. Clearly, it will be very costly to penetrate the U.S. and European consumer markets with an own-brand on the scale of Nike and Reebok. The expense for advertising and marketing will be enormous. My assessment, then, of this whole issue of firm strategy on the global scale is that it requires further political consideration and policy support in Korea. However, there are problems. Such an approach implies selective industry support, whereas, in fact, it may be more efficient to encourage individual companies with entrepreneurial ability (whatever their industry affiliation). There has been little analysis of this issue in Korea—industry policy remains opaque rather than known in this respect. It is apparent that, as Leipziger and Petri (1993) suggest, Korean industry policy has not kept pace with the rapid transformation of the Korean economy, its changing global position, and the competitiveness of its labor-intensive industries.

Perhaps the reunification of, or economic cooperation between, South Korea (the Republic of Korea) and North Korea (the Democratic People's Republic of Korea) will be the needed breakthrough in the search for a solution to the problems of Korean labor-intensive industries. The combination of the technology and capital of the South with the cheaper labor of the North could generate new opportunities for firms to restructure within Korea, thereby retaining their control over the structure of production. The geographical proximity of the North, and the absence of language barriers, could be an enormous advantage for both sides, even before any reunification. What is crucial, of course, is that the existing firms in the Pusan industry should survive until unification occurs. It is also worth noting that expectations are also critical in determining the future of the industry. As is the case in the security markets, expectations formed about a firm or an industry will drive the structure of prices. In the case of the footwear industry, pessimism about the future discouraged firms from establishing any constructive future plan while limiting public support for a coherent industry strategy. The ambiguous attitude of the central government also played a decisive, negative role in this process of destabilization of the industry. For too long, an indifferent and divided policy stance has been worse than having no policy at all.

EIGHT

Taiwan: Labor Shortage

Ching-lung Tsay

Taiwan's experience of rapid economic development and sustained growth during the past four decades has been widely discussed and frequently cited as a miracle (see, for example, Kuo 1983; Lau 1986). This miracle is considered to be primarily a result of success in export-oriented industrialization, one of the prime economic goals of the government. Throughout the period of economic transition from developing to more mature economy, it has been clear that small and medium enterprises (SMEs) have played an important role. The SMEs have contributed to the Taiwan economy in many ways, including the growth of industries in terms of number of firms and value of products, the creation of employment opportunities, and the expansion of foreign trade. For instance, in the earlier stage of Taiwan's development, the contribution made by SMEs to total manufacturing exports increased from 56 percent in 1972 to a peak of 74 percent in 1982. After that, the relative importance of SMEs gradually declined as Taiwan's economy began to shift toward technology-intensive activities. Although recent data suggest a tendency for SMEs to be superseded by large enterprises in terms of export performance, the SMEs remain important for overall Taiwanese economic performance (Taiwan 1992a, 1993d).

In its evolution to a more mature economy, Taiwan inevitably faces many problems at both local and international levels. Like other Asian newly industrializing economies (NIEs), Taiwan's industrial economy is being challenged by a number of factors, including labor shortage, rising real wages, currency value fluctuations, and increasing land and raw material costs. In pushing up production costs, these elements are reinforced by rising demands from labor unions and environmental protection regulations. As a consequence, Taiwanese producers find it more and more difficult to compete with low-cost producers in China and some countries of Southeast Asia. This gradual loss of world competitiveness for industrial products has created an urgent need for changes in Taiwan's industrial structure. To remain competitive in international markets, Taiwan's firms must restructure by moving into higher value-added, more skill-intensive and capital-intensive manufacturing and into business and services.

In this era of industrial upgrading, manufacturing enterprises are faced with various difficulties arising from a changing global environment. This observation is particularly true for those SMEs which are largely family-owned and family-managed. Although triggers of industrial restructuring have been identified and examined (Tsay 1993), relatively little is known about the various strategies manufacturing firms have adopted in this new phase of industrial development. Focusing on Taiwan, this chapter presents empirical evidence based on a nationwide survey regarding various adjustment routes national firms have chosen. For the purpose of comparative analysis of Asian NIEs, two specific types of manufacturing were selected: the electrical machinery and electronics industry and the textile and garment industry. The analysis attempts to relate the island's past economic success to rising living standards and aspirations among manufacturing workers for better living conditions. How might such phenomena affect corporate strategies, particularly in terms of labor utilization? What have been the consequences of, and responses to, the increasing shortage of industrial labor?

Manufacturing Competition and Economic Growth

Despite very limited natural endowments, Taiwan has achieved a high level of economic development within four decades. By 1990, the per capita GNP of the island was over US$10,000, and Taiwan ranked as the world's fourteenth largest trading country. This remarkable performance and economic transformation over such a short period is believed to be the result of many factors, including the successful implementation of land reform, the effective introduction of foreign capital, the government's encouragement of an export-oriented economy, and the efficient use of manpower (Wu and Lan 1991).

Following the period of import substitution (1950–62), the government of Taiwan promoted the export of manufactured goods, which proved to contribute significantly to the growth of the economy (Liu 1992). During the past four decades, the total volume of exports in creased substantially, from US$120 million in 1952 to US$76 billion in 1991. Moreover, the ratio of industrial products to total exports rose from 8.1 percent to 95.3 percent in the same period. The success in this phase of external orientation (1962–80) is reflected in the pronounced growth of the manufacturing industry on the island. The outstanding performance in exports and industrial production was the cause of the high economic growth during that period. As the island moved toward a more mature economy in the mid-1980s, the rate of economic growth slowed down (below 8 percent) and there was a significant decline in manufacturing. In 1986, manufacturing accounted for 39.7 percent of at Taiwan's gross domestic output. In 1992, that figure had dropped to 32.9 percent. The steep decline in manufacturing and the rise of the service sector are believed to be an inevitable process in the maturing of the economy. With rising living standards, there has been a growing demand for consumer services, and even the manufacturing industries have needed services to expand their development.

Despite the current labor force of over 8.18 million, Taiwan is experiencing a labor shortage, a phenomenon inferred from rising wages and the increase in foreign labor. Theoretically, a labor shortage means that job vacancies cannot be filled by applicants. Based on both a theoretical analysis and an examination of empirical data, Wu and Lan (1991) conclude that the labor market in Taiwan moved from a position of surplus to a labor-shortage condition, especially in low-skill employment categories. Citing results of a firm-level survey on labor mobility and working conditions of employees conducted by the directorate general of budget, accounting, and statistics, Wu and Lan found that the percentage of firms in the manufacturing industry facing a labor shortage rose steadily from 15.6 percent in 1982 to 55.5 percent in 1987. In the manufacturing sector, textiles and garments and accessories had relatively high ratios, but the figures for the construction industry were not as large, despite a labor shortage within that industry. Reasons given by the surveyed firms for not succeeding in hiring workers include "no applicant," "interest did not match," and "asked for too high wages."

After maintaining high economic growth rates for the past three decades, Taiwan has begun to experience rising real wages. For all types of industry, real domestic wages rose steadily during the last decade, the increase being about twofold (from NT$10,615 in 1980 to NT$21,989 in 1990). The largest increase appears to have been in the service sector, especially in the electricity, gas, water, and sanitation industry. Domestic wages also doubled in such industries as manufacturing and construction. The lowest increase in monthly real wages occurred in mining and quarrying and in social and personal services. A significant increase in real wages is no doubt one factor that has raised per unit production costs in manufacturing industries. Table 8.1 shows data on the ratio of labor costs to total (production) costs for various manufacturing industries. The ratio varies remarkably, from less than 5 percent to more than 20 percent, reflecting the differences between industries. In terms of changes in the ratio, more than half the twenty industries experienced an increase between 1976 and 1991, whereas only six experienced a small decrease. The industries of textiles, wearing apparel, and accessories, wood and bamboo products and nonmetallic furniture, rubber products, and plastic products are characterized by substantial increases in the ratio from an already high level. Given the increase in real wages, it is less likely that the industries would have increased their use of labor. The data in table 8.1 clearly illustrates the pressure applied by wage increases for restructuring of the labor-intensive manufacturing industries.

In response to the changed economic environment, a clear shift in the composition of manufacturing firms has occurred. The food-processing and textile industries' shares of total manufacturing production fell from 31.8 percent in 1952 to 7.9 percent in 1991, while the electronic and electrical products industry's share increased from 2.3 percent to 16.9 percent during the same period. It is clear that the electronics industry will play a leading role enhancing Taiwan's competitiveness in this new era. Since being designated a strategic industry, enormous efforts are being made by both the government and private firms to upgrade the technology in the electronics industry, particularly in the information-processing sector of the industry.

The development of the electronics industry in Taiwan began in the early 1960s, largely through foreign direct investment (FDI). Foreign companies were attracted to Taiwan for investment, particularly in its electronics industry, because of low-cost and preferential treatment. Initially, Taiwan's electronics industry produced mainly home electrical appliances, such as TVs, radios, and other consumer electronic products. Through these early operations, the industry accumulated ex-

Table 8.1 Share of Labor Cost in Total Costs (percentage)

Industry	1976	1981	1986	1991
Food processing	8.11	8.23	9.90	12.32
Beverage and tobacco	4.95	6.56	5.66	10.03
Textiles	14.86	16.46	16.06	15.84
Wearing apparel and accessories	18.49	20.88	20.46	24.74
Leather and fur products	18.49	18.75	18.35	17.24
Wood and bamboo products, printing, and nonmetallic furniture	16.33	17.21	17.72	19.63
Paper and products, printing and publishing	15.23	14.70	15.51	18.20
Chemical materials	9.01	7.60	9.01	11.60
Chemical products	12.21	13.62	13.90	16.42
Petroleum and coal	2.77	1.94	5.51	6.51
Rubber products	16.58	18.12	20.31	19.79
Plastic products	15.03	16.21	17.95	18.33
Nonmetallic minerals	16.13	14.33	16.68	17.56
Basic metal	7.39	7.53	8.59	10.82
Fabricated metal	20.82	18.88	18.67	20.73
Machinery and equipment	21.02	18.72	17.97	19.19
Electrical and electronic machinery and equipment	15.38	15.72	14.56	14.57
Transport equipment	12.98	13.08	13.36	13.33
Precision instruments	23.31	22.37	19.10	20.31
Miscellaneous	20.86	19.49	20.04	20.02

Source: Taiwan (1988, 1992a).

cellent labor resources, experience, and technologies. As the economy developed, home electrical appliance firms shifted their production to the more value added information technology products, such as monitors and microcomputers. It is obvious that information technology products will play an integral role in the development of Taiwan's electronics industry.

The government of Taiwan has been extensively involved in an effort to upgrade the electronics industry. It has provided subsidized credit, and government-sponsored research institutes have acted as conduits for the transfer of foreign technology to local firms. Hence, Taiwan's electronics industry grew rapidly in terms of employment, export, and GNP contributions. In 1991, the electronics and electrical industry accounted for 19 percent of total manufacturing employment. Moreover, electronics production constituted 26.6 percent of total exports and 18.4 percent of GNP. With regard to the information technology industry in particular, Taiwan ranked seventh in the world as measured by the value of computer hardware production.

It should be noted that small and medium enterprises have dominated Taiwan's manufacturing sector throughout different phases of industrial development. The share of SMEs (roughly defined as enterprises of fewer than 300 employees) in total manufacturing sales was over 47 percent in 1986 and 1987. Although the proportion decreased afterward, SMEs' share has remained at high levels (40 percent or higher). In terms of export performance, SMEs have undoubtedly played an important role. First, their contribution to total manufacturing exports was as high as 73 percent in 1982. This figure then dropped steadily to 65 percent in 1985 and to around 60 percent in the first three years of the 1990s, with exeptions in 1986 and 1987 (70 percent). Second, regarding the export ratio, the proportion for SMEs has remained around 45 percent, while the corresponding figure for large enterprises has been 20 percent or less. This difference persists despite the fact that the whole manufacturing sale accounted for by SMEs decreased from 47 percent in 1986 to 39 percent in 1992.

The importance of SMEs is also evident in terms of employment and number of firms. SMEs' share in the total manufacturing workforce has been on the rise since the 1970s (see table 8.2). The contribution made by SMEs with fewer than 100 employees increased continuously from 36 percent in 1971 to 48 percent in 1981, and to 59 percent in 1991 (Taiwan 1991b). With regard to number of firms, the share of enterprises of 10 to 100 workers increased rapidly during the period of export-oriented labor-intensive industrialization in the 1960s and early 1970s, reflecting the rise of factories and modern workshops (Liu, Liu, and Wu 1993). It has also been argued that these SME firms entered the market either by growing up from very small firms or by being newly established during that period (Schive 1993). As the manufacturing industry is realigning toward technology-intensive activities in the mid-1980s, large enterprises of over 100 employees are beginning to emerge. Similarly, the recent development of business groups has led the economy toward a modern economy oriented toward Chinese culture (Liu, Liu, and Wu 1993).

Past literature has discussed the strengths and weaknesses of SMEs in general. For example, it has been argued that theoretically, the advantage of SMEs lies in their quick reaction to market signals. Empirical evidence based on case studies of footwear and computer indus-

Table 8.2 Share of Manufacturing in Total Industry, by Enterprises and Employees, Selected Years 1954–1991 (number and percentage)

Firm Size (no. of employees)	1954	1961	1971	1981	1991
			Number of Enterprises		
N	42,388	51,567	45,636	92,381	143,459
1–9	38,369	46,145	29,274	65,789	94,262
10–29	2,904	3,872	10,785	16,260	33,202
30–49	488	737	2,028	4,550	7,381
50–99	289	426	1,600	3,948	5,171
100–499	210	318	1,628	1,326	3,072
500+	28	69	321	508	371
		As Percentage of Total Number of Enterprises			
1–9	90.7	89.5	68.7	69.6	65.8
10–29	6.9	7.5	25.3	17.2	23.2
30–49	1.2	1.4	4.8	4.8	5.2
50–99	0.7	0.8	3.8	4.2	3.6
100–499	0.5	0.6	3.8	1.4	2.1
500+	0.1	0.1	0.8	0.5	0.3
			Number of Employees		
N	309,887	454,272	1,201,539	1,978,161	2,634,145
1–9	113,445	141,121	113,507	244,197	380,827
10–29	61,112	63,985	126,429	267,420	536,240
30–49	22,520	27,430	77,267	172,200	275,926
50–99	19,121	29,052	110,785	273,744	351,858
100–499	46,351	63,723	339,389	496,522	580,820
500+	47,338	128,961	434,162	524,078	508,474
		As Percentage of Total Workforce			
1–9	36.6	31.1	9.4	11.2	14.5
10–29	19.7	14.1	10.5	12.3	20.4
30–49	7.3	6.0	6.4	7.9	10.5
50–99	6.2	6.4	9.2	12.6	13.4
100–499	15.0	14.0	28.2	22.8	22.0
500+	15.3	28.4	36.1	24.1	19.3

Source: Taiwan (1988, 1992a).

tries in Taiwan also points to SMEs' flexibility and their ability to respond rapidly to market niches (Levy 1990). Hence, the survival of SMEs depends, to a great extent, on the productivity effects of learning by doing (Schive 1993).

As Taiwan is moving toward a more technology-intensive economy, the question arises whether the small size of most Taiwanese firms will prove to be an obstacle to their survival in the international competition. As Schive (1993) argues, the ability to respond quickly to market changes makes it unnecessary for any SME to be an innovator. As a result, SMEs are often found to lack incentives to invest in R&D or to enjoy economies of scale in mass production or economies of scope in product diversification. Nevertheless, the predominance of SMEs in Taiwan indicates that this type of firm can compete successfully with large enterprises. It remains to be seen whether this pattern will continue in the later phase of industrial upgrading.

Aspirations of the Middle Class

The 1980s marked a turning point for Taiwan's labor-intensive enterprises as the competitive edge the island once enjoyed ceased to exist. In this transition to a new stage of development, changes in the composition of the manufacturing sector of the island have occurred. The most pronounced trend is the decline of textiles and the growth of the electronics and electrical products industry. Such intersectoral shifts in production have created new employment opportunities. As Fields (1992) argues, workers could leave the low-paying sectors of the economy and move into better-paying jobs, thereby improving their standards of living. In other words, this transformation of the economy toward higher technology coincides with the emerging middle-class aspirations among indigenous workers in Taiwan.

For many of the island's labor-intensive enterprises, the most difficult problem they face in maintaining their operations at home is the so-called shortage of labor. As expressed by some manufacturers, the hardship and poor environment in the production process are the major causes for local workers to shun certain jobs. Again, this selectivity of employment among native workers reflects some of their middle-class aspirations, a phenomenon which did not seem to exist in the earlier phases of development. In the past, the less educated workforce had very limited options for jobs. However, subsequent economic growth has resulted in rising income and accumulated wealth. Average workers in this new era of development can afford to be temporarily out of work if working conditions are unfavorable. Moreover, there are other employment alternatives in different sectors of the industry. An increasing number of workers are going into services and clerical work rather than shop-floor production.

Rising expectations among individuals in the process of economic development is reflected in investment in education. Over the years, there has been a sharp increase in school enrollment and years of schooling, particularly among females. At the same time, labor participation rates for young women (15–19 and 20–24 age groups) have dropped significantly (Tsay 1982, 1988). These changes have undoubtedly had some adverse effects on the supply of manual labor. According to different surveys conducted by various agencies in the late 1980s and early 1990s, about two-thirds of manufacturing firms surveyed reported having labor shortages (Taiwan 1987). The manufacturing industries with the most acute labor shortages are textile, garments and other textile products, plastic products, and electronics and electrical equipment. The main labor shortages are in the unskilled labor market.

Changes in the manual labor supply have also been viewed as a result of a shift in the class structure of Taiwan's society. Shen (1993), for example, bases his sociological analysis on Wright's class scheme of four major categories: capitalists, managers, workers, and the petite bourgeoisie. The nonagricultural self-employed, or petite bourgeoisie, can be considered as middle class in the sense that they own the means of production, but they neither purchase the labor power of others nor sell their own labor power. Focusing on the period between 1976 and 1987, Shen's data shows that the small rise in the numbers of nonagricultural, self-employed persons is overwhelmingly concentrated in the commerce industry. Increases in the proportions of this category are observed in industries such as public administration, social and personal services, and transport, storage, and communication. The proportion of petite bourgeoisie in the manufacturing sector is about 10 percent of the total number of nonagricultural self-employed persons in Taiwan, and this level remained relatively unchanged between 1976 and 1987. Various explanations have been offered to account for the rise of nonagricultural self-employment in Taiwan. The main explanations include the role of the informal economy and the emergence of

labor unions and labor regulations (which affect large-scale investments by capitalists), as well as the existence of subcontracting in the
production process.

In addition to changes in the class structure, a shift in the proportion of the workforce in various industries has also been observed. The
official statistics available show a substantial and steady increase in the
service sector's share of employed persons, from 35 percent in 1976 to
39 percent in 1981 and to 47 percent in 1991 (Taiwan 1993b). The
gains occur in categories such as commerce, financing, and social and
personal services. By contrast, the manufacturing industry recorded a
slow increase, from 29 percent in 1976 to a peak of 35 percent in
1987, and then a decrease, to 31 percent in 1991, in the proportions
of employed persons to the total workforce. As expected, the agricultural sector has experienced the largest decline in the share of labor
force (29 percent in 1976, 19 percent in 1981, and 13 percent in 1991).
Hence, it seems clear that as Taiwan has experienced higher levels of
economic development, there was first a shift of labor force from agricultural to manufacturing and then a shift from manufacturing to the
service sector.

Survey Results

The results of a national sample survey of manufacturing enterprises
in Taiwan conducted in 1992 provide useful information regarding issues that create difficulties in business activities and the policies or
strategies used by those enterprises to overcome constraints (Taiwan
1993c). Supplementary data were also drawn from other data sources
(i.e., Academia Sinica sources) in order to portray different types of
strategies, particularly location strategy (the move of the production
offshore or foreign direct investment) and varying labor strategies, including the use of foreign workers. The analysis controls for size of establishments, regional differences, and type of industry.

Business Environment

The perception of business conditions by firms in the two industries is
presented in table 8.3. In the survey, the two selected types of enterprises were asked to identify problems in management and technological development. With regard to management problems, it is clear that
manufacturing firms in Taiwan as a whole have lost past advantages in

Table 8.3 Problems in Management and Technological Development for Small and Medium Enterprises, by Industry and Region

	Textiles and Garments			Electrical Machinery and Electronics		
	Taipei Metro. Area	Other Metro. Areas	Rest of Taiwan	Taipei Metro. Area	Other Metro. Areas	Rest of Taiwan
Small corporations						
Management	(28)	(21)	(25)	(66)	(23)	(69)
Slow market	50.0	66.7	60.0	53.0	34.8	53.6
Rising labor cost	57.1	61.9	56.0	45.5	60.1	50.7
Lack of funds	42.9	33.3	40.0	36.4	34.8	43.5
Shortage of expertise	35.7	42.9	36.0	56.1	47.8	52.2
Technology	(13)	(12)	(11)	(35)	(9)	(20)
Parts production	7.7	0.0	27.3	22.9	22.2	40.0
Material	46.2	75.0	54.6	28.6	33.3	40.0
Product production	76.9	91.7	63.6	77.1	55.6	60.0
Product design	46.2	16.7	27.3	60.0	66.7	50.0
R&D	(13)	(12)	(11)	(35)	(9)	(20)
Knowledge	45.2	33.3	45.5	51.4	33.3	40.0
Funds and facilities	30.8	50.0	18.2	40.0	44.4	50.0
Shortage of expertise	23.1	25.0	54.6	62.9	66.7	40.0
Rapid changes	30.8	33.3	36.4	22.9	33.3	40.0
Medium corporations						
Management	(110)	(78)	(85)	(143)	(62)	(77)
Slow market	46.4	57.7	50.6	39.9	50.0	49.4
Rising labor cost	59.1	62.8	64.7	55.2	66.1	66.2
Lack of funds	31.0	23.0	27.1	26.6	19.4	31.2
Shortage of expertise	47.3	33.3	35.3	49.0	50.0	53.3
Technology	(81)	(48)	(45)	(106)	(36)	(70)
Parts production	4.9	18.8	6.7	21.7	22.2	22.9
Material	28.4	35.4	53.5	31.1	19.4	18.6
Product production	85.2	75.0	71.1	68.9	80.6	61.4
Product design	37.0	50.0	40.0	49.1	66.7	42.9
R&D	(81)	(48)	(45)	(106)	(36)	(70)
Knowledge	35.8	33.3	46.7	46.2	55.6	52.9
Funds and facilities	26.0	27.1	35.6	29.3	27.8	15.7
Shortage of expertise	45.7	47.9	46.7	56.6	52.8	62.9
Rapid changes	34.6	43.8	26.7	37.7	33.3	41.4

Source: Taiwan (1993d).

markets. This observation is particularly true for the labor-intensive textile and garment industry. In this industry, large proportions of both small and medium enterprises mentioned the problem of "insufficient and slow market activities." There appear to be regional differences in firms' perception. The larger percentage of textile and garment factories outside the Taipei metropolitan area indicates that they faced this particular problem of slow market activities.

Apart from the market demand, the problem of rising labor cost is evident within both categories in both industries. Moreover, rising labor costs affects all the enterprises under study, regardless of their size and location. Among textile and garment industries in the Taipei metropolitan area, 57 percent of small enterprises and 59 percent of medium enterprises identified the problem of rising labor cost. For plants located in other metropolitan areas and the rest of Taiwan, over 60 percent reported rising labor cost. Higher percentages of electronics firms outside the Taipei metropolitan area mentioned this specific problem. This difference holds true for both small and medium enterprises. This finding may reflect the fact that cheap labor is no longer available, even in areas outside the capital city.

In addition to problems in management, difficulties in technological development were identified by both types of industries. The statistics in table 8.3 clearly reveal that a large percentage of firms viewed problems in production technology as critical. This pattern is true regardless of size, location, and type of industry. In the electrical and electronics industry, the proportion of enterprises facing difficulties in product design technology is also substantial. The corresponding figures for the textile and garment industry are much smaller. Smaller proportions of firms in both the textile and garment industry and the electrical and electronics industry regarded the problem of parts production as important. Similarly, the difficulties related to improvement of materials have been relatively less acute.

With regard to problems related to R&D, generally higher percentages of responses came from the electrical and electronic industries. Problems such as lack of knowledge and shortages of experts, funds, and facilities were largely identified by small and medium firms located in the Taipei metropolitan area, other metropolitan areas, and the rest of Taiwan. For the firms within the Taipei metropolitan area, the problems regarding lack of knowledge and shortage of experts were perceived as important for both small and medium enterprises. However, no clear-cut pattern is observed for other regions. Surprisingly, low percentages of electrical and electronics firms viewed the rapid changes in the surroundings as a major obstacle to research and development. This fact may be due to the ability of SMEs to respond quickly to outside changes, as already mentioned.

Production and Technology

It is interesting to examine how manufacturing firms in Taiwan respond to business management, technological development, and R&D problems in order to compete in the world markets. The data are shown in table 8.4. Among electrical and electronics firms, responses to management difficulties are seen in policies aimed at developing new products, improving product quality, and promoting sales. However, no clear-cut pattern of response by size of enterprises and location is observed. For the textile and garment industry, major business strategies concentrate on improving product quality and promoting sales. Relatively smaller proportions of firms in the industry mentioned developing new products. This is true regardless of size and location of firms. Hence, it seems clear that there are differences in corporate strategies between the two types of industries.

Firms' responses to technological development are also presented in table 8.4. For both types of industries, corporations tend to rely on themselves by conducting their own research rather than contracting out the research or purchasing technology from other sources. Given the small size of manufacturing enterprises in Taiwan, the most feasible way to implement research would be joint ventures among firms. Other information, however, reveals that relatively small percentages of manufacturing enterprises in Taiwan are willing to go into joint ventures in R&D. This tendency is especially clear for the textile and garment industries, as substantial percentages of small factories (38.5 percent in the Taipei metropolitan area, 41.7 percent in other metropolitan areas, and 36.4 percent in the rest of Taiwan) indicated their unwillingness and inability to venture into joint R&D ventures, even though they are unable to conduct their own. More responses from manufacturing enterprises are observed for the category of "willing to be part of joint R&D venture if receiving assistance from the government." Hence, the results are consistent with what has been previously mentioned in the literature, that SMEs in Taiwan lack the desire and capability to venture into R&D and tend to rely on assistance from the state in this field.

Table 8.4 Strategies in Management and Technological Development for Small and Medium Enterprises, by Industry and Region

	Textiles and Garments			*Electrical Machinery and Electronics*		
	Taipei Metro. Area	*Other Metro. Areas*	*Rest of Taiwan*	*Taipei Metro. Area*	*Other Metro. Areas*	*Rest of Taiwan*
Small Corporations						
Management	(28)	(21)	(25)	(66)	(23)	(69)
Production	42.9	33.3	48.0	40.9	34.8	31.9
Sale	46.4	38.1	44.0	42.4	52.2	59.4
Quality	53.6	61.9	48.0	57.6	56.5	40.6
New products	28.6	14.3	20.0	36.4	47.8	59.4
Technology	(13)	(12)	(11)	(35)	(9)	(20)
Own research	76.9	83.3	63.6	91.4	77.8	85.0
Contract out	23.1	33.3	54.6	11.4	33.3	35.0
Purchase locally	30.8	33.3	45.5	25.7	33.3	15.0
Purchase abroad	15.4	0.0	9.1	8.6	11.1	30.0
R&D joint venture	(13)	(12)	(11)	(35)	(9)	(20)
Willing and affordable	0.0	0.0	0.0	11.4	0.0	30.0
Willing but need financial assistance	38.5	25.0	45.5	45.7	55.6	35.0
No need (doing own research)	23.1	16.7	18.2	31.4	33.3	30.0
Not willing and unable to do own research	38.5	41.7	36.4	5.7	0.0	5.0
Medium Corporations						
Management	(110)	(78)	(85)	(143)	(62)	(77)
Production	36.4	25.6	37.7	28.7	17.7	32.5
Sale	43.6	39.7	48.2	42.0	38.7	46.8
Quality	49.1	55.1	61.2	49.0	48.4	54.4
New products	20.0	37.2	21.2	51.8	56.5	74.0
Technology	(81)	(48)	(45)	(106)	(36)	(70)
Own research	87.7	93.8	86.7	89.6	91.7	97.1
Contract out	19.8	18.8	40.0	17.9	22.2	18.6
Purchase locally	13.6	18.8	11.1	5.7	16.7	7.1
Purchase abroad	33.3	29.2	17.8	24.5	27.8	22.9
R&D joint venture	(81)	(48)	(45)	(106)	(36)	(70)
Willing and affordable	8.6	10.4	8.9	24.5	22.2	21.4
Willing but need financial assistance	42.0	39.6	62.2	44.3	41.7	42.9
No need (doing own research)	26.0	39.6	22.2	26.4	30.6	25.7
Not willing and unable to do own research	22.7	10.4	4.4	3.8	5.6	7.1

Source: Taiwan (1993d).

Location Strategy

This particular survey of manufacturing enterprises does not contain information on location strategy, such as foreign direct investment (FDI), of the sample firms. However, it is possible to examine this corporate strategy at the aggregate level based on data from other sources, including the Taiwan Investment Commission and investment authorities of various countries. Beginning in the late 1980s, many of Taiwan's manufacturers moved their production offshore. Since 1986, the capital outflows from Taiwan to Southeast Asia have amounted to approximately US$13 billion (Kuo 1993; Yu 1992). The move offshore appears to be beneficial to Taiwan's economy. Profits from overseas operations have helped companies in their upgrading efforts at home. In many cases, offshore factories supply labor-intensive parts to home operations in Taiwan, thereby keeping production costs down and alleviating the chronic labor shortage. Many local manufacturers have worked out a division of labor between their operations at home and those overseas. For example, overseas plants tend to concentrate on low-end products, while Taiwan-based plants focus on high-end items. Many manufacturers, after setting up factories offshore, have transformed their Taiwan operations into headquarters for high-end production, R&D activities, receipt of orders, procurement of materials, and the provision of technical assistance and personal training for the overseas plants (Liu 1993a).

On the home front, efforts are being made by both government and private enterprises toward investment in industrial upgrading, which is essential for the continued development of the island's economy. While there are various ways to improve Taiwan's technological capability, the general trend is occurring at a slow pace. Past studies (San 1991; Mody 1990) have pointed out that many small and medium enterprises, which constitute the backbone of the economy, lack the desire or capacity to enter into the high-tech field. There is evidence of an overdependence on government-sponsored technology. Whether extensive intervention by the government will have favorable results in industrial upgrading remains to be seen.

Government Policy and Industrial Restructuring

The economy of Taiwan has been, to a great extent, directed by government policies. Recent state efforts are reflected in the Six-Year

National Development Plan (1991–96) designed to upgrade the island's infrastructure. The government is also trying to rejuvenate the island's declining manufacturing industries. As Liu (1993b, 52) puts it, "Because manufacturing has for decades been considered the driving force of the island's economic development, the government is deeply concerned over the recent decline in its share of Taiwan's economy." In 1986, manufacturing in Taiwan accounted for 39.7 percent of the island's gross domestic output, but the figure had dropped to 32.9 percent in 1992. However, it has been argued that this trend of declining manufacturing enterprises is not surprising, as the economy is entering the mature stage. As living standards improve, there is a growing demand for services; hence the shift of labor from manufacturing to the service sector. Similar patterns have also been observed in some developed countries, such as Japan and the United States. Nevertheless, the steep decline in manufacturing in Taiwan has caught the attention of the government.

To remedy the worsening situation, the government is facing a formidable challenge of creating an environment conducive to investment in industrial upgrading. Such an environment is vital to the long-term development of Taiwan's economy and its manufacturing industries. The proposed plan was an economic revitalization program, formally adopted by Executive Yuan (the cabinet) in July 1993. The major objectives are to accelerate industrial upgrading and to develop Taiwan into a regional operations center for the Asia-Pacific region. The program focuses on three specific areas: effective utilization of resources, promotion of cross-straits economic and trade links, and improvement of government administrative efficiency. Unlike the situation in Hong Kong (described in chapter 4), the government of Taiwan is making serious efforts to boost the island's industrial investment, especially in the manufacturing sector. The government has implemented various measures to help entrepreneurs overcome barriers to investment and is giving them additional assistance, as well as creating a more conducive investment environment.

With regard to the problem of land costs, the government's strategy is directed toward land rezoning, by releasing government-owned land and private farmland for use by industry and for building public infrastructure facilities. The government is also committed to help expedite the development of industrial zones and relax some restrictions on the use of land adjacent to factories. The revitalization program additionally includes the development of suburban industrial and commercial zones that will accommodate not only factories but also wholesale businesses and shopping centers, for which developers have encountered severe difficulties in procuring land.

The problems of rising real wages and chronic labor shortages have frustrated local enterprises, particularly those in the manufacturing industries and construction. To help alleviate this problem, the government has further relaxed its restrictions on the use of foreign workers. According to the statistics released by the Council for Labor Affairs, there are contract foreign workers in Taiwan. The economic benefits from the employers' perspective are clear: a solution to the labor shortage problem and reduced labor costs. But many scholars oppose the further opening up of the domestic labor market for diverse reasons, particularly relating to economic to social costs. For example, it has been argued by many scholars that the importation of foreign workers may retard the process of technological upgrading in Taiwan (Chang 1991; Lee 1992; Tsai and Tsay 1991). To strive toward a stage of full development, they argue, Taiwan should not allow labor-intensive industries to maintain production by using cheap foreign labor. Of course, the labor shortage and high labor costs are two sides of one coin. It is understandable that enterprises use the lack of local workers, rather than savings in labor costs, as their reason for hiring foreign labor.

Concern over the social consequences of the use of foreign workers have been frequently expressed. Kao (1992) summarizes the fears of social disorder associated with an influx of unskilled foreign workers. Given Taiwan's high population density, many people in Taiwan are concerned about the increasing land pressure brought about by a large influx of foreign people. Furthermore, possible crimes and racial conflicts, as well as infection by diseases carried by foreign workers, are often cited as possible negative impacts should the labor market become widely open to foreign labor (Tsai and Tsay 1991).

With a realization that relying upon foreign labor hinders long-term industrial upgrading, the government is pushing toward greater automation in the production process. Currently, the proportion of enterprises using automated equipment in production remains low—12 percent for all manufacturing industries at the end of 1991 (Taiwan 1992a). However, the trend is rising for the electrical and electronics industry. Incentive programs include the establishment of investment tax credits for procuring automation. To solve the problem of the deteriorating quality of the environment, the government is providing tax incentives for manufacturing industries to use pollution control equipment.

As was described earlier, SMEs have long been the backbone of the island's economy. However, they lack the desire or capacity to pursue long-term plans of transforming into high-tech industries. The government is, therefore, offering to provide financial assistance by extending loans and technical services to manufacturers and SMEs, through appropriations of NT$40 billion (US$1.54 billion) from the postal savings system. Other steps include increasing the development funds for SMEs, reducing the preferential interest rates on loans for the procurement of automation and pollution-control equipment, and allowing both government-run and private enterprises to pay for these imports by borrowing money or by issuing corporate bonds overseas.

Government strategies to promote the technology level of Taiwan's electronics industry have been evaluated elsewhere. San (1991) conducted an opinion survey of electronics firms regarding the role of the government in upgrading the island's electronics industry. The results show different views of the state by firms regarding what types of strategies should be adopted. The majority of electronics parts and components firms believe that the government should assist firms in acquiring foreign technology. The semiconductors industry, characterized by large capital investments and high risk, views the role of the government differently. They consider that the government should provide more technology transfers through government-sponsored research institutes. Moreover, they would like the state to coordinate joint research programs among firms. Finally, they emphasize the importance of educating more people in R&D. In the telecommunications equipment industry, firms believe that the government should offer joint research and technological transfers through government-sponsored research institutes. It should be noted that other strategies such as low-interest loans and tax exemptions on R&D expenditure are not considered to be the government's major tasks.

One obvious effort made by the government toward technological development was the establishment of the Hsinchu Science-Based Industrial Park in 1980. The purpose was to encourage foreign investment into the country and to attract back home those experienced and well-established Chinese engineers and technicians working abroad (mainly in the United States). The park is well equipped with necessary facilities, such as bilingual schools, buildings, and infrastructure, and the government offers cheap rent, tax exemption, and low-interest loans. In addition, the government established two research institutions to support the electronics industries, as most of Taiwan's electronics firms lack capital resources for research. One is the Institute for the Information Industry, founded in 1979. Its primary function is to promote the development and use of computer-related technologies. The other is the Industrial Technology Research Institution. The major objective of this organization is to help the government conduct R&D in industrial electronics technology for the public and private sectors. There is no doubt that the government has played a critical role in research and technology development.

The use of part-time employees may alleviate the rising costs of labor and the labor shortage, but this strategy is viewed differently according to the type of manufacturing firm. To many establishments, part-time employees are hired for reasons other than to reduce the cost of labor or to address the scarcity of workers. As has been found elsewhere, females play an important role in part-time employment in Taiwan (Shieh 1990). An increasing number of those industries intending to keep production in Taiwan are responding to the problem of labor shortage by employing foreign workers. This use of cheap, low-skilled foreign labor is likely to increase in the coming years. Although the short-term economic benefits are evident, such strategies may not produce long-term advantages. This is particularly true in speeding the industrial transformation toward a mature economy.

Investment by enterprises in workforce training is not widely practiced in Taiwan. However, such investments are becoming increasingly evident in high-technology industries. The majority of Taiwan's manufacturing firms, as small and medium enterprises, often face the problem of limited funds for the promotion of training and R&D. As a result, most high-technology-oriented enterprises consider the government's involvement in R&D to be extremely important. In this sense, the role of the government in shaping technological development is crucial. Continuing interventions by the state in various forms of assistance, particularly in relation to R&D, are likely, as SMEs are not willing to invest in this area on their own. Moreover, some incentive programs toward technology upgrading will be extended in the future. With regard to strategies related to overseas direct investment, the government is tapping new areas such as Vietnam and certain parts of Indonesia and the Philippines, in order to reduce reliance on investments from mainland China.

In the years to come, Taiwan will be in a good position to enter the high-fashion products sector of the light garment, textile ,and footwear industries. However, the island will lose its advantages in manufactur-

ing, which requires proficiency in mass production, to other NIEs, such
as Korea.

Conclusions

With the labor force's rising living standards and aspirations for a middle-class way of life, most Taiwanese manufacturers face the problem
of unskilled labor shortages. However, differences in enterprises' responses to the changing business environment emerge when size, type
of industry, and region are taken into account. The key question is how
to maintain strong competitiveness in international markets, given increasing challenges from the neighboring countries in Southeast Asia
and mainland China. One obvious goal Taiwan must achieve is to restructure its labor-intensive industries toward more technology-oriented activities. Whether the island succeeds will depend on many factors, including the various strategies adopted by enterprises in response
to changes.

As global competition accelerates, it remains to be seen how Taiwanese firms will cope with new challenges. Previous analysis has
pointed out some advantages of local enterprises. Being of small size,
Taiwanese manufacturers are flexible in their operations and can respond rapidly to market changes. Moreover, obtaining market information and tapping market niches enable Taiwanese manufacturers to
remain competitive in world markets. However, as technology and capital investments increasingly become competitive strategies, it is not
clear whether small firms will be impediments to industrial upgrading.
It may be necessary to complement the flexibility skills with technology and larger production.

PART THREE

Asian NIEs in Perspective

NINE

Patterns of Industrial Restructuring

Won Bae Kim

The fate of the Asian NIEs is closely related to the industrial restructuring process, the interplay of international imperatives and local responses. This chapter examines the interplay between firm strategies and firm attributes, on the one hand, and the international and local context, on the other. The success or failure of local restructuring depends greatly on the NIEs' firms, communities, and governments. Given their precarious position in the national and international economies (squeezed as they are by multinational firms in the upper-end markets and by competitors in developing countries with low-cost production in lower-end markets), labor-intensive industries in the NIEs are pressured to restructure for their survival.

Government-industry relations in the NIEs are known to be cooperative, although such cooperative relations have been strained recently by the increasing influence of private enterprises and the more complex economies of the NIEs. Another important factor that affects firms' strategy formulation, including relocation, is labor-management relations. A hard-working, docile labor force has been a characteristic of the Asian NIEs (as noted in chapter 2, this volume). In recent years, however, there have been increasing concerns about labor strikes, work stoppages, unreasonable wage demands, and the militancy of labor unions in the NIEs. Some observers believe that the Asian work ethic is being eroded by rising levels of income and consumption. The emergence of labor unions and their greater voice may also be a factor in

NIE firms' strategic choices. The future of labor-intensive industries in the NIEs will be limited if local management-labor relations are strained and firm managers consider unions' influence to be excessive. Cooperative labor-management relations are conducive to business growth and enhance firms' competitiveness in the long run.

Asian NIEs in Adjustment

After three decades of remarkable economic growth, Asian NIEs are facing difficult adjustment problems due to changes in the domestic and international environment. Rapid wage increases, labor shortages, exchange-rate fluctuations, protectionist tendencies in major world markets, pressure to open the NIEs' domestic markets, and increasing competition in export markets are triggering industrial restructuring in those countries. The NIEs no longer have a comparative advantage in low-tech, labor-intensive operations. Industrial upgrading and a shift to nonmanufacturing industries and service activities are necessary for their continued growth. The road to industrial upgrading and transformation is long and winding, however, because of difficulties involved in raising the capacity for technological innovation and production efficiency. Moreover, successful economic adjustment requires restructuring industrial organization, revamping economic infrastructure, and reforming institutions, none of which is easy to carry out. The approach taken during the years of the NIEs' comparative advantage, which was based on cheap labor, is no longer effective in the increasingly competitive international environment, in which a country's institutional creativity at all levels of institutions is called upon to excel. How successfully the Asian NIEs can succeed in the global competition will determine their position in the new global economic order.

The NIEs' transition from labor-intensive to technology-intensive economies is closely related to the restructuring of their labor-intensive industries, such as textiles, garments, footwear, and electronics, which have been the pillar export industries in the NIEs for the past three decades. With their well-disciplined and hard-working labor forces, those industries contributed substantially to the economic growth of the NIEs. During the 1980s, however, rising labor costs, appreciated exchange rates, labor shortages, and a changing work ethic eroded the competitive edge of the labor-intensive industries in the NIEs, especially in the Republic of Korea and Taiwan. Facing a grim prospect, they are muddling through for their survival. Differences in their local histories and institutional environments are producing diverse responses to similar problems. Different government policies in the NIEs affect the firms' strategies for expansion, conversion, and closure.

Government intervention in the economy has been pervasive in the NIEs, except perhaps for Hong Kong. As for the restructuring of labor-intensive industries, however, government policies have been unclear or inconsistent at best. With most government subsidies and supports for exports—direct and indirect—withdrawn, individual firms have been left largely on their own. Both the firms and the governments are in confusion: firms welcome deregulation but still expect government support, and the governments are trying to pull themselves out of the past interventionist mode but still find the need to regulate the industries to prevent their collapse. Examples are the footwear and textile industries in Korea; such equivocal government policies will only delay the restructuring process. Except for a few high-tech electronics industries, most labor-intensive firms in the NIEs are price takers in a competitive market, and therefore the assumptions of neoclassical models largely hold in this structure-dependent market. A short account of Korea's and Taiwan's footwear industries illustrates the differential effects of institutional and local factors on the evolution of the industry in the two economies.

Comparing the Taiwanese and Korean footwear industries reveals differences along four dimensions: the number and size of independent firms, the extent of subcontracting, the number and role of independent export traders, and product diversification. Unlike in Taiwan, where numerous small and medium enterprises partake of networks that link them backward and forward to suppliers and consumers, the export surge in Korea was accompanied by an expansion in the size of existing operations, not by the entry of new firms. There was no subdivision of orders among large numbers of independent manufacturers. A few large, vertically integrated firms accounted for most of Korea's footwear exports in the 1970s. During the 1980s, along with a decline in the average size of firms and an increasing number of smaller firms, there was a rise in the extent of subcontracting and the entry of export traders into Korea. The increased volume of marketing and exporting was handled mostly by large trading companies, although the number of export traders increased. In contrast to Taiwan, there was no product diversification in the Korean footwear industry; nonrubber athletic shoes continued to account for the majority of Korea's footwear exports. Taiwan, which began with plastic sandals (which comprised 40 percent of Taiwan's footwear exports in 1971), diversified into other products, such as nonrubber athletic shoes.

The different paths taken by the footwear industries of Taiwan and Korea—and also by their electronics industries (Mody 1990)—are attributed to institutional factors that created different configurations of transaction costs for the firms (Levy 1990). Markets were transactionally more efficient in Taiwan than in Korea at the outset of export-led industrialization in the early 1960s, because Taiwan had favorable initial conditions, such as higher per capita income, a higher level of education, and more commercial experience; South Korea's high costs of market transaction in its initial stage of export-oriented development forestalled the growth of small and medium operations. The Korean government's industrial policy also promoted the growth of large, vertically integrated firms by providing access to subsidized credit and tax concessions. The more pervasive hierarchical structure in Korea can be attributed to its strict form of Neo-Confucianism and uniformist culture under three decades of military rule.

The heavy dependence on one product (athletic shoes) and on a few contractors (Nike and Reebok), combined with the relative concentration and productive rigidity of Korean footwear producers, may have prevented Korea from breaking effectively into other segments of the world footwear market (Gereffi and Korzeniewicz 1990). South Korea did not achieve much industrial upgrading in the unit value of the footwear exports in the 1980s, whereas Taiwan's unit value steadily increased during the decade. The Taiwanese producers' greater organizational flexibility (resulting from their smaller size) enabled them to be responsive to design and fashion changes in the American market and helped them to achieve industrial upgrading through product diversification. In Korea, with the decline in the domestic footwear industry and rising concern over the decline, the government restricted capital outflows from the footwear industry and designated the industry as a target of its industry for rationalization (IFR) policy, which aimed at assisting the restructuring of labor-intensive industries (Lee 1993). Despite these differences, the contrast between Korea and Taiwan may not be as sharp as suggested by the example given above. Taiwan is also suffering from structural rigidities that have been reinforced by trade frictions. Taiwan's textile and garment industries exemplify many of the issues involved in adjustment. Outdated technology and skill have hindered progress in bleaching and dyeing. Success has not yet been achieved in producing fashionable textiles, which require a sensitive response to shifts in consumer preferences, an ability to produce in small lots with very tight delivery schedules, and precise quality control (Liang and Liang 1988c). Despite differences between Korea and Taiwan in their structures for subcontracting and their marketing networks, both countries provide a sharper contrast with Hong Kong, which took the route of flexible production specializing in niche markets.

The diversity in the restructuring of labor-intensive industries among the NIEs is closely related to each NIE's broad economic response to the changing international environment. Therefore, the success or failure of industrial restructuring must be assessed within this broad context of economic adjustment by the NIEs. The following developments account for macroeconomic adjustments by the NIEs in the 1980s and early 1990s. Facing the slowly growing American market and an increasingly protectionist tendency in the American and European markets, all the NIEs have been trying to diversify their export and import markets. The functioning of the European Community as a single economic entity and the formation of the North American trade bloc is bringing more pressure to bear on the NIEs to find alternative markets and to forge closer linkages with neighboring economies (W. B. Kim 1993b). Japan is clearly an alternative market that can supplement the slowly growing American market. But it is uncertain to what extent Japan can supplement America as a demand absorber in the region. Japan is not an easy market to penetrate for the NIEs' not-so-cheap, medium-technology goods.

Nonetheless, the NIEs will continue to depend on Japan for capital equipment and intermediate inputs, because technology gaps between Japan and the NIEs cannot be overcome easily in a few years' time. Recent trade figures prove that the NIEs have increased their trade with the countries in Pacific Asia, particularly with other NIEs themselves and with China, the ASEAN 4 countries, and Japan (Riedel 1991). This surge in intraregional trade reflects in part the NIEs' interest in the dynamic Asian market but more fundamentally the complementarities among the different components of the Pacific Asian economy—Japan, the NIEs, the ASEAN 4, and China. These complementarities, arising as they do from the diversity in industrial development levels and in the stages of demographic transition among Asian countries, cannot be maintained indefinitely because of the dynamics involved in economic growth, especially between the NIEs and other Asian economies (the ASEAN 4 and China). The ASEAN 4 will soon catch up with the NIEs in labor-intensive, low- and medium-tech products. So will China. Moving up the technology ladder will not be easy, given the relatively small size of the NIEs' economies. The arena for export competition is likely to become increasingly crowded in the next few years. Competition is inevitable, because the complementary relations portrayed above will be changing and past comparative advantages will no longer hold. Whether the NIEs can create a dynamic comparative advantage, perhaps in cooperation with neighboring economies, will largely determine their fate, because of the increasingly competitive environment they will face in the world market.

At the subregional level, the NIEs, especially the city-states of Hong Kong and Singapore, have been aggressively pursuing economic integration with neighboring economies. Given the reversion of Hong Kong's political control to China in 1997, the future of Hong Kong will depend on how it is integrated with the Chinese heartland. Hong Kong's foremost concern is to strengthen its function as the gateway between China and the outside world so as to maintain its preeminent position in China's economy. To hedge against future uncertainty, Hong Kong has been aggressively investing in China, particularly in neighboring Guangdong province. Hong Kong hopes to gain bargaining power with Beijing through economic expansion and integration with its immediate hinterland. Forging links at economic, physical, and social levels and thereby cultivating political constituents in China is considered to be the best bet for Hong Kong. Singapore has been equally aggressive in forming an integrated economic zone with neighboring economies. Linking Singapore with Johor in Malaysia and Riau in Indonesia symbolizes this effort. Securing a hinterland for essential supplies is vital to the survival of the Singaporean economy. Singapore is also active in hosting regional headquarters of large multinationals to enhance its position as a regional center for management and producer services.

Growing domestic demand is another source for sustaining productivity increases and achieving national economic growth; but given the small size of their economies, the NIEs cannot sustain the engine of growth by solely relying on domestic demand. Raising the share of labor income and thereby increasing domestic demand, however, would help them to achieve equitable economic growth. Huge investment projects, such as high-speed railroads, airports, and housing, may provide a short-run impetus for growth but may not be sufficient for long-term growth. Investing in R&D and higher education has been emphasized by the NIEs. Korea and Taiwan are in a relatively good position with regard to R&D, compared with Hong Kong and Singapore. As in the past, investment in human capital continues to be a viable option for resource-poor, small economies such as the NIEs.

The NIEs' broad economic adjustment process described above provides a background for industrial restructuring. Casual observations on the NIEs' industrial changes in recent years suggest that there have been three major types of response by NIE industries: offshore investment, upgrading technology and new products, and the flexible use of labor. The emphasis laid by each economy on these three strategies varies. Local history and industrial organization produce divergent paths to restructuring. States also play a role in industrial restructuring, and government policy affects firms' strategies. In this respect, the four NIEs provide interesting comparisons—especially between the two pairs: Hong Kong and Singapore, and Korea and Taiwan.

Hong Kong and Singapore share a few attributes that make them substantially different from Taiwan and Korea. They have no significant agricultural sector. Both have benefited from an organizational and marketing capability that was built up over decades by British-linked trading companies and was in place prior to industrialization. Their economic growth is a function of their service role in a wider regional economy, as entrepot traders, regional headquarters for multinational companies, and homes for nervous money. Their small size means that even with industrial and financial capital operating from a strictly international perspective, full employment and a wide diffusion of the benefits of growth can occur within their populations (Wade 1990a).

These two city-states, however, do not share the same approach to industrial development or the same strategy for industrial restructuring. Hong Kong's industrial strategy is not to upgrade its technology but rather to retain and modify its labor-intensive operations through the flexible use of labor (with outwork and homework, for example) while taking advantage of marketing networks and retailing channels. The city-state's physical compactness and highly developed infrastructure make such work arrangements possible. Its contractual work-group system uses capital intensively without requiring long-term commitments to workers (see chapter 4, this volume, and Krause 1988). Consequently, Hong Kong has developed a capability to produce labor-intensive manufactured goods at low prices and an ability to fill orders on short notice. The hallmark of Hong Kong's manufacturers is the responsiveness and adaptability of their small, domestic entrepreneurs (Krause 1988). The availability of abundant cheap labor in adjacent Guangdong province and the Pearl River Delta enables Hong Kong producers to remain competitive in international markets for fashion-oriented garments and electronics (see chapter 4, this volume). During the 1980s, many production facilities were located in neighboring Guangdong and southern China, and this practice continues. In contrast, Singapore focuses on upgrading its technology using its labor flexibly. The electronics industry exemplifies this strategy by shifting toward more technology oriented production processes while increasing its flexibility in the use of labor. Offshore direct investment is also becoming an important strategy for Singapore as well as for Hong Kong (see chapter 5, this volume). The government of Singapore has intervened in the nation's economic development and is still playing an active role in industrial development.

Taiwan and Korea also share several attributes. Both are former colonies of Japan, and both are divided countries. Each has experienced a rapid transition from an agrarian to an industrial economy. Both countries are at a crossroads. Higher labor costs, slower growth, and stiffer competition make it difficult for their businesses to make profits. Companies that assumed heavy debts to invest in real estate in the hope of making quick profits are in trouble. The changed environment demands that enterprises modify their production, financing, investment, and marketing strategies. Although the increasing complexity of the two countries' economies demands greater decentralization in economic decision making, their industries have not always been in a position to effect adjustments without government aid. The private sector clearly acknowledges the role of industrial policy: to provide information about changes in industrial structure, to help remove structural rigidities, in coordination with macroeconomic policies to assist industries in adapting to new conditions so that they can perform more efficiently, and to promote the flow of resources to activities in which they can be most productively employed (Liang and Liang 1988c).

In contrast to Hong Kong's and, to a lesser extent, Singapore's emphasis on the flexible use of labor, Taiwan and Korea place greater emphasis on technological upgrading. The size of their economies is certainly one factor enabling these two countries to pursue technological upgrading rather than the flexible use of labor. Korea's emphasis on technological upgrading through increased investment in research and development can be attributed to a characteristic of its industrial organization—the existence of large conglomerates—whereas Taiwan's private sector has a lesser ability to make large investments in R&D. Both countries have recently increased their outward foreign investment. Taiwan, with its huge current account surplus, has become a big investor in Asia and North America. These two countries' investments in Asia have been mostly in small-scale, labor-intensive, export-oriented operations, whereas their investments in North America have had the purpose of securing new technology and on-site production plants to circumvent trade and nontrade barriers in North American markets. It is likely that South Korea and Taiwan will make investments in larger, capital-intensive operations as they learn more about the host economies—primarily those in Southeast Asia and China. In sum, shifting comparative advantages in Asia and the Pacific and increasing competition in the region suggest that the NIEs do not have much future in labor-intensive operations. China and Southeast Asia will increasingly house low-tech, labor-intensive operations. It is therefore imperative that labor-intensive industries in the NIEs either move to upscale markets or convert to other operations.

How fast and smooth such a transition will be depends on each NIE's growth performance, the initiatives its industries take, and their strategies for restructuring. The role played by the state in this process will also affect the outcome. The roles being played by NIE states in the 1990s are more complex and diverse than the East Asian model portrayed in the recent World Bank (1993a) study. In both Korea and Taiwan, the state is seeking a new role because of political and economic liberalization started during the late 1980s. Changes in state-society relations in the two countries are inevitable as the state undergoes transformation. Singapore and Hong Kong also face these changes, though on different scales. Partial democratic reform has caused Hong Kong to shift from a state supported by big-business to one supported by the middle-class, which is pushing toward a regulatory welfare state (So 1993). Singapore, on the other hand, has taken a route toward a social-corporatist state, in which the city-state plays a key role in securing its hinterland across the national boundary.

Development policies implemented by a capable bureaucratic machinery during the heydays of Japan's and the Asian NIEs' development are generally known to have contributed to the success of Asian economies. Industrial policy targeted for particular industries helped the NIEs achieve fast economic growth by providing subsidies and special privileges. The effectiveness of such growth-focused industrial policy, however, is in question now, because industrial restructuring is not a simple process of extension or expansion. Restructuring requires changes in industrial organization, market structure, and state policies. A vertically integrated organization suitable for the mass production of a single product (e.g., athletic shoes in Pusan) may not be appropriate for niche markets or differentiated products. Markets regulated to protect certain industries (such as heavy industries in Korea and Taiwan) may become an obstacle for restructuring. Growth-oriented policies may not facilitate firms' restructuring efforts and industrial upgrading, let alone meet the increasing demands for equity and economic justice (for example, in Korea). The state with bureaucratic inertia can no longer be an authoritative actor in increasingly complex global competition. Indeed, the importance of enterprises, both big and small, in such competition is increasingly recognized in the NIEs. The NIEs' corporations have grown in size and capability during the past three decades and now play a significant role in international markets. Conflicts between them and the state are sometimes inevitable—especially when corporate goals clash with state regulations and indirect guidance, as has happened especially in Korea in recent years. Given the importance of economic interests in global politics, countries where government, enterprises, and workers cooperate with one another may have a better chance to beat the competition—approximating what Lester Thurow (1992) dubbed "communitarian capitalism" for Japan.

Patterns of Firm Strategy

The major aim of the East-West Center project was to map the differences among the Asian NIEs in their firms' responses to the competitive challenges that face labor-intensive industries. The survey focused on the firms' strategies with respect to the adoption of new technology, product extension, overseas investment, and the use of labor. By employing these strategies, either singly or in combination, NIE firms are restructuring so as to secure flexibility in the organization of their production. Flexible production, in turn, enables firms to deal with risk and uncertainty. Obviously, different strategies imply differing paths for the future of a firm. For example, new technology and product diversification are geared to increasing labor productivity through increased capitalization, which may or may not entail a restructuring of the workplace. In contrast, more direct strategies for managing labor, such as the use of temporary and part-time workers, are adopted to reduce labor costs. Through subcontracting, firms can not only achieve reductions in labor costs but also avoid the capital investments that would be required if subcontracted functions were internalized. These different responses by firms to intensified competitive pressure are conditioned by internal factors including institutional structure.

The industries included in the survey are primarily labor-intensive—textiles, apparel, footwear, and electronics—although the samples varied depending on the survey locality. Most of the firms were locally owned and independent, except in Singapore, where the proportion of foreign-owned, joint-venture, and branch firms is substantial. A majority of the sample firms were also unlisted (i.e., not in the stock market), except for about one-fifth of the firms in Seoul. The Hong Kong firms were very small compared with those of the other NIEs. Larger than average size was found in the Pusan sample, which contained particularly large footwear firms. Most of those labor-intensive firms were export-oriented, especially in Hong Kong and Singapore. The level of unionization was generally low, particularly in Hong Kong, where small, independent, local firms predominate.

The performance of the firms, measured by changes in their sales in the previous two years, reflects the difficulties in remaining competitive in world markets. Those in Pusan appear to have had the worst performance among the firms sampled (table 9.1). Among the Korean firms, business decline was attributed to high wages and salaries and high costs of raw materials, in addition to stiff competition and decreased demand. High wages and salaries and high costs of raw materials not only lower the profit level of NIE firms but also erode the price competitiveness of the NIEs' products. Competition was ranked as another important factor in business decline for the Singaporean, Hong Kong, and Seoul firms. Competition arising from the entry of new firms, especially those in China and the ASEAN countries, may lead to decreased profits or decreased sales revenues, or both, for the NIE firms. As the reasons given for sales increase or decrease indicate, the NIEs' comparative advantage, based on low wages and low production costs, appears to be lost. Realizing this loss, the firms (except for those in Hong Kong) were pursuing new products, better-quality products, or specialized products. Those whose sales had increased attributed their success to product quality, niche marketing, and flexible pricing. It is noteworthy, however, that some of the Hong Kong firms' business growth still depended on low wages and salaries and low costs of raw materials.

Table 9.1   Business Change and Major Reasons

Change and Reasons	Hong Kong	Singapore	Seoul	Pusan
Change in sales volume (%)				
Increase	54	48	61	32
Decrease	24	30	33	58
Same	22	22	6	10
Reasons for sales decrease				
(rank in order of importance)[a]				
High wages/salaries	3	3	1	1
High costs of raw materials	4	4	3	3
High prices of main products	—	—	—	4
Product quality	—	—	—	—
Stiff competition	2	1	2	2
Decrease in demand	1	2	4	2
Reasons for sales increase				
(rank in order of importance)[a]				
Low wages and salaries	3	—	—	—
Low costs of raw materials	4	—	—	—
Product quality	2	1	1	1
Flexible pricing	—	4	4	4
Niche marketing	—	3	3	2
Increase in demand	1	2	2	3

Source: East-West Center Survey on Enterprise Strategy.

[a] Averages of ratings given by responding firms; 1 = most important, 4 = least important

Rapid wage increases in the NIEs are thought to be one factor responsible for the declining competitiveness of their firms in the global market. About three-quarters of the responding firms in Korea considered recent wage increases to be steep, whereas about two-thirds of those in Hong Kong and Singapore considered them to be moderate (table 9.2). The firms in Pusan appear to have experienced the worst situation, if we take into account the high rate of labor turnover, especially among young, female workers who support those labor-intensive firms. The deteriorating labor market conditions in Pusan's labor-intensive industries have encouraged workers to move out of manufacturing jobs, perhaps mainly to service jobs. Although this tendency is less pronounced in Seoul and Singapore, the trend is likely to continue because of high mobility among young, female workers in the labor-intensive industries of the NIEs.

Table 9.2   Labor Market Characteristics (percentage of firms)

Characteristic	Hong Kong	Singapore	Seoul	Pusan
Wage increase in the past 3 years				
Steep increase	24	33	76	75
Moderate increase	68	62	24	24
No change	5	3	0	1
Decrease	3	3	0	0
Rate of labor turnover (%)				
0–9	52	43	28	19
10–29	18	34	44	45
30–49	15	11	23	19
50–69	6	9	3	11
70+	9	3	1	6
Ratio of labor turnover by sex, ratio, skill, and age				
Female to male	3.5:1	2.9:1	1.3:1	3.5:1
Unskilled to skilled	1.5:1	2.4:1	2.8:1	1.2:1
Young to old	1.4:1	4.5:1	15.3:1	5.7:1
Job shift destination				
Other firms in same industry	—	46	64	55
Other manufacturing firms	—	34	24	15
Nonmanufacturing jobs	—	9	10	26
Other	—	11	3	4

Source: East-West Center Survey on Enterprise Strategy.

Given a tight labor market and firm attributes, the most prevalent strategy adopted by the NIEs' enterprises was subcontracting by which means they were able to cope with labor shortages and fluctuating demand. This strategy was used by respectively 68, 75, 76, and 64 percent of the responding firms in Hong Kong, Singapore, Seoul, and Pusan (table 9.3). The second most popular production strategy was product diversification or new products. The adoption of new technology was another important choice made by the firms. The low rate of new-technology adoption by the firms in Hong Kong and Pusan may reflect the more labor-intensive nature of those firms.

A more direct strategy to ensure flexibility in the use of labor is the use of temporary workers and part-time workers, which can be characterized as external, or numerical, flexibility—that is, the option of adjusting the size of the workforce through nonstandard forms of employment—in contrast with internal, or functional, flexibility, which

Table 9.3 Strategies of NIE Firms (percentage of firms)

Characteristic	Hong Kong	Singapore	Seoul	Pusan
Product diversification	45	52	64	45
Overseas investment	40	37	15	15
New technology	34	63	65	37
Subcontracting	68	75	76	64
Temporary workers	34	52	49	38
Part-time workers	20	16	32	17
Plans to reduce employment	11	19	21	33
Foreign workers	3	80	10	4
Worker retention	46	85	74	58
Worker training	33	69	52	53

Source: East-West Center Survey on Enterprise Strategy.

enables management to make changes in work organization and the evolution of job tasks (Storper and Scott 1990). Slightly more responding firms in Singapore and Seoul than in Hong Kong and Pusan used temporary workers as a strategy, indicating perhaps a tighter labor market in these localities (table 9.3). Overseas investment was not widely practiced by the Korean firms but was used by substantial proportions of those in the smaller economies of Hong Kong and Singapore. The higher frequency of worker retention and worker training in Singapore and Korea relative to Hong Kong may also be an indication of a tighter labor market in those two countries. Another interesting comparison can be made between Singapore and Seoul, on the one hand, and Hong Kong and Pusan, on the other, with respect to the strategy of product diversification. The higher proportions of the firms using the strategy in Singapore and Seoul than in Hong Kong and Pusan indicate a more technology-oriented route of adjustment by the former group of firms.

Major reasons for adopting the above strategies were similar among the three economies. For example, the most important reason for overseas investment given by firms in all four cities was lower wage costs, although the second and third most important reasons varied according to the local environment (table 9.4). Easier market access and cheaper land were other important reasons for overseas investment. Fewer labor problems were an important reason only for the Singaporean firms, which are subject to rigorous labor laws and regulations within the state. Increasing output and improving product quality were

Table 9.4   Major Reasons for Adopting Specific Strategies

Characteristic	Rank in order of importance[a]			
	Hong Kong	Singapore	Seoul	Pusan
Overseas investment				
Lower wage costs	1	1	1	1
Easier market access	—	3	2	3
Cheaper land/availability	2	4	3	2
Cheaper components/ parts production	—	—	—	—
Fewer labor problems	—	2	—	—
Business expansion	3	—	—	—
New technology				
To increase output	1	1	1	1
To improve product quality	2	2	2	3
To cut labor costs	3	3	—	2
To produce new products	—	—	3	—
Subcontracting				
Lower administrative costs	—	5	1	5
Labor shortage	—	1	2	1
Lower wage costs	—	4	5	3
Specialized skills	—	2	3	2
Fluctuating demand	—	3	4	4
Temporary workers				
Labor shortage	—	1	1	—
Fluctuating demand	3	2	2	2
Market uncertainty	—	3	3	1
Lower wage costs/benefits	4	4	—	3
Labor flexibility	2	—	—	—
In-time delivery	1	—	—	—
Lower administration costs	—	—	4	4
Part-time workers				
Shortage of suitable workers	—	1	1	1
Flexible deployment of labor	1	2	2	2
High wage/non-wage costs of regular workers	—	3	3	3
In-time delivery	3	—	—	—
Not required as full-time	2	—	—	—

Source: East-West Center Survey on Enterprise Strategy.

[a] 1 = most important, 5 = least important

the first and second most important reasons, respectively, for adopting new technology in the sampled NIE labor-intensive firms (except in Pusan), whereas cutting labor costs was less important.

Production and design technologies were the types of new technol-

Table 9.5   Characteristics of Technology Introduced 1990–1992, by Region
(percentage of firms)

Characteristic	Hong Kong	Singapore	Seoul	Pusan
Type of technology				
Production	74	35	58	60
Design	17	21	18	19
Quality control	5	21	17	12
Office	5	12	7	8
Inventory control	—	10	—	2
Other	—	1	—	—
Source of technology				
Imported	53	49	40	36
Developed domestically	37	17	35	38
Developed in-house	10	34	25	26
Impact on employment				
Increased	23	16	27	8
Decreased	12	30	18	47
No change	65	54	56	45
Range of tasks				
Increased	—	46	25	28
Decreased	—	21	36	47
No change	—	33	39	25
Complexity of knowledge required				
Increased	—	71	41	19
Decreased	—	11	32	68
No change	—	18	27	13

Source: East-West Center Survey on Enterprise Strategy.

ogy adopted by the largest percentages of NIE firms (table 9.5). Quality control was another type of technology invested in by these firms.
Firm size, which crudely represents financial ability and time horizon,
appears to account for the different patterns observed in Hong Kong
and Singapore from those in Seoul and Pusan. The higher proportion
of imported technology in Hong Kong and Singapore can be attributed
to the small size of their economies and the less active role of their governments in R&D activities. Local conditions, especially at the industry level, seem to have influenced the choice of technology and in turn
had differential effects on employment. For the declining labor-intensive industries of Pusan, adopted technologies have had, on balance, a
negative impact on employment and skills, but they have not had a
pronounced negative impact for those in Seoul and Hong Kong. Sin-

gapore illustrates a positive case, wherein the adopted technologies were labor-saving but skill-increasing. Again, the reasons for these differences may be related to the firms' time horizons: firms in a declining industry are not likely to invest in upgrading the skills or increasing the job scope of their workers. It is possible that the introduction of labor-saving technologies, together with lowering the skill level of the workforce, is the least desirable strategy from the perspective of the local economy in question, a process Pusan appears to be facing.

The flexible use of labor has been a major strand of firms' strategies in labor-intensive industries for coping with increasing wage rates and market uncertainty (Liemt 1992). As we have seen (tables 9.3 and 9.4), most of the responding firms decided to cope with labor shortages, fluctuating demand, and increasing costs by subcontracting. Subcontracting was both production-related and labor-related, although it appears to have been mainly a strategy to secure functional and numerical flexibility in the labor process. Subcontracting was done mainly for the production of components and parts. An exception was Singapore, where other activities, such as maintenance and employees' welfare, were subcontracted to outside specialized firms. The employment of temporary workers and part-time workers gives firms numerical flexibility, although it is used much less frequently than other strategies, according to the survey results. Timely delivery of products constitutes an important reason for hiring temporary and part-time workers in Hong Kong. Most of the temporary workers belong to the unskilled workers category, although the clerical-service category accounted for about 30 percent in Singapore. Most of the surveyed firms were not considering any significant workforce reduction in the near future. The exception was Pusan, which faces a difficult economic situation. Not only business decline but also rising wages and salaries were listed as reasons for expected layoffs.

The use of part-time workers, which enables firms to reduce labor costs as well as to retain flexibility, is common among firms in advanced economies. The majority of responding firms in the NIE sample had not resorted to using part-time workers, however. For the firms that did use part-time workers, the most important reasons were a shortage of suitable workers, the desire for a flexible use of labor, and a need to cut high wage and nonwage labor costs (table 9.4). Using more shift work was not a popular option for these firms, although about 20 percent of these in Singapore had resorted to shifts (chapter 5, this volume). The employment of foreign workers appears to be a prevalent practice in Singapore, where it is legal (table 9.3). In contrast, the number of firms hiring foreign workers in Seoul and Pusan was small, because it was not a legal option in Korea. Among the Korean firms, the major reason for hiring foreign workers was the ability to pay them lower wages and benefits, whereas in Singapore the major reasons were the labor shortage and the need for workers to work during unpopular shifts. The use of foreign, unskilled labor may not be an attractive option for the labor-intensive Hong Kong firms, given the availability of abundant, cheap labor in nearby Guangdong.

Interestingly, a large number of the sampled firms had worker-retention and training schemes (table 9.3). Worker-retention schemes, more prevalent in Singapore and Seoul than in Hong Kong or Pusan, represent the firms' desire to retain workers, particularly skilled workers, in a tight labor market. The major programs offered by the firms to the workers were higher wages and benefits and better working conditions. Although there were variations among the NIEs, training and retraining, stock sharing and profit sharing, and information sharing and consultation were other programs offered to retain workers. Training was done mainly within the firms, except for Singapore, where outside training and financial assistance were equally important.

In sum, the survey results indicate that some of the NIEs' labor-intensive firms pursue industrial upgrading through the introduction of new technology and product diversification. Foreign direct investment is also becoming an important strategy for these industries, at least for the sample firms, to regain their price competitiveness. Subcontracting is indeed a popular strategy among the firms, indicating that these firms do secure a certain level of flexibility in the labor deployment through subcontracting. As indicated in the reasons given for subcontracting and using temporary and part-time workers, the firms consider labor shortages to be the most important factor. Because of the recent slowdown of labor force growth in the NIEs and anticipated aggravated labor shortages, firms engaged in labor-intensive operations will pay more attention to such options as foreign direct investment and the flexible use of labor. But use of temporary and part-time workers is not yet widespread in the NIEs, partly because employment contracts are less explicit in the NIEs than in more developed economies. Unlike American and European corporations, whose strategies depend on the numerical flexibility of labor that often results in reductions in force, the NIE firms appear not to be resorting to such drastic employment practices. The majority of the responding firms do not intend to reduce their workforce in the immediate future. Instead, they seem to be paying close attention to retaining and training their workers. In this regard, their approach resembles that of Japanese firms, which emphasize internal flexibility and long-term employment (Koike and Inoki 1990). The contrast between American and Asian NIE firms stems from both institutional and social differences. Manipulation of the labor process is more prevalent in contract-oriented individualistic capitalism than in trust-oriented communitarian capitalism, such as is found in the Asian NIEs and Japan.

Firm Attributes and Strategic Decisions

The following logistic regression analysis of the reasons why certain firms tend to adopt a particular strategy takes into account the size of the firms, the types of industry, the types of firms, and a host of other firm attributes. Specifically, the following characteristics are included as explanatory variables in the analysis of firms' responses to the survey:

SIZE: measured by the logarithm of a firm's sales value;

LCOST: labor cost as a proportion of total production cost;

EXPORT: exports as a proportion of total sales;

DSALE: change in sales during the past two years;

DFTYPE: whether a firm is independent (a single-plant company) or a branch-subsidiary;

DFOWN: whether a firm is locally-owned or foreign-owned or joint venture;

DGAR: whether a firm belongs to the garment industry;

DTEX: whether a firm belongs to the textile industry;

DGATEX: whether a firm belongs to the garment-textile industry (for Singapore only).

Other potentially important explanatory variables, such as the level of union activity at the firm and the firm's membership in the stock market, were omitted because not all the country samples had information on these variables. The firm's binary choice of each strategy listed in table 9.3 is estimated by using the explanatory variables. The dependent variables used in the analysis are:

PRODUCT: whether a firm adopts product diversification strategy;

NEWTECH: whether a firm introduces new technology;

INVEST: whether a firm makes overseas investments;

SUBCONT: whether a firm does subcontracting;

TEMPORARY: whether a firm employs temporary workers;

PARTIME: whether a firm hires part-time workers;

EMPLOYEE: whether a firm expects to reduce the number of workers in the next two years;

RETENTION: whether a firm has a retention strategy;

TRAINING: whether a firm has training programs.

The analysis was first performed separately for each industry and then for all the sample industries together with industry dummy variables. Since the analysis for each industry produced many equations with low levels of overall significance (measured by goodness-model fit) and the results were not significantly different from those for the combined sample of industries except for a few equations, only the latter results are discussed here. Table 9.6 shows the results of the regression analysis for the sampled firms in Hong Kong, Singapore, Seoul, and Pusan. The coefficient in each equation describes the influence of the listed explanatory variable on the probability of a firm's adopting the specified strategy. On the whole, the size of a firm (SIZE), its export orientation (EXPORT), and business performance (DSALE) appear to have had significant effects on a firm's decision with respect to both production (PRODUCT, NEWTECH, INVEST, SUBCONT) and labor-related strategies (TEMPORARY, PARTIME, EMPLOYEE, RETENTION, TRAINING). Among these firm characteristics, firm size was most important across the strategies and countries. Larger firms, which have greater financial ability than smaller ones, tended to adopt strategies of product diversification, new technology, and overseas investment. Larger firms were also more likely than smaller ones to implement worker retention and training programs, although they were more inclined to reduce the size of their work force in the next two years. The influence of firm size on the use of temporary and part-time workers was not significant except for Seoul firms, which were less likely to use temporary and part-time workers.

The business performance of a firm appears to have had more influence on its production-related decisions. A firm's business performance, approximated by the direction of change in its sales in the past two years, had a positive effect on its adoption of new technology and product diversification across countries. Growing firms were more likely than others to employ training programs (except in Seoul), implying a positive cycle of growth in those firms. The negative effect of firms' growth performance on overseas investment (especially in Pusan) seems counterintuitive and is not consistent with the results of other studies. (For example, Chen 1992, using data on Taiwan's foreign direct investment, found that growth performance had a positive effect on a firm's propensity to invest abroad.) One possible explanation is that growing firms in labor-intensive manufacturing may feel less need to go abroad because they are able to compete with others from their home locations.

The export orientation of a firm seems to have had a significant effect on a few of its decisions related to production and labor deployment. Export orientation is presumed to have a positive influence on decisions regarding numerical labor flexibility, because export-oriented firms are more subject to fluctuating demand than domestic-oriented firms. Although this expectation was confirmed in Hong Kong and Pusan, the opposite was found in Seoul. Interestingly, no consistent pattern between export orientation and overseas direct investment emerged across countries. Only in Pusan was the degree of a firm's export positively and statistically associated with overseas investment. Although failing to reach statistical significance except in Pusan, a positive association was found consistently across countries between the degree of export orientation and plans to reduce the size of their workforce in the future.

Labor intensity measured by labor cost as a proportion of total production cost does not seem to have had a significant effect on firms' strategic choices, except for product diversification. Firms with higher proportions of their total production costs in labor were less likely than other firms to invest in product development. Likewise, the expectation that labor intensity would have a negative effect on the decision to adopt new technology was not borne out in Seoul, where a significant positive effect was found. This finding suggests that some firms could upgrade their technology and use automation to reduce their heavy dependence on labor. The lack of statistically significant associations between labor intensity and firms' other strategies indicates that labor intensity within these labor-intensive industries is not a good predictor of strategy.

Table 9.6 Logistic Regression of Firm Strategy

Dependent variable and locale	CONSTANT	SIZE	LCOST	EXPORT	DSALE	DFTYPE	DFOWN	DTEX	DGAR	DGATEX	MODEL FIT
PRODUCT											
Hong Kong	-5.8100	.3192	-.5532	-.00189	.7680	.9875	1.0801		-.5732		18.651
	(.0459)	(.0521)	(.1371)	(.7717)	(.1435)	(.2966)	(.1958)		(.2835)		(.0094)
Singapore	-.9253	.1419	-.0278	.00039	.0759	1.6035	.2744			-1.5399	19.489
	(.5791)	(.3387)	(.0731)	(.9557)	(.8868)	(.0319)	(.6311)			(.0333)	(.0068)
Seoul	-.4897	.2463	-.0922	-.00377	.6484	1.2003	-1.0313	.5336	-.5173		21.731
	(.6293)	(.0347)	(.4208)	(.3867)	(.0529)	(.0478)	(.1515)	(.2976)	(.1748)		(.0054)
Pusan	-3.7565	.2608	-.3135	.00300	1.3227	.2515	-.1619	.4800	.1997		32.620
	(.1838)	(.0476)	(.0754)	(.5617)	(.0020)	(.7144)	(.9147)	(.3156)	(.7214)		(.0001)
NEWTECH											
Hong Kong	-6.5475	.3646	-.1419	-.00460	1.3438	.4573	.1503		-1.4699		21.383
	(.0443)	(.0468)	(.7087)	(.5426)	(.0300)	(.6207)	(.8552)		(.0154)		(.0032)
Singapore	-2.7721	.3316	-.0133	-.00298	.8925	1.0625	-.7914			.1785	16.281
	(.1106)	(.0359)	(.3583)	(.6638)	(.0977)	(.08491)	(.1616)			(.7807)	(.0227)
Seoul	-1.1562	.4566	.3686	-.00628	.8495	-.6687	-.5726	-1.0010	-.2711		34.294
	(.3360)	(.0014)	(.0049)	(.1842)	(.0182)	(.3610)	(.4325)	(.0471)	(.5206)		(.0001)
Pusan	-18.8769	.3558	.0158	.00315	.4117	-.4929	-25.1678 [a]	.7180	-.4929		22.407
	(.0001)	(.0068)	(.9260)	(.5320)	(.3204)	(.4657)		(.1303)	(.4657)		(.0042)
INVEST											
Hong Kong	-10.2217	.5655	-.1314	-.0088	.3511	.7777	-.5556		-.3323		19.352
	(.0026)	(.0026)	(.7227)	(.8965)	(.5134)	(.4301)	(.5316)		(.5442)		(.0072)
Singapore	-9.3565	.7056	.0124	.0113	.7506	1.1251	.8522			.3669	25.541
	(.0003)	(.0015)	(.4289)	(.1516)	(.2837)	(.0741)	(.1896)			(.6081)	(.0006)

Seoul	-6.6003 (.0002)	.6601 (.0001)	-.0816 (.6072)	-.00588 (.3808)	-.0481 (.9241)	1.1067 (.3185)	.6591 (.5758)	.1217 (.8645)	.4708 (.3848)		31.283 (.0001)
Pusan	-4.6393 (.3328)	.3716 (.0845)	.3750 (.3004)	.0229 (.0254)	-1.5848 (.0431)	-3.4566 (.0019)	-2.0257 (.3814)	-1.3624 (.1525)	3.4566 (.0019)		44.561 (.0001)
SUBCONT											
Singapore	-3.3751 (.1154)	.4287 (.0310)	-.00109 (.9454)	-.00156 (.8431)	.4025 (.5018)	.5059 (.4461)	.3127 (.6175)			-.0283 (.9692)	10.619 (.1561)
Seoul	.2074 (.8474)	.1634 (.2174)	-.0222 (.8693)	-.00570 (.2573)	-.3452 (.3747)	.6537 (.2538)	-.00350 (.9958)	-.7992 (.0918)	1.0646 (.0280)		18.643 (.0169)
Pusan	-3.6653 (.2010)	.1811 (.1671)	-.0300 (.8610)	.0105 (.0334)	-.0654 (.8440)	.2086 (.7673)	.8819 (.5907)	-.4635 (.2999)	.8567 (.1315)		18.623 (.0170)
TEMPORARY											
Hong Kong	-.6116 (.8149)	-.0561 (.7233)	-.3208 (.3848)	.0175 (.0111)	-.4498 (.3992)				1.2092 (.0317)		13.284 (.0209)
Singapore	-1.5321 (.3503)	.1609 (.2690)	-.0188 (.1936)	.00615 (.3636)	.5118 (.3151)	.5776 (.3066)	.0505 (.9625)			-.7079 (.2555)	15.705 (.079)
Seoul	.9014 (.3587)	-.0947 (.3819)	-.1128 (.3398)	-.0113 (.0161)	-.5842 (.0902)	-.5625 (.3271)	.8215 (.2120)	1.8568 (.0007)	.1885 (.6248)		22.925 (.0035)
Pusan	25.9090 (.0001)	-.1074 (.4027)	.0635 (.7092)	.0146 (.0030)	-.1074 (.4027)	-.1363 (.8431)	-25.9284 [a]	.3103 (.5159)	.9361 (.0653)		19.490 (.0124)
PARTIME											
Hong Kong	-1.4887 (.6220)	.0097 (.9545)	.0732 (.8519)	.00675 (.3391)	-.4242 (.4559)	.0304 (.9764)	-.1413 (.8688)		-.3213 (.5854)		1.667 (.9760)
Singapore	-2.0572 (.4030)	-.0866 (.6701)	.0154 (.4806)	.008590 (.4696)	.4336 (.5925)	-2.1240 (.0488)	3.3289 (.0088)			-2.4200 (.0326)	15.550 (.0296)
Seoul	2.4642 (.1548)	-.3479 (.0542)	-.1885 (.3434)	-.00012 (.9861)	.9125 (.0774)	.2047 (.8134)	-2.7695 (.0201)	.3055 (.6370)	1.4315 (.0217)		15.869 (.0443)
Pusan	-3.6402 (.5413)	.0673 (.8279)	.1880 (.6105)	-.0082 (.4926)	1.4519 (.1647)	-1.9127 (.3115)	0 [a]	3.3493 (.0167)	1.8438 (.2014)		13.386 (.0631)

Table 9.6 Logistic Regression of Firm Strategy (continued)

Dependent variable and locale	CONSTANT	SIZE	LCOST	EXPORT	DSALE	DFTYPE	DfOWN	DTEX	DGAR	DGATEX	MODEL FIT
EMPLOYEE											
Hong Kong	1.7362 (.6922)	-.2462 (.3093)	.0842 (.8897)	.00879 (.3652)	-.8667 (.3203)	.6199 (.6906)	-2.4191 (.0461)		1.4735 (.1449)		10.158 (.1798)
Singapore	-7.1595 (.0078)	.4533 (.0428)	.00229 (.8940)	.0118 (.2472)	.0344 (.9556)	-.1503 (.8911)	-.1503 (.8399)	-.1503		.7418 (.3929)	11.347 (.1242)
Seoul	-3.2831 (.0205)	.1707 (.1741)	.1421 (.2912)	.00423 (.4274)	-.4291 (.2934)	-.5841 (.3516)	1.3639 (.2204)	.6634 (.2056)	-.3502 (.4619)		10.145 (.2550)
Pusan	-4.5091 (.1123)	.2477 (.0573)	.1103 (.5335)	.0106 (.0408)	.1303 (.7585)	-.3286 (.6112)	-.6944 (.6403)	.0189 (.9686)	-.5520 (.3112)		16.691 (.0335)
RETENTION											
Hong Kong	-4.0835 (.1531)	.2306 (.1499)	.1393 (.6991)	.0137 (.0368)	-.0520 (.9199)	.1925 (.8336)	-.9033 (.2563)		-.6279 (.2398)		15.401 (.0312)
Singapore	-1.9490 (.3511)	.2251 (.2237)	.0312 (.1846)	.00408 (.6415)	.5785 (.4168)	1.2181 (.1229)	-1.0644 (.1640)			.4053 (.6215)	7.292 (.3992)
Seoul	1.9358 (.1519)	.0200 (.8719)	-.0974 (.4526)	-.00756 (.1368)	.5832 (.1388)	.5612 (.3705)	-1.1702 (.2933)	-.1956 (.7167)	.0585 (.8970)		.8743 (.4193)
Pusan	-16.2807 (.0001)	.4535 (.0010)	.1923 (.2738)	-.00697 (.1712)	.4645 (.2799)	.2181 (.76734)	-24.0333 [a]	.6773 (.1490)	1.7166 (.0037)		24.488 (.0019)
TRAINING											
Hong Kong	-5.6889 (.0543)	.3821 (.0267)	.3928 (.3019)	-.0122 (.0756)	.3239 (.5649)	.2899 (.7697)	-1.8304 (.0291)		.0584 (.9180)		14.390 (.0047)
Singapore	-3.1234 (.1104)	.3693 (.0384)	.00430 (.7877)	.00747 (.3332)	1.1773 (.0631)	-.2706 (.6951)	-.1946 (.7610)			-.5048 (.4735)	31.875 (.0001)

Seoul	.2027 (.8364)	.2688 (.0213)	-.00362 (.9744)	-.00104 (.8120)	-.00173 (.9958)	-.2805 (.6265)	-.6031 (.3461)	-.3242 (.4948)	-.4912 (.1989)	9.647 (.2907)
Pusan	-7.5063 (.0080)	.4517 (.0007)	.1831 (.2744)	-.00361 (.4530)	.7128 (.0877)	-.7991 (.2831)	.6707 (.6529)	-.0458 (.9214)	.2557 (.6220)	21.047 (.0070)

Source: East-West Center Survey on Enterprise Strategy.

Definitions of explanatory variables

SIZE: measured by the logarithm of a firm's sales value

LCOST: labor cost as a proportion of total production cost

EXPORT: exports as a proportion of total sales

DSALE: change in sales in the past two years; if increase, DSALE = 1

DFTYPE: whether a firm is independent or branch/subsidiary; if independent, DFTYPE = 1

DFOWN: whether a firm is locally owned or foreign-owned/joint venture; if locally owned, DFOWN = 1

DGAR: whether a firm belongs to the garment industry or not; if garment industry, DGAR = 1

DTEX: whether a firm belongs to the textile industry or not; if textile industry, DTEX = 1

DGATEX: whether a firm belongs to the garment/textile industry (for Singapore only); if garment or textile industry, DGATEX = 1

Definitions of dependent variables

PRODUCT: whether a firm adopts product diversification strategy

NEWTECH: whether a firm introduces new technology

INVEST: whether a firm makes overseas investment

SUBCONT: whether a firm does subcontracting

TEMPORARY: whether a firm employes temporary workers

PARTIME: whether a firm hires parttime workers

EMPLOYEE: whether a firm expects to reduce the number of workers in the next two years

RETENTION: whether a firm has a retention strategy

TRAINING: whether a firm has a training program

[a] No significance level is attached because of the redundancy of the variable.

Two variables depicting the organizational characteristics of a firm were included to shed light on their influence on a firm's strategic decisions related to production and labor use. Firm type (DFTYPE) distinguishes between an independent firm (i.e., a single-plant company) and a branch-subsidiary of a mother company. Firm ownership (DFOWN) refers to whether a firm is owned by local capital or not. Since the firms surveyed in Hong Kong were mostly local, independent, and unlisted, their strategic choices were not greatly affected by these firm attributes. In the other three NIE locations, firm type appears to have had some influence on the choices. Independent firms were in general more likely to adopt product diversification, and the relationship was statistically significant in Singapore and Seoul. The result was mixed for the effect of firm type on new technology. Independent Singaporean firms were more likely to adopt automation and other new technologies than were dependent firms. Given the stronger need for independent firms to stay ahead of their competition, compared with branch firms or subsidiaries, which are functionally specialized and dependent on corporate headquarters for major decisions, it was expected that independent firms would be more likely to seek investment opportunities abroad. The regression of firm type on the decision to invest overseas partly supports this expectation, except in Pusan, where the result indicates the opposite. The lower likelihood of overseas investments by independent firms in Pusan could reflect the peculiar circumstance in which Pusan's labor-intensive firms, particularly footwear firms, are situated. As discussed in chapter 7 in this volume, an older technology is used to produce footwear in Pusan. Pusan's footwear firms make overseas direct investment primarily on the advice of major buyers such as Nike and Reebok. Since these buyers place orders directly to the overseas factories, home manufacturers (the footwear firms in Pusan) do not have much control over their foreign subsidiaries. Thus these independent but "captive" firms are less likely than truly independent enterprises to make commitments of overseas investment.

As described in the chapters on Hong Kong and Singapore (chapters 4 and 5), locally owned firms were expected to be less likely than foreign-owned firms to adopt new technology and new products, owing to their lesser capacity to make capital investments. Our results, however, do not firmly support this hypothesis. Although the findings were inconsistent across countries, firm ownership seems to have had a negative effect (significant in Singapore) on firms' decisions to retain and train employees. The use of part-time workers by firm ownership differed in Singapore and Seoul. Locally owned firms in Singapore were more likely than foreign-owned firms to use part-time workers as a response to a labor shortage, whereas locally owned firms in Seoul were less likely to do so. These different responses by firms facing similar problems of labor shortage and wage increases may reflect differences in local labor regulations and practices between the two countries.

The effect of industry type is apparent in some strategic choices. In comparison with firms in the electronics industry (or the footwear industry, in the case of Pusan), firms in the garment industry (garment-textile industry in Singapore), which is most labor-intensive among the sample industries, were less likely to invest in new technology or new products, but they were keen about increasing labor flexibility through the employment of temporary workers (or foreign workers, in the case of the Singaporean firms). Firms in the garment industry (in Seoul and Pusan) tended to use subcontracting more than did firms in the electronics and textile industries. Seoul firms in the garment industry were more likely to use part-time workers, whereas Singaporean firms were less likely to do so. The industry effect varies across countries, however, and even within a country (compare Seoul and Pusan), indicating that the same industry has various structures. This finding suggests the use of a more disaggregated industrial classification, perhaps four-digit classification, to control for within-industry variation across locales.

The above analysis suggests that firms' strategic decisions are significantly associated with firm characteristics such as size, growth performance, and export orientation, and with the organizational features such as firm ownership and type. Larger firms tend to adopt new technology, make overseas investment, and introduce new products more readily than do smaller ones. Export-oriented firms are less likely to adopt new technology and new products. Instead, they tend to seek less costly options, relying mainly on labor-related strategies, for their survival. The industry effect is substantial even among these relatively labor-intensive industries. We found no major differences among the four NIE locales in the effect of firm attributes on strategy choices. Firm size appears to have significant effects across countries. A few firm attributes, such as export orientation, firm type, and firm ownership, were found to have differential effects between countries, which suggests a need for in-depth analysis of the local context.

Local Environment and Firms' Responses

The consequence of industrial change and restructuring has been geographically uneven. The decline of certain industries—especially labor-intensive ones—can have a serious impact on localities where such industries are heavily concentrated. The example of the footwear industry in Pusan reveals how adjustment failures in one or two industries can damage a local economy of almost five million people. In fact, the entire Korean economy suffered a loss of 208 establishments in the three labor-intensive industries of textiles, garments, and footwear in 1992 (Korea 1993). This number accounted for 47 percent of total closures in the manufacturing sector in that year. Since those labor-intensive industries are concentrated in Pusan, the impact of firm closure has been particularly acute in that city. Why have so many labor-intensive firms in Pusan closed down their operations? Was it the best choice for those enterprises? How did government policy (or its absence) affect the closures? Was government support for those firms justifiable? Answers to these questions require a more in-depth analysis of firms' strategic choices in relation to their attributes, market structures, and policy environments. The survey results as reported in this chapter provide some clues. State-industry relations in the NIEs are known to be cooperative, since the state usually provides various supports for the industries. The textile, garment, and electronics industries received export subsidies and low-interest credits in the past.

The situation changed during the 1980s, however, and those labor-intensive industries no longer enjoy preferential policies. Consequently, many enterprises in labor-intensive industries in the NIEs consider public policy to be less supportive in various areas than formerly. Surveyed firms in Pusan were most critical of government policies toward industry, whereas those in Singapore rated government support neutral (table 9.7). The opinion of firm managers in Hong Kong and Seoul fell between the two. Of the various types of government support, management regarded government support for R&D as least satisfactory. Hong Kong entrepreneurs also considered government support for information and consultation to be weak, whereas Singaporeans thought government support for industrial relations and regulations, and laws favoring industry (specifically labor regulations), were insufficient. Among the firms in Seoul and Pusan, government support for infrastructural provision was rated low. Pusan's capital-short entrepreneurs gave a low score to access to loans. Domestic-oriented, smaller textile

Table 9.7. Management Opinions of Labor-Management Relations and Government Support for Industry

Characteristic	Average Score[a]			
	Hong Kong	Singapore	Seoul	Pusan
Labor-management relations	4.2	4.4	4.0	4.0
Union's influence on firm strategy	1.2	2.6	2.7	3.7
Industrial relations compared with the past	—	—	2.8	3.2
Public sector support				
Access to loans	—	3.1	2.6	1.9
Infrastructure provisions	3.0	3.6	2.1	2.0
Industrial relations	2.2	3.3	2.4	2.2
Marketing	3.1	3.0	2.5	2.0
Information and consultation	2.0	3.2	2.6	2.0
R & D support	2.3	2.9	2.1	1.8
Regulation and law	2.7	2.8	2.7	2.0

Source: East-West Center Survey on Enterprise Strategy.

[a] Averages of ratings given by responding firms; 5 = most favorable, 1 = least favorable. Average scores were computed by adding all the weighted scores and dividing the sum by the total number of responses.

and garment firms were more likely to consider public-sector support to be lacking than were export-oriented, larger electronics firms (chapter 5, this volume).

The local business environment is an important determinant of a firm's competitiveness. Two aspects of local environment are particularly important: government policy and labor-management relations. Since the NIEs have been undergoing a period of labor movement and rapid wage rises, firms' perceptions of local industrial relations, including labor-management relations, may have significant influence on their corporate strategies. On the whole, the sample firms in the NIEs considered their labor-management relations to be cooperative (table 9.7). Perhaps, because of low levels of unionization, management did not consider unions to have substantial influence on corporate strategy. However, the perceived degree of unions' influence on corporate decisions seems to have been directly associated with the level of unionization in each locality. In Hong Kong, where there is virtually no union activity, unions' influence on corporate strategy was considered to be negligible, while it was considered to be more than moderate in Pusan, where the level of unionization approaches 30 percent. The survey results indicate that unionization of workers was not a deterrent to the adoption of new technology. This finding is interesting because unions are generally perceived to be resistant to technological change (Bemmels and Reshef 1991), and it may simply be due to the low level of unionization in the NIEs' labor-intensive enterprises. Interestingly, too, a majority of surveyed firms in Seoul and Pusan regarded wage increases in the last two years as too high, whereas a majority of Singaporean firms considered the increases to be moderate. This difference may lie in differential changes in productivity and wages in the two countries, which may stem partly from past government policies with respect to wages and labor. During the 1960s and 1970s, the Korean government held industrial wages to minimum levels, whereas Singapore adopted the policy of boosting wages in the early 1980s to raise the skill levels of its workers.

The above findings suggest that firms operating in a more favorable local environment—that is, where there are good management-labor relations and strong support from the government—will have a better chance to endure a difficult period of adjustment. It is argued here that cooperative triangular relations among the state, industry, and labor are fundamental to sustaining the national competitiveness of a country. The state has clearly taken the initiative to reconfigure the past state-dominant triangular relations in Taiwan and Korea. Singapore, however, remains in the state-dominant mode, with the state having the added role of transnational corporatist. The reversion of Hong Kong to China in 1997 complicates state-society relations there. The business community and the middle class have divergent attitudes and approaches to Hong Kong's current British government and its future governance from Beijing.

Conclusion

As the Asian NIEs are growing out (or being crowded out) of labor-intensive manufacturing and moving (in fits and starts) toward more skill-intensive and capital-intensive production processes, the ASEAN countries and China are replacing the NIEs in labor-intensive, low-tech export markets. The accumulation of capital and technology has enabled the NIE economies to compete with Japan in an increasing number of skill-intensive and technology-intensive industrial products, even though the technological gap between them and Japan has not been narrowed significantly yet (see also Young 1994). Now the issue is the adaptiveness and flexibility of the NIEs' firms and industries—the strategies of restructuring and change.

The results of the East-West Center's study indicate that subcontracting is the most popular strategy used by the NIEs' labor-intensive enterprises, which face tight labor-market conditions and volatile markets. The major rationale for the heavy dependence on subcontracting, outwork, and internal contracting is to maintain a flexible production system by shifting risks to small subcontractors, internal contractors, and outworkers. Although subcontracting is common in all the Asian NIEs, the structure of subcontracting networks differs somewhat among them. The existence of a network of interdependent, small-scale producers, present in Hong Kong's garment industry, has given rise to an efficient network of subcontracting with low transaction costs. Small and medium firms in Korea, in comparison, are dependent on their subcontracting relations with giant *chaebol* companies (business conglomerates) or are often integrated into them as part of their vertical integration process. The agglomeration of related industrial activities in the Seoul metropolitan area helps Seoul-based firms to extend their network of subcontracting into a wider area. Taiwan's subcontracting networks are based on a complex web of linkages between larger and smaller firms. Business arrangements in Taiwan are based on patrilineal ties rather than on corporate patriarchy (Ellison and Gereffi 1990). Taiwan's subcontracting system approximates that of Hong Kong rather than those of Korea or Japan (Amsden 1991). Underlying these subcontracting networks within the Asian NIEs and Japan are social networks and personal contacts, which nurture mutual trust and reciprocity.

Together with product diversification and the development of new products, new technology is another popular strategy adopted by NIE enterprises. The technology route contrasts with the subcontracting strategy, which aims at spreading risks and reducing production costs. Even though a desire to reduce labor costs is an important reason for adopting new technology, production considerations such as increasing output and improving product quality provide the major incentive for this strategy among the NIEs' labor-intensive industries. This finding suggests that upgrading product quality is one means by which the NIEs' labor-intensive enterprises maintain their competitive edge through productivity increases. Hong Kong firms, however, are an exception to this approach, for they tend to remain labor-intensive rather than investing in technology and labor-saving methods of production. Technological investment as revealed in the cases of Singapore and

Seoul is accompanied by upgrading the skills of workers, and hence it enhances local productivity. Where technology investment is labor-reducing or lowers the skill level of workers, as observed in Pusan, it is detrimental to the local economy.

Foreign direct investment is another important option for the NIEs' labor-intensive enterprises. Obviously, lower labor costs in overseas locations are the major reason for this strategy. Despite the negative employment implications for home localities, overseas direct investment is a predominant response of Hong Kong electronics enterprises, and it is likely to be so for the low value-added industries in other NIEs. Hong Kong firms' extensive investment in China (especially in nearby Guangdong province) reflects their interest in the lowest-labor-cost solution rather than in increasing labor productivity through capitalization. To a certain extent, the other NIEs' firms are interested in this option, which is basically to form international subcontracting networks via foreign direct investment. Within the hierarchy of international subcontracting arrangements, the NIEs are moving away from component subcontracting to commercial subcontracting or even to independent exporters, relegating component subcontracting to China and other Asian countries (Gereffi 1993). Breaking free from the commercial subcontracting role is, however, difficult for the NIEs' firms without their own internationally recognized company brand names, a substantial advertising budget, and appropriate marketing and retailing networks. As noted by Lim (chapter 7, this volume), Pusan's footwear industry clearly demonstrates the difficulties facing firms engaged in "captive" commercial subcontracting.

The employment of foreign workers is also an option for labor-deficit economies such as Singapore and Hong Kong. Indeed, these two small economies have been importing foreign workers to compensate for their domestic labor shortages. The firms surveyed in this study used foreign workers to meet their labor needs, especially in unpopular jobs. Taiwan also recently accepted unskilled foreign workers in limited sectors despite arguments against importing them, such as their dampening effect on industrial restructuring and their contribution to rising social burdens. In spite of the interest expressed by many small-scale manufacturing firms in importing foreign workers, the Korean government, following the Japanese approach, seems to prefer overseas direct investment to the importation of foreign workers because of perceived high social costs associated with their importation. In all the labor-short NIEs, the state plays a role in mediating the conflicting interests of industry and labor unions (or the general public). A closed-door policy toward foreign labor forecloses lower labor costs for labor-intensive firms in home locations.

The survey results suggest that such firm attributes as size and export orientation have some influence on firms' decisions about production and the management of labor. The size of a firm is an important variable in determining its strategic choices. We can infer from this finding that the size distribution of firms in a labor-intensive industry should have a considerable impact on the aggregate performance of the industry. The entry and exit of firms and traders are easier in Hong Kong and Taiwan, where numerous small and medium firms form a less vertically integrated network, than in Korea, where large, vertically integrated firms characterize the industrial structure of the country. A large, vertically integrated industrial organization tends to produce a rigid productive structure, whereas a small, vertically disintegrated industrial organization tends to promote productive flexibility. Hong Kong's garment and electronics industries, which consist of numerous small and medium firms, demonstrate the advantage of flexibility in industrial organization. Korea, however, probably has more potential than Hong Kong to enter the independent export market because its large, vertically integrated industrial conglomerates have the capital and technology to set up overseas production facilities and marketing networks.

Another lesson that can be learned from the East-West Center's project is related to state-business, or, more broadly, state-society, relations. As seen in the comparison of local environments among the five city economies, supports for local businesses including government labor policies, credit (Korean firms are in the worst position among the three NIEs in terms of the interest rates they have to pay for loans), and R&D, seem to help shape firms' competitiveness, especially that of small and medium enterprises. Whether such small-scale, labor-intensive firms tend to adopt a short-term or a long-term perspective in their business planning depends partly on what kind of social relations they develop with the local community. Those social relations, in turn, are partly determined by the local physical and institutional context. Building up supportive social infrastructure for firms and constructing cooperative management-labor relations are conducive to enhancing not only firms' ability to compete but also national competitiveness in the global market. As Wade (1993) points out, as world trade becomes more politicized, maintaining national competitiveness is an important task for the government, as well as for firms.

Asian NIEs in Transition

Gordon L. Clark and Won Bae Kim

Whereas much of the literature on the East Asian development experience has stressed the role of the state in promoting export-led economic growth, this book emphasizes the importance of corporate strategy in industrial restructuring and encourages a broader perspective: that is, we take a step beyond accounting for past growth of the Asian NIEs and focus on the patterns and processes of industrial restructuring during the early 1990s. This whole analysis is premised on two suppositions. First, the growth of the Asian NIEs over the past few decades has been so significant that each NIE, consistent with its particular history and economic structure, is at a point where the competitiveness of its low-valued-added labor-intensive industries cannot be sustained over the coming decade. On the evidence assembled here, in general and in particular case studies, the international competitiveness of these industries is being squeezed from below (from the ASEAN 4 and China) and above (from the major Western markets). The second supposition is that state development policy may be less important than before in these circumstances, as individual firms and enterprises are forced to respond to international competition outside the broad growth parameters previously set by the development state. The future of the Asian NIEs, singularly and together, depends a great deal on how individual corporations adapt and respond to the economic transition now taking place in those economies.

The East-West Center project was originally conceived to test empirically and develop in detail the veracity of these two suppositions. The results of the project reported here and elsewhere tend to confirm the suppositions; there can be no doubt about the tenuous nature of the NIEs' competitiveness in labor-intensive industries, just as it is clear that the relationship between the state and markets has become both more complex and, at the same time, more attenuated in all cases (compare Young 1993). It is important to remember, of course, that the project was also premised on a particular methodological claim: that the interaction between global economic processes and local circumstances has been mediated and sustained through the institutions and circumstances of each Asian NIE. Thus, the generality of our conclusions regarding NIEs' international competitiveness in labor-intensive industries should be tempered by our concern for the distinctiveness of local outcomes. By holding constant the focus of our analysis—the NIEs' labor-intensive industries, the industry survey, the questions asked, and the analytical framework used to evaluate responses—it was hoped that we would be able to show just how different the Asian NIEs are at the level of firm strategy and state policy. So, for example, Ho's case study of Singapore (chapter 5, this volume), when compared with Chiu and Lui's case study of Hong Kong (chapter 4, this volume), demonstrates just how different industry restructuring is between the two city-states. The historical legacy of colonialism is not the same: differences in the size, ownership, and market focus of individual corporations in the Singaporean and Hong Kong electronics industries (for example) contribute to distinctive paths of restructuring, just as very different state institutions have created (and closed off) alternative paths of growth.

Given these observations (at the empirical level and the methodological level), the final topic to be considered is the future of the Asian NIEs. Here, there are a variety of related issues. For a start it should be asked whether, in twenty years time, the current round of industrial restructuring will be judged to have been a significant turning point in the development of the NIEs or an aberration given the likely evolution of the global economy. This question, and the possible futures it puts in play, can not be easily answered. History will be the ultimate judge of any predictions made at this point in time. It is fair to say, however, that on the basis of our cross-economy case study research we are convinced that the current round of restructuring is very significant for the long-term economic structure of the Asian NIEs. So many global economic forces have conspired at this time that it is practically impossible to imagine that the Asian NIEs will be able to sustain their low-value-added, labor-intensive industries in their current form and configuration. In this chapter, we consider a set of possible scenarios regarding the future of each of the Asian NIEs, emphasizing the inherited dilemmas of growth. In doing so, we first consider the possible long-term relations between the NIEs and China before looking at a series of related but economy-specific issues.

The New International Order

Recognizing the limits of local, export-based economic growth, the Asia-Pacific economies have encouraged firms to shift labor-intensive production facilities to other sites in Southeast Asia and China. As noted in chapter 3, the Japanese government has suggested that this policy of geographical diffusion has a number of advantages, not the least of which is the development of regional markets for leading producers located in Japan and the NIEs. At a time when North American and European markets are resisting the expansion of trade with the developed economies of Asia, investment in the ASEAN 4 and China by Japan and the NIEs may be a mechanism for mutual growth and economic expansion. In this context, bilateral economic development agreements, such as those between Singapore and Malaysia and between Singapore and Indonesia, are a means of expanding markets and building economic alliances. Although the effectiveness of state development policy in the NIEs may have diminished in recent years (compared to firms' market strategies), state-to-state alliances may be vital for increasing the opportunity set of NIE's firms. Each of the case studies recognizes the potential importance of this option for future economic growth, just as each case study also recognizes the sensitivity of this issue for domestic politics and the new international order.

Since the collapse of the Soviet Union, the world economy has moved toward a multipolar economic and political structure. The United States, Germany, and Japan have become the three principal actors, although the United States remains the primary leader in this triangular system of influence and global policy making. The dynamic growth and fast development of the Asian-Pacific economies, in particular Japan and the Asian NIEs, over the last three decades has added momentum to the formation of a "fortress Europe" and the creation of the North American Free Trade Agreement (NAFTA). The world's largest market, the United States, has been contracting in relative terms; the American economy is not likely to regain its past dominance over the rate of growth of the world economy. Instead, casual observation suggests that protectionist impulses will be in the ascendancy in U.S. policymaking, focused on both the European Economic Community and the Asian economies. These factors are promoting the internal integration of Asia. Indeed, economic integration is accelerating at the regional and subregional levels, especially centred around city economies like the growth triangle, dependent on Singapore, and the Hong Kong-Guangzhou-Pearl River Delta. Closer links are also being developed between Korea's west coast and China's Shandong and Liaodong peninsula, including the possible formation of a Yellow Sea Economic Zone and the formulation of a Japan Sea Rim Economic Circle (Kanamori 1993).

In Asia, Japan's influence has been gradually expanding and now appears to dominate most of the Asia-Pacific region. Notwithstanding historical experience and apprehension about Japan's increasingly hegemonic position in Asia, many countries in the region realize they cannot compete with Japan in any head-to-head economic competition; the Asian NIEs accept Japan's predominance in Asia. But not in political terms. There is increasing awareness among Asian countries that regional security should be sustained by the countries in the region. Recognizing that an Asian security arrangement led by Japan would not be welcomed by its neighbors—in particular, China and both Koreas—Japan has proposed the establishment of a multilateral regional security institution (Sekiguchi and Noda 1992). While quietly modernizing its defense capacity and forging closer political alliances with small Asian countries, China is now striving for faster economic growth. With the assistance of its ailing former foe and friend Russia, China is expanding its military capacity, presumably for self-defense purposes. Ironically, the economic complementarity between the two countries places Japan foremost in China's economic modernization process (Whiting 1992). Although Beijing has sought to diversify its sources of capital and foreign exchange, Japan remains essential to China's latest phase of economic growth. Japan also has a strategic interest in seeing a stable and prosperous China, recognizes China as a formidable regional power, and is concerned with the possible external effects of internal political instability (e.g., the potential for massive refugee movements).

As Wong (1988) notes, the future of the Asia-Pacific region is held by four major countries or economic coalitions: Japan, China, the Asian NIEs, and the ASEAN 4, including the Indochina states. The metaphor of flying geese in a sense portrays the symbiotic relations

Table 10.1   Selected Economic Indicators of Major Provinces in China, 1984–1991

	Annual Average Growth of National Income (%) 1984–1991	GNP 1991 ($US million)	Population 1991 (millions)
Jiangsu	10.8	27.289	68.4
Shanghai	7.7	16,113	13.4
Zhejiang	13.2	18,477	42.0
Total		61,879	123.8
Guangdong	14.0	33,450	64.4
Fujian	12.8	10,479	30.8
Total		43,929	95.2
Hebei	8.9	18,046	62.2
Beijing	8.4	10,494	10.9
Tianjin	6.8	6,338	9.1
Total		34,878	82.2
Shandong	11.0	29,464	85.7
Lioning	7.7	20,161	39.9
Sichuan	8.0	24,128	109.0

Source: People's Republic of China (1985–92).

among the Asian market economies headed by Japan. Implied by the metaphor is a vision of Japan leading the Asian market economies, each located in the formation in accordance with its recent history of growth and place in the growth process (see chapter 3, this volume). Before 1979, however, China could be thought to have been a giant sitting duck, estranged from the flying geese. But China is no longer a sitting duck. Parts of China, mostly the coastal provinces, grew very rapidly over the 1980s. One province, Guangdong, has already joined the ranks of dynamic Asian economies (see table 10.1 on the rates of growth of Chinese provinces). The middle coast of China (Jiangsu, Shanghai, and Zhejiang), for example, has a larger GNP than either Malaysia or the Philippines, while the combined GNP of Guangdong and Fujian approaches that of each of those two countries. This geographical segment of the Chinese economy will be the leading edge of Chinese development and will interact with other component parts of the Asia-Pacific region. The questions now are: (1) How many Chinese "geese" will join the Asian economic growth process? and (2) How will they compete with the Asian NIEs and the would-be NIEs of the ASEAN 4 (Indonesia, Malaysia, Philippines, and Thailand)?

The economic and demographic diversity of the Asia-Pacific region provides an important basis for sustaining the symbiotic relations among the countries of the region. Japan and the Asian NIEs have either completed or are about to complete an extraordinary demographic transition, while China and the ASEAN 4 are themselves undergoing a slower demographic transition toward a stable and mature population structure. The different stages of demographic and industrial transition in each economy enable (perhaps by chance) these economies to interact in a complimentary fashion with one another. For example, the availability of cheap labor in Southeast Asia and China was very conducive to the increased inflows of capital from Japan and the Asian NIEs to these countries during the 1980s. Increased cross-national but intraregional flows of capital, labor, goods, and information, in turn, have contributed to the demographic and industrial transition in Southeast Asia and China (W. B. Kim 1993a).

As has been noted throughout the book, compared with Japan the Asian NIEs are facing difficult adjustment problems due to changes in the domestic and international environments. Rapid wage increases, shortages of unskilled workers, exchange-rate fluctuations, and rapid rises in urban land prices are common to the NIEs. The labor-intensive industries of the NIEs are no longer crucial to the success of those economies nor do they hold their comparative advantages when compared to the ASEAN 4 and China. The Asian NIEs, their corporations and states, have had to rethink their places in the global economy and their relations with the competing trading blocs of the global economy.

The relatively contracting U.S. market and rising protectionist tendencies in North America and Europe have encouraged the NIEs to plan for the diversification of their export markets. Japan, which clearly is an alternative market to supplement the shrinking American market, is not an accessible or an easy market for the NIEs to penetrate. Securing new and larger export markets has become critical for these small market economies in the 1990s. Growing economic interdependency in Asia is partly a reflection of the survival strategies adopted by the NIEs; each have complimentary relations with both China and the ASEAN 4. However, unlike Japan and China, or Japan and ASEAN 4 relations (where technology gaps cannot be closed over the long term) the NIEs' complimentary relations with China and the ASEAN 4 are more competitive, because the technological gap between

Table 10.2   Asian NIEs' Trade in the Asia-Pacific Region

	Value of Trade ($US million)			Annual Growth Rate (%)	
	1981	1986	1992	1981–1986	1986–1992
NIES-China	8,188	20,014	91,680	16.1	24.3
NIEs-Japan	32,374	44,998	106,568	5.6	13.1
NIEs-United States	39,996	68,076	133,536	9.3	10.1
NIEs-ASEAN4	15,044	15,644	53,249	0.7	19.1
NIEs-others	90,760	100,421	293,309	1.7	16.5
China-Japan	10,930	17,542	25,374	8.2	5.4
China-United States	6,187	7,381	17,485	3.0	12.2
China-ASEAN4	1,182	1,589	5,179	5.1	18.4
China-others	24,808	48,102	119,921	11.7	13.9

Source: IMF (1988, 1993); Taiwan (1989, 1993a).

Note: Taking country sources in reversed order (e.g. Chine-NIEs), one may obtain different totals and rates, but discrepancies are small, except for "China-Japan" and "China-United States," for which discrepancies are large.

the NIEs, China, and the ASEAN 4 is neither large nor stable. Moreover, the rapid growth of China (with a population of 1.2 billion) and Southeast Asia (with more than 400 million in population) are great potential markets for the NIEs. This uneasy and transitional form of cooperation underlines the problematic nature of the NIEs' relations with China and the ASEAN 4.

Economic Relations between China and the NIEs

The complimentary economic relations between China and the NIEs have been well documented; the trade data clearly demonstrate burgeoning trade relations between the NIEs and China. During the 1980s, trade between the NIEs and China grew at a rapid pace, topping the growth rates of all other country-region trade-flow combinations (see table 10.2). Lowered social and political barriers in China are an obvious cause of the rapid increase in trade. But also, the need for the NIEs to form closer connections with economies other than the United States is an important factor behind NIEs' rising trade with China and other countries in the Asian-Pacific region. As indicated in the trade matrix, the emerging economic interdependency of the Asia-Pacific region will be multitiered, and cooperation mixed with competition will prevail. The international division of labor will no longer be centered around a single country (like the United States in the past, or perhaps Japan in the near future) but will be spread out along the matrix including Japan, the NIEs, the ASEAN 4, and China. Japan, of course, will be the most important absorber of demand, next to the United States, in the region. At the same time, the NIEs themselves are becoming an important market. As trade friction with the United States increases and the Japanese yen continues to appreciate, the NIEs' role of demand absorber in the region is likely to increase. Interdependency will become more prevalent in the region through active foreign investment by the NIEs (Watanabe 1991).

As noted by many observers, the pattern of trade between the NIEs and China is becoming competitive as well as complimentary. And competition is likely to grow as intraindustry trade gradually supplants interindustry trade (as seen in recent trade statistics). The more competitive trade becomes, the greater the possibility that the NIEs will become more insecure about their position in the new international division of labor. Taipei is indeed concerned with the prospect that Taiwan may well become Beijing's economic hostage, due to its increasing trade and investment relations with mainland China (Yen 1991). This pessimistic outlook has resulted in cautious and conservative behavior on the part of the NIEs' policy makers and investors.

Since 1985, NIE investment in the Asian region has increased significantly. This intraregional investment is a product of changes in both the domestic conditions of and international environment surrounding the NIEs. As we have shown, the NIEs are experiencing shortages of unskilled labor and sustained wage-rate increases; it is difficult for the NIEs to remain competitive in low-value-added, labor-intensive industries. The NIEs are also under pressure to open up their domestic markets and to readjust the value of their currencies. Foreign direct investment to lower-labor-cost locations is one important strategy of restructuring. The NIEs began investing in the ASEAN 4 in the early 1980s and in China in the late 1980s. Since 1988, the NIEs' investment in China has exceeded that of both Japan and America (table 10.3). Up to 1991, the investment pattern of the NIEs in China seems to suggest that NIEs investors have been cautious and risk-aversive. The overwhelming majority of investment has been in small-scale, export-oriented, labor-intensive industries. In comparison, investment in China by Taiwanese and Korean firms is smaller than Taiwanese and Korean investments in the ASEAN 4. However, considering the similarities between China and the ASEAN 4 in terms of investment potential, abun-

Table 10.3 Foreign Direct Investment in China, by Country or Region, Selected Years, 1979–1992 (US$ million)

	Cumulative 1979–1983	1984	1985	1986	1987	1988	1989	1990	1991	1992
Japan	955	203	471	210	301	276	439	457	812	2,173
NIEs	4,373	2,238	4,210	1,586	2,017	4,127	3,718	4,872	8,897	47,001
Hong Kong	4,319	2,175	4,134	1,449	1,947	3,467	3,160	3,833	7,215	40,044
South Korea	—	—	—	—	—	3.4[a]	9.8[a]	46	138	417
Singapore	54	63	76	137	70	137	111	103	155	997
Taiwan	—	165	—	—	100[b]	520[b]	437[b]	890	1,389	5,543
United States	860	—	1,152	527	342	370	641	358	548	3,121
Total	7,453	2,875	6,333	2,834	3,709	5,297	5,600	6,596	11,977	52,295

Source: "Foreign investment in China," 1992; "Foreign investment in the PRC," 1991–92; Bank of Korea (1992); and W.B. Kim (1993a).

[a] Bank of Korea (1992); W. B. Kim (1993a).

[b] Chiu (1993).

dancy of natural resources, and availability of relatively cheap labor, it is likely that NIEs' investment in China will grow as the learning process continues. The key factor differentiating China and the ASEAN 4 is economic system compatibility, which may partly explain the difference in the average size of investment. Indeed, China's policy of regulating foreign investment is partly responsible for small-scale, short-run, profit-motivated investment. As both sides learn about each other and gradually build confidence, it is likely that more investment will be made in large-scale, long-term projects.

In a sense, not only is China experimenting with its open-door policy, the fact is that the Asian NIEs and other countries are experimenting with their investment strategies in China. The future of foreign direct investment into China, however, will depend greatly on, first, how fast China adapts its institutions to prevailing global (or at least regional) market institutions and, second, more importantly, how predictable China's political and economic transition will be to the outside world. Investment motivation and behavior, however, appear to vary among the NIEs. Hong Kong is differentiated from other NIEs because of the looming consequences of 1997. Hong Kong has been the leading foreign direct investor in China. It has invested in diverse projects involving many provinces and many sectors. Hong Kong investors have also been involved in large infrastructure projects. Hong Kong entrepreneurs started their investment activity in labor-intensive, small-scale operations in Guangdong province. While large numbers of Hong Kong residents are looking abroad in preparation for 1997, many Hong Kong businesses are also looking to China, and in particular, Guangdong, as a rich business frontier. Hong Kong entrepreneurs have made significant investment in this region—a key strategy in their efforts to restructure and to survive. The process of integration between Hong Kong and China is not occurring solely through Hong Kong investment in China. Chinese corporations have also invested in Hong Kong and have been engaged in capital acquisition, joint ventures, and corporate buyouts.

Hong Kong's future depends on how the integration process with China proceeds. For its part, Hong Kong will have to enhance its functions in the areas of finance and producer services and strengthen its gateway functions to the international economic networks (Watanabe 1990). Obviously, Hong Kong will gain bargaining power with Beijing through its economic expansion and integration with the immediate hinterland and with China as a whole. Once sovereignty is no longer a negotiation issue, however, Hong Kong's only option will be to forge economic linkages with Chinese consumers, producers, and decision makers as widely and tightly as possible in order to secure its future. Hong Kong's strategy may be explained as follows. Hong Kong investors believe that closer linkages with China (especially Guangdong) through investment and trade will be the only way to sustain their leverage with Beijing and to guard their position against an uncertain future.

Relations between Taiwan and mainland China have changed significantly and continue to change. The trade, economic ties, communications, and human interaction between the two have expanded enormously since the late 1980s due to a host of factors, including public policy commitment in both Beijing and Taipei. Despite these heightened interactions across the strait, Taiwanese investors still seem cautious and hesitant to move forward. Unlike Hong Kong firms, Taiwanese firms have been reluctant investors in China. Moreover, Taiwanese investment in China has been subject to government control and attempts to balance Taiwan's outward investment by country and region. For example, Taiwanese investment in China has been balanced against its investment in Southeast Asia (Baum 1993). Political considerations have also influenced the direction of investment flows. Large firms that have close connections with the Taiwanese government and greater latitude in their investment location decisions have tended to follow the direction set by the government, whereas smaller firms tend to invest wherever they find profitable opportunities. The data reveal that Taiwanese investment toward the mainland is primarily carried out by small and medium enterprises, resulting in an average size of investment of around US$1.0 million. In contrast, the average size of Taiwanese investment toward the ASEAN 4 is larger (table 10.3). Political stability and a better business environment in the ASEAN 4 countries are two reasons for this larger average investment size.

Korea's relations with China are more complex. Before the normalization of diplomatic relations between the two countries, South Korea used China as a key go-between in its negotiations with North Korea (the Democratic People's Republic of Korea). This strategic political interest determined the basic direction of South Korea's economic relations with China. However, South Korea now finds its economic interests to be more important than its strategic political interests. At any rate, South Korean investment in China has been predominantly in export-oriented, labor-intensive, small-scale operations. Very recently, however, large firms (including the four giants, Hyundai, Samsung, Lucky-Goldstar, and Daewoo) have begun to expand their branch offices in China and are considering investing in major projects targeted for China's domestic market. In South Korea, as in Taiwan, both outward and inward investment have been regulated; in Korea, Foreign Exchange Control regulations have been the primary means of controlling the volume, nature, and direction of foreign direct investment.

While Hong Kong, Taiwan, and Korea have close and intimate relations with China (though different in each case according to their very different historical relationships), Singapore's future relations with China are uncertain. Like a number of other Asian countries, China is a destination for Singaporean investment. At present, that investment is principally focused on labor-intensive industry and is linked to Singapore's extended global trading network. In the long term, of course, it is doubtful that Singapore could supplant Hong Kong as the favored point of entry into the mainland economy. Moreover, given developing relations between Hong Kong and individual provinces, Hong Kong's significance seems to be growing relatively more important. Given the extraterritorial alliances initiated by Singapore with Malaysia and Indonesia, and given the apparent specificity of knowledge so essential for stable long-term investment relationships (see, generally, Tesar and Werner 1992), it is doubtful that China will play the same role for Singapore as the mainland plays for Taiwan and Hong Kong. On the other hand, if their extraterritorial alliances are not so successful or if political tensions make the growth of these alliances difficult, China and Indochina may become more important for Singaporean firms.

In sum, the outflow of FDI from the Asian NIEs has been principally due to the changing comparative advantage of the NIEs—as forecast by K. Kojima (1973, 1978) and reformulated by C. H. Lee (1990). The NIEs' investment pattern resembles Japanese FDI in the 1960s and 1970s, which focused on small-scale, labor-intensive, low-technology industries in which Japan's competitive edge had been eroded by rising wage rates. In these cases, FDI strategy has been simply to exploit the location-specific advantages of the host country, utilizing firm-specific assets such as production technology and external market channels. Adjustments to changing comparative advantage at home, however, are not limited to just transferring entire industries offshore. Adjustments can be made through the intrafirm division of labor by multinational enterprises across national boundaries (see Kojima and Nakauchi 1988). This is actually what happened with Japanese FDI during the 1980s and thereafter, with Japan closely following the behavior of Western multinationals. Since the early 1980's, Japanese FDI has undergone significant changes in emphasis. First, the volume of FDI has increased substantially; second, it has shifted from resource development and a cheap-labor orientation to market-oriented and technology-based investment; and third, large multinationals have become major investors in Southeast Asia and the United States (Yoon 1990). The fact that the NIEs' investment in China has been primarily carried out by small and medium enterprises indicates that the majority of investments are single production units, with little firm-level integration. This is quite different from Japanese FDI, which has tended to form intrafirm linkages (Hayashi 1992).

China's open-door policy—in particular, the special economic zones (SEZs) and the FDI policy—was conceived to build a diversified industrial base through the transfer of new technology and managerial and labor skills by the importation of foreign capital. It was also designed to increase the rate of exports. Even so, the overall thrust of China's FDI policy has been in effect inward oriented and is not aimed at export-led growth in the manner of Japan and the Asian NIEs (Kamath 1990). After more than ten years of the open-door policy, the major objectives of technology enhancement and technology transfer appear not to have been met. Rather, FDI has been mostly in low to intermediate technology. China's FDI policy has discouraged whole foreign ownership and has restricted access to the Chinese domestic market. As a consequence, it has failed to attract large investors who are able to bring in advanced technology. The lack of domestic market access also helps explain why Hong Kong firms have been such aggressive investors in China; Hong Kong will have unlimited domestic market access once it becomes integrated into China after 1997. In this regard, China's FDI policy will need to be rethought. Indeed, in recent years it appears that China has been using market access as leverage in its business deals with foreign investors. The admission of China into the GATT, however, will mean a more open market for foreign suppliers. To prepare for this eventuality, China may begin to open up its market with the NIEs first and then other countries.

The host country's policy regarding inward foreign investment often determines the sectoral composition and geographical location of foreign investment. As manifested in China's coastal development strategy, China adopted a containment strategy of foreign investment, that is, foreign investment is allowed only in designated areas and specified sectors. Coastal areas are favored over interior provinces. The heavy concentration of FDI in Guangdong indicates a deepening integration process between Guangdong and Hong Kong. On the whole, the regulated open-door policy favoring coastal areas has brought about uneven regional development and has revived a culture of competitive regionalism, which, according to some observers, may lead to a de facto federation of economically independent provinces (Chang 1992). After more than a decade of economic reforms, China is increasingly a polycentric and economically differentiating system of regions and industries (Chang 1992). Personal relations developed through business channels with local government officials and investors are often considered important by foreign investors as a means of securing their interests against the not-so-transparent political system and frequent policy changes (most of all, a small guarantee against uncertain future) (S.J. Kim 1993). Whether these relations will be resilient enough in the face of rapidly changing economic circumstances remains an open question (compare Shleifer and Vishny 1993).

Contingent Economic Growth

Clearly, the place of individual Asian firms in the world economy has significantly changed since the early 1980s. With the increasing significance of other Asian competitors and the increasingly hostile political economy of trade, the performance of individual firms in labor-intensive industries is now more than ever dependent on enhancing the quality of production and maximizing the rate of labor productivity. The sheer volume of production is now an inadequate basis for maintaining market position. In theory, we might expect a settled landscape of comparative advantage rather separate and distinct from these issues of market demand and corporate performance. But the idea that economic growth and market competition are separable is increasingly untenable, even in theory. For example, the work of Plosser (1989) and others on real business cycles suggests that firms' decisions with respect to unanticipated shifts in demand may affect labor productivity and, if permanent, then affect the path of firms' (and economies') capital accumulation. Thus, in understanding the future growth of whole economies it becomes vital also to understand how the inherited institutional structure of firms affects decision making with respect to the nature and organization of production, the temporal profile of labor productivity, hence capital accumulation, et cetera. A number of issues specific to each of the Asian NIEs illustrate the contingency of economic growth.

Contested Exchange and Neocolonialism

In their work on Hong Kong (chapter 4 in this volume), Chiu and Lui emphasize time and again the small scale, production networks, and export market dependence of labor-intensive industries in the colony. They also argue that Hong Kong is a special case of Asian development, an instance of disorganized capitalism built around entrepreneurial families and community networks, rather than state-based industrial policy. Their field surveys of garment and electronics manufacturing suggest that over the past few years (the early 1990s) local firms have tended to remain labor-intensive rather than investing in technology and labor-saving methods of production. As well, many Hong Kong firms are restructuring so as to extend their entrepreneurial functions to include representing Chinese producers and foreign buyers. As Chiu and Lui note, local firms' Hong Kong production base is becoming less important than their connections with the growing manufacturing base of China. Small Hong Kong firms are becoming spatially elongated production functions (see also Clark 1993b).

Given the declining significance of labor-intensive production in Hong Kong, the future growth of the colony is, in part, dependent upon ensuring the stability and maintenance of those new production networks. At the same time, it remains true that the competitive edge of any garment firm (production or network based) depends on at least matching the costs of production of competitors, whether located in Hong Kong, China, or the ASEAN 4 countries. With limited ability or apparent interest in increasing labor productivity through increasing capitalization, the lowest-labor-cost solution (given a desired quality of production) is an essential ingredient in any firm's competitive strategy. Here, though, there are a set of opposing economic imperatives, which may be resolved in ways that set off vicious cycles of exploitation and decline. One imperative is to maximize profits, most likely short-term profits (i.e., wealth). To do so, Hong Kong entrepreneurial firms have to bargain for the highest final prices from foreign buyers and the lowest prices from mainland Chinese producers. Too high a final price will drive foreign buyers to other suppliers, too low a production price will encourage mainland producers to find other representatives. On the other hand, the knowledge base of Hong Kong producers and merchants is often quite extraordinary; foreign buyers may extract a low final price only if they know of other offers to produce similar products at lower prices. The 1990s world of Hong Kong labor-intensive firms is, as Bowles and Gintis (1993) would describe it, a world of "contested exchange." One consequence of this harsh environment may be that Hong Kong firms leapfrog one another across China, exploiting one site after another in their efforts to remain competitive with other producers located in countries that offer equivalent goods at very competitive prices over the long term.

At the heart of this process of spatial leapfrogging (as opposed to spatial filtering) is a process of exploitation. This process could be thought to have three subprocesses, which are related and interact in an additive fashion. First, it involves a process of institutional (firm) design whose objective it is (on the part of Hong Kong entrepreneurs) to conserve power rather than share power in a bilateral manner. Why? The conservation of power is the means by which entrepreneurs maximize their flexibility in the face of changing market conditions. Second, it involves a process of distributing market risk. Hong Kong entrepreneurs strive to minimize their risk exposure and the potential costs of relying on other external market agents; they do so by distributing market risks, as much as possible, to other parts of the production network located away from the home base of entrepreneurs. Third, it involves a process of short-term alliance building and alliance destruction. This is a political process, based upon local political elites. It is also a process of accommodation and exchange, involving (in some instances) corruption of one form or another. The acknowledged instability of these alliances promotes the exploitation of third parties (local producers or their workers) in circumstances where only one party (entrepreneurs) has the capacity to remove itself from the relationship. In these ways, spatial leapfrogging is consistent with Bowles and Gintis's notion of contested exchange.

Inevitably, Hong Kong and Singaporean firms have had to respond to the burgeoning competition from other Asian producers. And yet, the two city-states are very different in terms of the strategies used by corporations to restructure in the face of new sources of competition. While Singaporean firms have indicated a considerable degree of frustration over the apparent inability of the government to control land and labor costs (relative to their competitors), the relationship between the private sector and the public sector remains very close compared to Hong Kong and perhaps compared to Korea. Even though it is difficult to summarize that relationship in terms that are both fair to the city-state and intelligible to outside readers, the relationship is a mixed form of Western and oriental corporatism involving multinational and domestic companies and the state in a political process of accommodation designed (including other objectives) to maximize economic growth. Like Hong Kong firms, to remain competitive Singaporean firms have had to restructure in an extraterritorial manner, incorporating other cheaper sources of land and labor into their networks of production and exchange. Incorporation of land and labor, though, has been orchestrated by the city-state, planned and arranged between the city-state and the governments of Malaysia and Indonesia. In Miyoshi's (1993, 728) terms, the Singaporean incorporation of land and labor is colonialism in the guise of "transnational corporatism." Here, again, the contrast with Hong Kong is very revealing about firm strategies and the consequences of those strategies for regions and nations. While many Hong Kong firms have embarked on a short-term strategy of spatial leapfrogging, the involvement of the Singaporean state in territorial incorporation has been conceived as a long-term development strategy for the region.

In the short term, the exploitation of land and labor is arguably less important than the establishment and maintenance of long-term collaborative economic relationships. Thus, Miyoshi's supposition that transnational corporatism is inevitably exploitive is an instance where his theoretical disposition takes analysis too quickly to its logical conclusion. That is, although Singaporean firms are profit-maximizing agents concerned with obtaining land and labor at the right price (relative to their competitors), short-term exploitative behavior is mediated by the city-state in the interests of stable long-term collaboration between Malaysian states and Indonesia. The necessary spatial stability of this transnational economic and political alliance mitigates against "excessive" spatial leapfrogging. At the same time, the continued differentiation of the territorial complex (in terms of relative land and labor prices) is vital for its long-term stability; the convergence of wages and prices between the jurisdictions that make up the growth triangle would, over the long term, actually cut against its value to Singaporean firms. Colonialism as transnational corporatism is, in many respects, unstable if the long-term effect of such collaboration is development of the incorporated periphery.

Three other issues may also undercut the long-term stability of the emerging Singaporean territorial complex. First, there is the issue of race and religion. It should be remembered that the post-World War II era of decolonialization involved the formation (by the British) of a federated nation-state including Singapore and Malaya. The federation was, however, quickly fractured by racial and religious rivalries. The growth triangle is another version of the process of federation, being driven this time by economic imperatives, not geopolitical interests or administrative convenience (a spatial economic strategy that seems to be increasingly important in Asia; see Tang and Thant 1993). Notwithstanding the impact of economic imperatives, the underlying racial and religious rivalries remain. Will development be sufficient (and equitably spread) to blunt the force of those rivalries? Second, there is the issue of modernity or what M. Miyoshi calls the "neocolonial practice of [cultural] displacement and ascendancy" (Miyoshi 1993, 728). Again, cultural displacement and ascendancy may have racial and religious overtones. But this is not simply the reflection of simmering tensions. It is also the result of new transnational elites coalescing around common ideas and cultural icons that are used to display their successful inclusion into metropolitan culture (Said 1993). At one level, cultural displacement and ascendancy are means of consolidating power; they include and exclude others. At another level, however, such cultural transformations are the ingredients for local resistance, active and passive. Third, there is the issue of firm sovereignty: that is, the extent to which the interests of Singaporean firms are subsumed within the corporatist compact. Territorial incorporation provides firms the arena in which to seek out and form other alliances outside of those maintained in the city-state. It seems more than possible that as the growth triangle develops, the city-state will not be able to hold the loyalty of its firms once gaps open up between the (private) economic and the (public) political objectives behind territorial incorporation.

Corporate Restructuring and Finance

The issue of neocolonialism is significant for all the Asian NIEs and is especially sensitive for Japan and its economic relations with Asia. Foreign direct investment in Asia by the NIEs and Japan has been closely scrutinized by indigenous elites concerned about losing control of the development process, its structural configuration, and its equitable consequences (relative to the home of investment). While foreign direct investment played only a limited role in domestic Korean development (SaKong 1993), it is now an important strategic option for firms in Korean labor-intensive industries. In this volume, Park (chapter 6) and Lim (chapter 7) have noted for Seoul and Pusan respectively that overseas investment in new production facilities (replacing or adding to domestic Korean production capacity) has been important for both the electronics and footwear industries. But other important strategies have been used by Korean firms concerned about labor costs, labor shortages, and higher rates of labor turnover. Many Seoul-based electronics firms have extended their sourcing networks, extensively utilizing female labor, and have sought to increase the capitalization of production so as to lessen their dependence on labor power.

These are common enough strategies, easily recognized in other Asian NIEs (see chapter 9, this volume). Here, however, the focus is on a couple of other related issues that are important in the Korean context. The first issue concerns the actual form of the modern corporation. The labor-related restructuring strategies noted above take as given the form of the firm and seek to affect the combination of inputs in production. Instead of treating the firm as given, as a shallow conduit for organizing production, there is evidence that the firm itself is increasingly the object of restructuring strategies designed to enhance its international competitiveness. For larger firms, competitiveness has come to be understood as an issue of flexibility; that is, it enhances the responsiveness of the firm to shifts in market preferences and the actions of market competitors. In Korean labor-intensive industries, the firm is typically organized around large-scale commodity manufacturing using routine and well-defined production systems. For many of these firms, Fordism is both metaphorical, in the sense that it represents firms' relations with labor, and real, in the sense that it represents the character of assembly-line production. Clearly, this is changing with the introduction of advanced manufacturing systems that aim at increasing the rate of capital utilization across a broader range of related products. But it is also clear that these firms are being restructured so as to increase their organizational flexibility—in effect, to increase the proportion of their assets that can be switched and reswitched to match the pace of innovation in export product markets.

There are a variety of ways of theorizing this kind of restructuring, including reference to Storper's (1992) notion of product-based technological learning in industrial districts. Here, though, we wish to emphasize a different aspect of the same process: the systematic shedding of sunk costs by firms concerned about their long-term strategic flexibility, not only their short-term adjustment of production costs. Simply, sunk costs are those costs that are irrevocably commited even if production were to cease and the plant closed. In Clark and Wrigley (forthcoming), this point is expanded to include a variety of different sunk costs including setup costs, accumulated sunk costs, and exit sunk costs. It is also suggested through a series of related theoretical propositions that the notion of sunk costs is especially useful in understanding the logic of corporate restructuring. Park's work on Korean labor-intensive firms (chapter 6 in this volume) suggests that long-term strategic flexibility is being sought by a combination of strategies—by outsourcing to cater for new demand of existing products (thereby minimizing any new set-up sunk costs), by utilizing networks of related firms to develop new products (thereby minimizing accumulated sunk costs), and by utilizing foreign plants and producers (thereby minimizing exit sunk costs). As an ideal type, Korean firms that have followed this recipe for corporate restructuring have, in effect, sought to both externalize the costs of commitment and dominate strategic alliances with their partners.

More generally, pressures to restructure the form of the modern Korean corporation has involved rethinking the advantages and disadvantages of *chaebols*—conglomerates of related firms organized in a hierarchical fashion with respect to bureaucratic power and corporate autonomy. Whereas many Western analysts have associated high rates of Korean economic growth with the distinctive benefits of this institutional arrangement of related firms, critics of the *chaebol* have questioned whether it is now an efficient institution with respect to the changing place of Korea in the world economy. For instance, the centralized and vertically arranged nature of bureaucratic power in *chaebols* may have, in effect, homogenized participating firms' cultures, encouraging an internal focus and mitigating against an external market-driven focus. Consequently, some firms have been unable to take full advantage of alliances with outside and overseas firms; often corporate officers have faced mixed and competing incentives (inside and outside of the *chaebol*), encouraging conservatism rather than innovation. The fact that *chaebols* often carry inefficient and uncompetitive firms (with respect to global competitors) within their organizations also drains resources and investment potential at the center of the *chaebol* while limiting the power of individual firms' corporate officers to take investment risks. If the *chaebol* was an efficient institutional arrangement of interfirm relations twenty years ago, heterogeneity, rather than homogeneity, of corporate cultures is, perhaps, a necessary ingredient for success in a world where innovation in high-valued-added products is the likely future for Korean firms. Thus, there are increasing pressures to decentralize corporate power and fracture inter-firm linkages. In doing so, there are increasing pressures to restructure the internal organization of constituent firms.

However, significant local constraints appear to exist with respect to the process of corporate restructuring. Lim's study of the Pusan economy and the changing fortunes of the footwear industry (chapter 7, this volume) points to three important constraints. One is obviously, but significantly, political. The process of minimizing sunk costs in the Pusan region is also clearly a process of corporations reducing their commitment to the local industry. Given the immediate past history of economic growth in the industry and the extraordinary sacrifices by workers (of their wages and benefits) in the interests of fostering that growth, the process of restructuring can be easily interpreted as an act of disloyalty to the local community. Not surprisingly, there has been dispute within the community over plant closings and firm restructuring. A second constraint on the process of corporate restructuring is the relations between local footwear producers and the international owners of the brand-name products that are, after-all, their primary market. The prospect of expanded local long-term strategic options (via reduced sunk costs) has not been altogether welcomed by brand-name owners. Increased long-term options cut against the power of brand-name owners to dominate the exchange relations between footwear buyers and sellers. Here, again, Bowles and Gintis's (1993) world of "contested exchange" has great relevance in helping to understand the scope and limits of corporate strategy.

But the most important constraint on the process of corporate restructuring is financial. Chapter 7 also shows that many of Pusan's footwear firms are caught in a triple bind: as markets shrink for their locally produced footwear products and as they attempt to formulate strategies that may allow for greater flexibility over the long-term, their financial capacity to do so is being undercut by existing sunk costs and declining residual income available for investment. Strong and Meyer (1990), writing about corporate acquisitions and restructuring in the U.S. context, capture neatly the elements of the problem facing Korean firms. In the absence of both alternative sources of income for investment and an adequate and well-designed public policy for economic restructuring, the Korean footwear firms have been unable to obtain sufficient residual income to finance discretionary investment. Indeed, given the enormous exit costs involved in corporate restructuring, many of these larger firms have faced bankruptcy. Even without bankruptcy, the inability of local footwear firms to finance discretionary investment, which would enhance their long-term strategic options, has made these firms increasingly hostage to the interests of brand-name owners. In this respect, the community interest in the performance of footwear firms has been practically discounted and replaced by the international interests of brand-name owners. Restructuring in the NIEs is very much related to the logic of corporate finance.

Equity Markets and International Finance

The discussion so far has concentrated on the structure and organization of commodity production in the Asian NIEs, reflecting the focus of the East-West Center's project on corporate restructuring in labor-intensive manufacturing industries. We have been concerned with the "real" factors of production—land, labor, and capital—in the context of global economic competition. While this focus is obviously important, reflecting the historical evolution of Asian economies, it is also increasingly apparent from recent studies of the growth of the Asian NIEs that other factors have come to be important in affecting their performance. Indeed, if we were to assess the relative importance of the various factors affecting the performance of the Taiwan economy over the 1980s, commodity production and trade would be judged by some to have been much less significant than the astonishing speculative "bubble" that dominated local equity markets over much of the decade. For many economic theorists, bubble economies are hardly ever significant. Bubbles would not exist if markets were efficient; for bubbles to be more than just a momentary phenomenon, "asset prices [can] not reflect fundamentals" (Stiglitz 1990, 13). More generally, economic theorists are reluctant to accept that equity markets could affect the performance of the "real" economy, except in the sense these markets are sometimes thought to be important for capital formation (but see Mayer 1990).

Recent studies of the causes and consequences of the 1987 stock market crash have gone some way to changing theorists' views about the importance of bubble economies for the "real" economy. As well, there has been a reevaluation of the most recent generation of economic models, which presume rational expectations drive actual economic agents (see Shiller 1992). With respect to the Asian NIEs, chapter 3 argues that the Taiwanese bubble economy was very important for the evolving social and economic structure of the local economy. The Taipei stock market index increased from about 1,000 points in 1985 to about 12,000 points in 1990 before crashing in 1990–91 back to 2,000 points at the end of 1991. More recently, the index has again accelerated. For many of the middle class, their active participation in the stock market was an amazing gamble matching in volatility shifts and changes in land and property prices. Over the 1980s and 1990s, there have been extraordinary changes in middle-class perceptions and values, in particular the discounting of conventional values attributed to commodity trade and the rise of competing values associated with financial transaction, speculation, and international arbitrage. While it is difficult to show the effects of these rapid shifts in values and asset prices, many commentators suggest that the problems facing labor-intensive firms (increasing wages and prices, limited labor supply, and escalating labor turnover) are, in part, derived from the burgeoning social significance of the finance sector in Taiwan.

How could stock market performance be so (negatively) significant for the "real" economy of commodity production and trade? What are the patterns of stock market performance across the Asian NIEs? Imagine that individual entrepreneurs, instead of investing in their commodity-producing firms, switched their residual funds from discretionary investment in plant and equipment to a portfolio of stocks designed to reflect the performance of the local equity market. If entrepreneurs invested in market-specific index funds, what would be the likely returns from such a passive investment strategy? Over the period 1983 to 1993, investment in the Taipei TSE index would have returned 40 percent per annum, albeit involving an annualized risk of 80 percent. While the Taipei equity market is generally acknowledged as a gamble in any circumstances, it is also instructive to note that over the same period passive investment in the Hang Seng (Hong Kong) and Korean KOPSI would have returned between 20 and 25 percent per annum, with a risk of about 30 percent per annum. Over the period, 1990 to 1993, Asian equity markets have increasingly performed less well compared to the U.S. Dow Jones Industrial Average, although the Hang Seng remains an opportunity for investors seeking a high risk-adjusted return. Just as high returns encouraged rampant local speculation, very low returns (and relatively high risk) have dampened speculation in individual markets. Still, it is more than possible that a passive, index-based investment strategy could be a superior corporate strategy compared to investment in plant and equipment in local labor-intensive industries.

Index funds are valuable to individual investors for a variety of reasons. They are designed to mimic the overall performance of local equity markets, matching the performance of an optimal diversified portfolio without having to carry the information costs involved in constructing a portfolio and the transaction costs involved in buying individual stocks. Moreover, index funds allow individual investors to avoid the commitment implied by owning individual stocks and thus the necessity of monitoring the performance of those stocks and those that manage the companies listed on the local stock exchange. In essence, index funds are very useful for investors who wish to avoid the complexities associated with corporate strategy in the "real" economy. Index funds allow for short-term investment, hedging against the risks associated with individual investments, and participation in bull markets across the world. While it might be argued that the recent experience of Asian investors in local equity markets must have encouraged greater caution with respect to the risks inherent in bubble economies, the available evidence suggests that investment in index products is now even more important than before, although investment is increasingly across markets rather than in single-market products. Put slightly differently, many Taiwanese entrepreneurs have adjusted to recent experience by seeking global index funds rather than returning to the "real" economy of commodity production (see Obstfeld 1992).

Two qualifications should be taken into account before the reader accepts or rejects the argument made above about the increasing social and economic significance of equity markets in the Taiwanese economy. One concerns the potential value of expanding equity markets for small and medium enterprises (SMEs). Soohyun Chon has pointed out (in conversation) that some SMEs have benefited from the expanding equity market by using increases in their listed stock prices as a means of attracting equity investment, rather than paying a premium on loans from financial institutions. This appears to be an important alternative source of financing, which was not available ten years or so ago, even if stock prices are extraordinarily volatile. A second qualification concerns the increasing significance of Asian equity markets for overseas investors. In the case of Taiwan, the relatively well developed equity market has attracted the interest of many Western institutional investors, thereby adding to the flow of investment in the economy, if not necessarily adding to the stock of capital. At issue is the extent to which equity value has been translated into production plant and equipment. The rate of translation (as it were) appears to be driven by entrepreneurs' objectives, which in turn are driven, in part, by expectations. Equity adds to corporate capital stock if enterpreneurs are confident about the long term future of their firms and industries; equity adds to entrepreneurs' wealth if they are not so confident. In the case of Taiwanese labor-intensive firms, equity appears to translate into a wealth effect rather than an investment effect.

Clearly, the risk and return profiles of Asian equity markets are not only of significance for local investors and production companies. The growth and volatility of these equity markets has been increasingly important for Western (especially U.S., U.K., and European) institutional investors. Since the late 1980s, returns on fixed income investments, like government bonds and money market products, have greatly declined, encouraging investment managers to take more seriously the potential value of Asian markets. Given that these markets seem to have their own internal dynamics, quite distinct from U.S. and European stock markets, conventional notions of portfolio diversification have also encouraged investment managers to shift significant resources into Asian equities. Mutual funds, pension funds, and large institutional investors now offer a wide variety of global investment products, many of which are composites of Asian equity indexes weighted according to investment managers' assessments of risk and return. These kinds of funds are typically open ended. That is, individual investors (more likely their agents) normally trade in and out of these funds on the basis of relative returns and their own assessments of the likely path of Asian equity markets. In this sense, the Asian NIEs have been incorporated by financial institutions into the global arbitrage economy. Financial incorporation has been in the interests of investment managers; it remains to be seen how incorporation will affect the paths of growth of each of the Asian NIEs over the coming decades.

Conclusion

Throughout this book we have sought to highlight both the commonalities and differences between the Asian NIEs. With respect to commonalities, the reference point has been the recent performance of the NIEs' labor-intensive industries, arguing that they face many common problems all of which threaten the international competitiveness of these industries. Given the structural transformation of the Asian NIEs over the past decade, these industries are now less important for the future growth of the NIEs. With respect to differences, the reference point has been corporate strategy and (to a lesser degree) institutional context, arguing that how firms have adjusted to these common problems has been quite different between economies, reflecting the very different histories and circumstances of these economies as well as the strategic options available to sustain competitiveness. In these ways, it has been argued that the Asian NIEs face separately a very different world than that of twenty years ago. For all the Asian NIEs, the era of labor-intensive, locally manufactured commodity production and trade has ended. While export-led growth was a vital element in the mix of policies and circumstances that contributed to their extraordinary growth over the past few decades, the future of the Asian NIEs is more uncertain and contingent than ever before.

We have focused on corporate strategy in the belief that understanding firms' economic performance is an essential ingredient in any overarching study of the growth of the Asian NIEs. This microeconomic perspective inevitably intersects with a variety of theories and arguments about the crucial variables behind the growth of the Asian NIEs. While not wishing to deny the importance of understanding the relative contribution (relative to other economic and institutional factors) of industrial policy to the past growth of the NIEs, we have also argued that the relevance of industrial policy to their future growth may be much less than that supposed by advocates of policy-driven growth. In Korea, for example, industrial policy seems to be unrelated to the predicament facing labor-intensive industries. In the case of Taiwan, there are good reasons to suppose that financial liberalization has had an enormous impact on the available scope of private economic agents, an impact that arguably has swamped the effect of conventional industrial development policies. Of course, in Singapore, there remains a close, corporatist connection between the public and private sectors, but even this relationship is undergoing change as indigenous Singaporean firms venture into production and trade relations with the rest of Asia. There are now many reasons to rethink the now conventional emphasis on development policy as opposed to the strategies of firms.

If it is important to rethink the relevance of the prevailing orthodoxy with respect to the study of the growth of the Asian NIEs, it is also important to reflect again on the applicability of the Asian experience to other countries and regions of the globe. In the literature, it is common to compare their experience with Latin American countries, perhaps because what is being compared are two very different development policies that were initiated in the 1950s and early 1960s: in Latin America, a number of countries used an import-replacement development strategy, whereas in the Asian NIEs, the common strategy was export-led growth. Here, the applicability of the Asian experience is considered by referring to the experience of a set of African countries. In comparative (and even, in a couple of instances, in absolute) terms, the selected African economies performed poorly over the period 1960 to 1990. But does this mean that the Asian NIEs are an appropriate model for planning their future growth? To the extent that there are sufficient commonalities between the Asian NIEs (compared with other sets of countries and regions) to speak of an Asian model of development, something that Barro and his colleagues may dispute, the applicability of such a model to other regions also depends on the capacity of political institutions to implement such a program of development. It also seems to us that there has been insufficient analysis of the political foundations of Asian development to make strong policy recommendations concerned the applicability of export-led models of development to other regions with different cultural traditions.

With respect to the future of the Asian NIEs, the conditions leading to past rapid economic growth have substantially changed—the NIEs will not reach the same high rates of growth apparent over the past couple of decades. Why? The international competitiveness of local labor-intensive firms, the pressures to shift investment overseas to less developed Asian countries, the decreasing gap between imports and exports consistent with domestic higher-value-added production, and the emerging slowdown in labor productivity growth (relative to escalating real wages). Whereas many recent studies of the success of the Asian NIEs have focused on the factors that initiated and sustained high rates of growth, it is now important to also ask how growth might be maintained when many of these factors are not so important for each NIE. If the Asian NIEs are to continue to grow at comparatively high rates of growth, each NIE (but more particularly, its firms and corporations) must resolve a series of economy-specific challenges.

Survey on Enterprise Strategy

Preamble

This survey is part of a large, comparative international project on industrial restructuring in the Asian NIEs. The project is sponsored and coordinated by the East-West Center's Population Institute in Honolulu. At the local level, the project is being conducted by the local institutions listed in the acknowledgments. The aim of the project is to better understand the changing conditions facing local companies and enterprises, and the kinds of responses of businesses to those economic pressures. The survey asks questions related to technology, labor costs, labor supply and turnover, investment decisions and future plans in relation to market conditions.

Information obtained from the survey will be treated as CONFIDENTIAL. No information will be released to the public which could identify particular companies or enterprises. Your participation in this survey is gratefully appreciated. Copies of the final report will be available upon request.

I. Basic Firm Data

1. Name and address of your firm: _____

2. Year of establishment at the above address: _____

3. Type of industry: _____

4. Principal products: 1. _____   2. _____   3. _____

5. Is your firm: 1. Fully locally owned   2. Fully foreign owned
   3. Joint venture

6. Is your firm: 1. Listed   2. Unlisted

7. Is your firm: 1. Independent firm 2. Branch/subsidiary of another organization

   7-1. If independent, is it owner managed: 1. Yes   2. No

   7-2. If a branch or subsidiary, where is the headquarters of the parent company located?

8. Is your firm operating mainly by subcontracting?   1. Yes   2. No

   8-1. If yes, what is the ratio of subcontracting to the total sales?___

9. How large was your enterprise as of the year end 1991:
   1. Value added _____   2. Sales _____
   3. Gross fixed assets _____   4. Employees _____
   5. Percent of labor compensation to sales volume _____

II. Enterprise Size and Markets

10. How many persons including management are working in your enterprise as of July 1992 (include those temporarily absent and on sick leave)?

	Male	Female
1. Full-time	____	____
2. Part-time	____	____
3. Temporary	____	____
4. Total	____	____

11. What is the distribution of employees by occupation?

	Male	Female
1. Managerial/administrative	_____	_____
2. Professional/technical	_____	_____
3. Clerical/sales/service	_____	_____
4. Skilled operatives (3 years and more experience)	_____	_____
5. Unskilled workers	_____	_____
6. Apprentices	_____	_____
7. Total	_____	_____

12. What is the proportion of production for export?_____ %

12-1. If any "export," where does your enterprise export to (percent of total exports):
1. Japan _____   2. Asian NIEs _____
3. Southeast Asia (except Singapore) _____
4. North America _____   5. European Community _____
6. China _____   7. Other (specify) _____

III. Business Conditions and Plans

13. In the last two years, how has your business changed in terms of sales volume?
   1. Increased   2. Decreased   3. Remained same

14. How well has your enterprise been doing over the past three years? (percent change/year)

	1989	1990	1991
1. Sales	_____	_____	_____
2. Production costs	_____	_____	_____

14-1. If business has decreased, what factors are responsible? (if more than one, list them in descending order of importance)
_____ _____ _____ _____
1. Higher wages/salaries
2. Higher costs of raw materials and inputs
3. High prices of main products due to currency revaluation
4. Product quality

5. Stiffer competition
6. Labor disputes
7. Decrease in demand
8. Other (specify _____)

14-2. If business has increased, what factors are responsible?
(if more than one, list them in descending order of importance)
____ ____ ____ ____

1. Low wages/salaries
2. Low material costs
3. Product quality
4. Flexible pricing
5. Specialization in niche markets
6. Increase in demand
7. Other (specify)

15. Has your enterprise extended its range of products (including diversification of products, multiple products, and new products) in the last two years?   1. Yes   2. No

15-1. If yes, has that led to any changes in employment?
1. Increased   2. Decreased   3. No change

15-2. If yes, have the new products changed skill requirements
in production?   1. Increased   2. Decreased   3. No change

16. In the last five years, has your enterprise invested in overseas
plants/factories?   1. No   2. Yes

16-1. If yes, what year/years has the investment been made?
____ ____ ____ ____

16-2. If yes, what were the main reasons for investing overseas?
(if more than one, list them in descending order of importance)
____ ____ ____ ____

1. Lower wage costs
2. Easier access to markets
3. Cheaper component/parts production
4. Fewer labor problems
5. Currency revaluation

6. Cheaper land/availability of land
7. Other (specify _____)

16-3. If yes, where were those investments made?
1. Japan _____ 2. Asian NIEs _____
3. Southeast Asia (except Singapore) _____
4. North America _____ 5. European Community _____
6. China _____ 7. Other (specify) _____

16-4. If yes, what was the value of investments made for the years 1987 through 1991?
1987 _____ 1988 _____ 1989 _____ 1990 _____ 1991 _____

16-5. If yes, what is the size of employment in overseas plants? ___
17. For the next three years, is your enterprise planning to invest in overseas plants/factories? 1. No 2. Yes

17-1. If yes, what is the main reason? (if more than one, list them in descending order of importance) ____ ____ ____ ____
1. Lower wage costs
2. Easier access to markets
3. Cheaper component/parts production
4. Fewer labor problems
5. Currency revaluation
6. Cheaper land/availability of land
7. Other (specify _____)

17-2. If yes, where will those investments be made?
1. Japan _____ 2. Asian NIEs _____
3. Southeast Asia (except Singapore) _____
4. North America _____ 5. European Community _____
6. China _____ 7. Other (specify) _____

IV. Labor Market Conditions

18. What proportion of total costs of production in 1991 are attributable to labor costs?
1. 0–9% _____ 2. 10–19% _____ 3. 20–29% _____
4. 30–39% _____ 5. 40–49% _____ 6. >50% _____

19. What are the average monthly wage rates of production workers in 1992 according to the following categories?
  1. Supervisors/foremen _____
  2. Skilled operatives _____
  3. Unskilled operatives _____

20. In the last three years the wage rates of production workers in your enterprise have had:
  1. Steep increases   2. Moderate increases
  3. Decreases   4. Remained the same

21. What is the rate of labor turnover (percent of workforce per year) in your enterprise in 1991?

1. 0–9% _____   2. 10–29% _____   3. 30–49% _____
4. 50–69% _____   5. 70% and more

22. What was the average rate of separation for production workers in your enterprise in the past three years?

23. Which groups have higher labor turnover rates?
  1. Male _____ or Female _____
  2. Skilled (more than 3 years of experience) _____ or Unskilled _____
  3. Young (less than 25 years old) _____ or Old _____

24. When workers leave your enterprise, do they leave for
  1. Other firms in the same industry
  2. Other firms in the manufacturing business
  3. Non-manufacturing sector jobs
  4. Others (specify _____)

V. Enterprise Strategy (Technology)

25. Has your enterprise introduced new technology in the last two years?   1. No   2. Yes

  25-1. If yes, what kind of new technology?
  1. Production
  2. Design
  3. Office

4. Quality control
5. Inventory control
6. Other (specify _____)

25-2. If yes, are those technologies imported, domestically developed, or in-house developed?

25-3. If yes, has that caused any change in employment?
1. Increase   2. Decrease   3. No change

25-4. If yes, did the new technology:
a. change the range of tasks required of production workers?
    1. Increase   2. Decrease   3. No change
b. change the complexity of technical knowledge required?
    1. Increase   2. Decrease   3. No change
c. change the demand for certain occupations?   1. No   2. Yes
d. If yes for c, specify _____

26. What were the main purposes of introducing new technology? (see below codes and list three major ones in descending order)

____   ____   ____

Codes:
1. To increase output
2. To cut labor costs
3. To cut material/energy costs
4. To reduce the need for skilled labor
5. To improve product quality
6. To reduce wage costs
7. To reduce supervisory costs
8. To save space
9. To produce new products
10. Other (specify _____)

VI. Enterprise Strategy (Contract Work, Part-Time, and Shift)

27. Does your enterprise contract-out work to other establishments?
    1. No   2. Yes

27-1. If yes, which activities are contracted-out?
1. Maintenance (including security)
2. Employees' welfare (transport, food, etc.)
3. Components/parts production
4. Other (specify _____)

27-1a. If your enterprise contracts-out components/parts production to overseas, where are those subcontracting units located?
1. Japan _____   2. Asian NIEs _____
3. Southeast Asia (except Singapore) _____
4. North America _____   5. European Community _____
6. China _____   7. Other (specify) _____

27-2. If yes, how many workers are involved in contract work?
Female _____   Male _____

27-3. If yes, what are the main reasons for contracting-out work? (see codes below and list the major reasons in descending order of importance) _____ _____ _____
1. Lower administrative costs
2. Lower training costs
3. Lower wage costs
4. Specialized skills
5. Fringe benefits
6. Fluctuating demand
7. Labor shortage
8. Labor union
9. Other (specify _____)

27-4. If yes, what is the proportion of contract costs to total production costs? _____

27-5. If yes, is contract work mainly done on your enterprise's premises or in other locations?
1. On the premises
2. Outside the premises but within the locality
3. Outside the locality within the country (not applicable to Hong Kong and Singapore)
4. Outside the locality in neighbor country
5. Overseas

28. In the last two years has your enterprise hired temporary or casual workers? (Temporary workers are those hired for short period of time, with temporary contracts or no contract)   1. No   2. Yes

28-1. If yes, for what types of work?
1. Unskilled, general
2. Skilled production
3. Clerical/service
4. Other (specify _____)

28-2. If yes, what are the major reasons for employing temporary or casual workers? (see codes below and list three major ones in descending order) ____ ____ ____
1. Lower administrative costs
2. Lower training costs
3. Lower wage costs
4. Fringe benefits
5. Labor shortage
6. Fluctuating demand
7. Market uncertainty
8. Labor union/laws
9. Other (specify _____)

28-3. Where do temporary workers come from?
1. Within the locality
2. Outside the locality but within the country (not applicable to Hong Kong and Singapore)
3. Neighboring country
4. Overseas

29. Does your enterprise employ more or fewer part-time workers compared with two years ago?
   1. More   2. Fewer   3. Same

29-1. If more, what are the major reasons for that? (see codes below and list up to three major ones in descending order)

____ ____ ____
1. Shortage of suitable workers
2. High wage costs
3. High non-wage labor costs

4. Quality/productivity control
5. Flexible deployment of labor
6. Other (specify _____)

29-2. If fewer, what are the major reasons for that (see codes below and list up to three major ones in descending order)

____   ____   ____

1. Company preference for full-time employees
2. Products do not require part-time workers
3. Union resistance
4. Labor laws
5. Other (specify _____)

30. How many shifts has your enterprise been operating?

	Per day	Per week
In July 1992	_____	_____

31. If the number of shifts changed in the last year, what was the direction of change?
   1. Increase   2. Decrease   3. Same

31-1. If increase, what was the main reason?
1. Limited production capacity
2. Saving in wage costs
3. Increase in demand
4. Other (specify _____)

31-2. If decrease, what was the main reason?
1. Union resistance
2. Labor law
3. Decrease in demand
4. Other (specify _____)

32. Does your enterprise currently employ foreign workers?
   1. Yes   2. No

32-1. If yes, what is the major reason for hiring foreign workers?
1. Low wages/benefits
2. Willing to work unpopular shifts/assignments

3. Younger and nimble
4. Other (specify _____)

32-2. If yes, how many foreign workers in the following categories?
a. Skilled   Male ____ Female ____
b. Unskilled   Male ____ Female ____

32-3. If no, would your enterprise like to use foreign workers?
1. Yes   2. No

VII. Enterprise Strategy (Redundancy, Retraining, and Retention)

33. Does your enterprise expect or plan to increase or reduce the number of employees in the next two years?
    1. Increase   2. Reduce   3. No change

33-1. If any change, what are the main reasons? (if more than one list them in descending order in importance) ____ ____ ____
1. Business change
2. Work reorganization
3. Automation
4. New product
5. Shortage of qualified workers
6. Company restructuring
7. Rising wage/salary costs
8. Plant capacity
9. Rising non-wage labor costs, e.g., fringe benefits
10. Business uncertainty
11. Export quota
12. Labor union
13. Labor laws
14. Other (specify _____)

34. Does your enterprise have retention strategies now?
    1. No   2. Yes

34-1. If yes, what kind of retention strategies do you have?
  1. Higher wages and benefits (pensions, health care,
     and education)
  2. Stock sharing and profit sharing
  3. Earlier promotion
  4. Training and retraining
  5. Better working conditions
  6. Shortening working hours
  7. Information sharing and consultation
  8. Other (specify _____)

35. Does your enterprise offer any training schemes for the currently
employed?   1. No   2. Yes

  35-1. If yes, what kind of retraining schemes do you have?
  1. Financial assistance
  2. In-house training
  3. Outside training
  4. Other (specify _____)

  35-2. If yes, did your enterprise receive any financial assistance
  from public authorities?   1. No   2. Yes, Amount _____

VIII. Labor Unions

36. What is the level of unionization in your enterprise? _____%

37. Labor-management relations in your enterprise can be described
as:

1	2	3	4	5
Cooperative		Neutral		Confrontational

38. To what extent do labor unions affect your enterprise strategy?

1	2	3	4	5
Considerably		Moderately		Negligibly

IX. Management Opinions

39. Are there any industry-wide efforts to improve production efficiency and/or product quality (e.g., R&D in design, process, etc.) in your locality?   1. No   2. Yes (specify _____)

40. Do you think industrial relations in general in your locality compared to the past are favorable to management?

1	2	3	4	5
Favorable		Neutral		Unfavorable

41. In the last two years, do you think the public sector including government was supportive of enterprise management in terms of:

	Very supportive		Neutral	Not supportive	
a. access to loans	1	2	3	4	5
b. infrastructure provision	1	2	3	4	5
c. industrial relations	1	2	3	4	5
d. marketing	1	2	3	4	5
e. information and consultation	1	2	3	4	5
f. R&D support	1	2	3	4	5
g. regulation and laws	1	2	3	4	5

42. What programs would your enterprise like provided by the public sector to facilitate enterprise development? _____

References

ADB (Asian Development Bank). 1991. *Asian development outlook*. Manila: Asian Development Bank.

Alchian, A. 1950. Uncertainty, evolution, and economic theory. *Journal of Political Economy* 58:211–21.

Amsden, A. 1989. *Asia's new giant: South Korea and late industrialization*. New York: Oxford University Press.

———. 1990. Third world industrialization. *New Left Review* 182:5–31

———. 1991. Big business and urban congestion in Taiwan: The origins of small enterprise and regionally decentralized industry (respectively). *World Development* 19:1121–35.

Andrews, K. R. 1971. *The concept of corporate strategy*. Homewood, Ill.: Dow Jones Irwin.

Ariff, M., ed. 1991. *The Pacific economy*. Sydney: Allen and Unwin.

Australia. 1993. *Quarterly Economic and Trade Review*. April. Canberra: Department of Foreign Affairs and Trade.

Bailey, T. 1993. Organizational innovation in the apparel industry. *Industrial Relations* 32:304–8.

Bank of Korea. 1991. *Korea overseas investment yearbook*. Seoul: Bank of Korea.

———. 1992. *Financial statement analysis*. Seoul: Korean Footwear Industry Association.

———. 1993. *Korean investment yearbook*. Seoul: Bank of Korea.

Bardhan, P. 1988. Alternative approaches to development economics. In *Handbook of development economics*, vol. 1, ed. H. Chenery and T. N. Srinivasan, 39–71. Amsterdam: North Holland.

Barnes, T. 1992. Reading the tests of theoretical economic geography. *In Writing worlds: Discourse, text, and metaphor in the representation of the landscape*, ed. J. Duncan, 118–35. London: Routledge.

Barro, R. 1991. Economic growth in a cross section of countries. *Quarterly Journal of Economics* 106:407–43.

———. 1992. Industrial policy, a tale of two cities. *Wall Street Journal.* 1 April.

Barro, R., and X. Sala i Martin. 1990. *Economic growth and convergence across the United States.* Working Paper 3,419, National Bureau of Economic Research, Cambridge, Mass.

Baum, J. 1993. Taipei's offshore empire. *Far Eastern Economic Review* 156, no. 11 (18 March): 44–45.

Beauregard, R. A. 1989. Space, time, and economic restructuring. In *Urban Affairs Quarterly Annual Reviews,* vol. 34, *Economic restructuring and political response,* ed. R. A. Beauregard. Newbury Park, Calif.: Sage.

Bello, W., and S. Rosenfeld. 1990. *Dragons in distress: Asia's miracle economies in crisis.* San Francisco: Institute for Food and Development Policy.

Bemmels, B., and Y. Reshef. 1991. Manufacturing employees and technological change. *Journal of Labour Research* 12:231–46.

Birnbaum, D. 1993. *Importing garments through Hong Kong.* Hong Kong: Third Horizon.

Bowles, S., and H. Gintis. 1993. The revenge of homo economicus: Contested exchange and the revival of political economy. *Journal of Economic Perspectives* 7:83–102.

Brace for Japan's hot new strategy. 1992. *Fortune.* 21 September, 24–31.

Bradford, C. I. 1990. Policy interventions and markets: Development strategy typologies and policy options. In *Manufacturing miracles: Paths of industrialization in Latin America and East Asia,* ed. G. Gareffi and D. L. Wyman, 34–51. Princeton: Princeton University Press.

Bryant, R. C. 1989. The evolution of Singapore as a financial centre. In *Management of success: The moulding of modern Singapore,* ed. K. S. Sandhu and P. Wheatley, 337–72. Singapore: Institute of Southeast Asian Studies.

Business Times. 1989a. *Asian NIEs' labour costs provide the edge in world trade: Report.* 24 April.

———. 1989b. *Seven workers lost for every eight hired: MNCs report high turnover of staff.* 25 January.

———. 1991a. *DBS land joins Pernas to build JB township.* 7 May.

———. 1991b. *BG Lee urges moderation in wage rises, hiring of foreign workers.* 15 October.

———. 1991c. *Batam shaping up as production centre.* 28 October.

———. 1991d. *Strategic investments abroad mostly by govt-linked firms.* 13 December.

———. 1992a. *Government can help companies go regional.* 25 September.

———. 1992b. *EDB makes investing abroad easier.* 12 October.

———. 1992c. *S'pore govt unveils first major investment in China.* 29 November.

Castells, M., L. Goh, and Y. W. Kwok. 1988. *Economic development and housing policy in the Asian Pacific Rim.* Monograph 37, Institute of Urban and Regional Development, University of California, Berkeley.

Chang, Ching-hsi. 1991. An economic analysis of guest workers in Taiwan. Paper presented at workshop, Labor Flows to Taiwan, 6–8 June, Institute of Economics, Academia Sinica, Taipei.

Chang, M. H. 1992. China's future: Regionalism, federation, or disintegration. *Studies in Comparative Communism* 25:211–27.

Chapman, K., and D. F. Walker. 1991. *Industrial location.* 2d ed. Oxford: Basil Blackwell.

Chen, E. K. Y., and K. W. Li. 1991. Industry development and industrial policy in Hong Kong. In *Industrial and trade development in Hong Kong*, ed. E. K. Y. Chen, M. K. Nyaw, and T. Y. C. Wong, 3–47. Hong Kong: Centre of Asian Studies, University of Hong Kong.

Chen, Jieh-Shyuan. 1991. *Economic structure and social characteristics of small and medium enterprises in Taiwan: A case study of textile, footwear, machinery, and information industries* (in Chinese). Ph.D. diss., Tung Hai University, Taiwan.

Chen, T. J. 1992. Determinants of Taiwan's direct foreign investment. *Journal of Development Economics* 39:397–407.

Chen, T. J., and D. P. Tang. 1990. Export performance and productivity growth: The case of Taiwan. *Economic Development and Cultural Change* 38:577–85.

Cheng, T. J. 1990. Political regimes and developmental strategies: South Korea and Taiwan. In *Manufacturing miracles: Paths of industrialization in Latin America and East Asia,* ed. G. Gereffi and D. L. Wyman, 139–78. Princeton: Princeton University Press.

Chia, S. Y. 1989. The character and progress of industrialisation. In *Management of success: The moulding of modern Singapore*, ed. K. S. Sandhu and P. Wheatley, 250–279. Singapore: Institute of Southeast Asian Studies.

Chinloy, P. T., and E. Stromsdorfer, eds. 1987. *Labor market adjustments in the Pacific basin.* Boston: Kluwer-Nijhoff.

Chiu, Lee-in Chen, and C. Chung. 1993. An assessment of Taiwan's indirect investment toward mainland China. *Asian Economic Journal* 7(1):41–70.

Chiu, S. 1992. *The state and the financing of industrialization in East Asia: Historical origins of comparative divergences.* Ph.D. thesis, Princeton University.

Chiu, S., and T. L. Lui. 1993. Neither state nor market: Development theories and industrial restructuring in Hong Kong. Department of Sociology, Chinese University of Hong Kong.

Cho, L. J., and Y. H. Kim. 1991. Political, economic, and social developments in the 1980s. In *Economic development in the Republic of Korea*, ed. L. J. Cho and Y. H. Kim, 603–19. Honolulu: East-West Center.

Choi, Y. P., H. S. Chung, and N. Marian. 1985. *The Multifibre Arrangement in theory and practice*. London: Frances Pinter.

Chow, P. C. Y., and M. Kellman. 1993. *Trade: The engine of growth in East Asia*. New York: Oxford University Press.

Chu, Y. W. 1988. *Dependent industrialization: The case of the Hong Kong garment industry*. Master's Thesis, University of Hong Kong.

Clark, G. L. 1981. The employment relation and spatial division of labor: An hypothesis. *Annals, Association of American Geographers* 71:412–24.

———. 1993a. Costs and prices, corporate competitive strategies and regions. *Environment and Planning A* 25:5–26.

———. 1993b. Global interdependence and regional development: Business linkages and corporate governance in a world of financial risk. *Transactions, Institute of British Geographers* N.S. 18:309–25.

———. 1993c. *Pensions and corporate restructuring in American industry: A crisis of regulation*. Baltimore: Johns Hopkins University Press.

———. 1994. Strategy and structure: Corporate restructuring and the scope and characteristics of sunk costs. *Environment and Planning A* 26:9–32.

Clark, G. L., M. S. Gertler, and J. Whiteman. 1986. *Regional dynamics: Studies in adjustment theory*. London: Allen and Unwin.

Clark, G. L., and N. Wrigley. Forthcoming. Sunk costs: A framework for economic geography. *Transactions, Institute of British Geographers*.

Coffee, J. C. 1991. Liquidity versus control: The institutional investor as corporate monitor. *Columbia Law Review* 91:1277–368.

Collingsworth, T., J. W. Goold and P. J. Harvey. 1994. Time for a global New Deal. *Foreign Affairs* 73(1):8–13.

Collis, D. 1991. *Corporate strategy: A research agenda*. Harvard Business School, Boston Mass.

Corbo, V., and S. M. Suh, eds. 1992. *Structural adjustment in a newly industrialising country: The Korean experience*. Baltimore: Johns Hopkins University Press.

Cumings, B. 1988. World system and authoritarian regimes in Korea, 1848–1984. In *Contending approaches to the political economy of Taiwan*, ed. E. A. Winckler and S. Greenhalgh, 249–69. New York: M. E. Sharpe.

Daly, M. T., and M. I. Logan. 1989. *The brittle rim*. Ringwood, Victoria, Australia: Penguin.

Deyo, F. C. 1987. Coalitions, institutions, and linkage sequencing: Toward a strategic capacity model of East Asian development. In *The political economy of the new Asian industrialization*, ed. F. Deyo, 227–47. Ithaca: Cornell University Press.

Dicken, P. 1992. *Global shift*. 2d Ed. New York: Guilford.

Dixon, C. 1991. *Southeast Asia in the world economy*. Cambridge: Cambridge University Press.

Donaghu, M. T., and R. Barff. 1990. Nike "just did it": International subcontracting and flexibility in athletic footwear production. *Regional Studies* 24:537–52.

Douglass, M. 1993. *Putting the region back into regional planning.* Department of Urban and Regional Planning, University of Hawaii. Mimeographed.

Durlauf, S. 1992. International differences in economic fluctuations. In *Technology and the wealth of nations,* ed. N. Rosenberg, R. Landau, and D. Mowery, 121–47. Palo Alto: Stanford University Press.

Easterly, W. 1994. Explaining miracles: Growth regressions meet the Gang of Four. Policy Research Working Paper 1,250, World Bank, Washington, D.C.

Economic Daily News. Various years. *Annual economic yearbook of the Republic of China.* Taipei: Economic Daily News.

Economic Planning Council. Various years. *Annual Taiwan statistical data book.* Taipei: Economic Planning Council.

EIU (Economist Intelligence Unit). 1989. *Country Reports: Korea.* London: EIU.

———. 1990. *Singapore: Country profiles 1989–90.* London: EIU.

———. 1992a. *Singapore: Country profiles 1991–92.* London: EIU.

———. 1992b. *Taiwan: Country profiles 1991–92.* London: EIU.

Eisinger, P. K. 1988. *The rise of the entrepreneurial state.* Madison: University of Wisconsin Press.

Ellison, Christopher, and Gary Gereffi. 1990. Explaining strategies and patterns of Industrial development. In *Managing miracles: Paths of Industrialization in Latin America and East Asia,* ed. Gary Gereffi and Donald L. Wyman, 368–403. Princeton: Princeton University Press.

Federation of Hong Kong Industries. 1992. *Hong Kong industrial investment in the Pearl River Delta.* Hong Kong: Federation of Hong Kong Industries, Industry and Research Division.

Fields, Gary S. 1992. Living standards, labor markets, and human resources in Taiwan. In *Taiwan: From developing to mature economy,* ed. Gustav Ranis, 395–433. Boulder, Colo.: Westview.

Florida, R., and M. Kenney. 1992. Restructuring in place: Japanese investment, production organization, and the geography of steel. *Economic Geography* 68:146–73.

Foreign investment in China, 1992—Statistics. *JETRO China Newsletter* 105:19–24.

Foreign investment in the PRC, 1991–1992. *JETRO China Newsletter* 102:16–19.

Frankel, J. 1992. Is Japan creating a yen bloc in East Asia and the Pacific? Working paper 4,050, National Bureau of Economic Research, Cambridge, Mass.

Frankel, J., and M. Mussa. 1980. The efficiency of foreign exchange markets and measures of turbulence. *American Economic Review* 70:374–81.

Friedman, M., and R. Friedman. 1980. *Free to choose.* Harmondsworth, U.K.: Penguin.

Frobel, F., J. Heinrichs, and O. Kreye. 1980. *The new international division of labour.* Cambridge: Cambridge University Press.

Gamer, R. E. 1972. *The politics of urban development in Singapore.* Ithaca: Cornell University Press.

Garnaut, R. 1989. *Australia and the Northeast Asian ascendancy.* Canberra: AGPS.

Gereffi, Gary. 1993. International subcontracting and global capitalism: Reshaping the Pacific Rim. In *Pacific-Asia and the future of the world system,* ed. Ravi Arvind Palat, 67–81. Westport, Conn.: Greenwood Press.

Gereffi, Gary, and M. Korzeniewicz. 1990. Commodity chains and footwear exports in the semiperiphery. In *Semiperipheral states in the world economy,* ed. W. G. Martin, 45–68. Westport, Conn: Greenwood.

Germidis, D., ed. 1980. *International subcontracting.* Paris: OECD Development Centre.

Gerschenkron, A. 1966. *Economic backwardness in historical perspective.* Cambridge: Harvard University Press.

Ghadar, F., W. H. Davidson, and C. C. Feigenoff. 1987. *U.S. industrial competitiveness, the case of the textile and apparel industries.* Lexington, Mass.: Lexington Books.

Giordano Holdings Ltd. 1991. *Giordano Holdings Limited: New issue.* Hong Kong: Giordano Holdings Ltd.

Gold, T. B. 1988. Entrepreneurs, multinationals, and the state. In *Contending approaches to the political economy of Taiwan,* ed. E. A. Winckler and S. Greenhalgh, 175–205. New York: M. E. Sharpe.

Goodstadt, L. 1969. Profits in pawn. *Far Eastern Economic Review* 64, no. 16: 224–26.

Greenwood, J. 1990. Hong Kong: The changing structure and competitiveness of the Hong Kong economy. *Asian Monetary Monitor* 14:21–31.

Haddon-Cave, P. 1984. Introduction to *The business environment in Hong Kong.*: 2d ed., ed. D. Lethbridge, xi–xix. Hong Hong: Oxford University Press.

Haggard, S. 1988. *Policy, politics and structural adjustment: The US and the East Asian NICs.* Paper presented at Conference on Economic Development Experiences of Taiwan and Its Role in an Emerging Pacific Area, 8–10 June, Institute of Economics, Academia Sinica, Taipei.

Hamilton, C. 1983. Capitalist industrialisation in East Asia's four little tigers. *Journal of Contemporary Asia* 13:35–53.

Han, Y. S. 1990. Korea: A newly industrialising economy market opening, internationalisation, and international competition. In *The newly industrialising economies of Asia*, ed. M. Kulessa, 21–31. Berlin: Springer Verlag.

Harrison, B. 1994. *Lean and mean: The changing landscape of corporate power in the age of flexibility*. New York: Basic Books.

Harvey, D. 1982. *The limits to capital*. Oxford: Blackwell.

———. 1989. *The condition of postmodernity*. Oxford: Blackwell.

Hayashi, T. 1992. *Intrafirm transfer of production of Japanese multinational enterprises: A case study in electric machinery industry*. Paper presented at seminar, The Role of Foreign Investment in Structural Change in East and Southeast Asia, 18 September, Honolulu, Hawaii.

Hayter, T., and D. Harvey, eds. 1993. *The factory and the city: The story of the Cowley automobile workers in Oxford*. London: Mansell.

Helliwell, J. F. 1992. *International growth linkages: Evidence from Asia and the OECD*. Working paper 4,245, National Bureau of Economic Research, Cambridge, Mass.

Henderson, J. 1989. *The globalisation of high technology production*. London: Routledge.

———. 1991. Urbanization in the Hong Kong South China region: An introduction to dynamics and dilemmas. *International Journal of Urban and Regional Research* 15:169–79.

Ho, D. K. L. 1989. *The political economy of public housing in Hong Kong*. Master's thesis, University of Hong Kong.

Ho, K. C. 1991. Studying the city in the new international division of labor. Working paper 107. Department of Sociology, National University of Singapore.

———. 1993. Industrial restructuring and the dynamics of city-state adjustments. *Environment and Planning A* 25:47–62.

———. 1994. Industrial restructuring, the Singapore city-state, and the regional division of labour. *Environment and Planning A* 26:33–51.

Ho, K. C., and A. So. 1993. Borderland integration in Asia: Hong Kong and Singapore compared. Department of Sociology, National University of Singapore.

Ho, L. S., P. W. Liu, and K. C. Lam. 1991. *International labour migration: The case of Hong Kong*. Hong Kong: Hong Kong Institute of Asia-Pacific Studies.

Ho, Y. P. 1992. *Trade, industrial restructuring, and development in Hong Kong*. London: Macmillan.

Holmes, J. 1986. The organization and locational structure of production subcontracting. In *Production, work, territory: The geographical anatomy of industrial capitalism*, ed. A. J. Scott and M. Storper, 80–106. Boston: Allen and Unwin.

Hong, M. S. 1987. Competition between NICs and ASEAN. *East Asia International Review of Economic, Political and Social Development* 4, 130–44.

Hong Kong. 1979. *Report of the Advisory Committee on Diversification.* Hong Kong: Government Printer.

———. 1982. *Hong Kong 1981 census, main report.* vol. 1, *Analysis.* Hong Kong: Government Printer.

———. 1988. *Hong Kong 1986 census, main report,* vol. 1, *Analysis.* Hong Kong: Government Printer.

———. 1990. *Hong Kong's manufacturing industries.* Hong Kong: Industry Department.

———. 1991a. *Estimates of gross domestic product: 1966 to 1990.* Hong Kong: Government Printer.

———. 1991b. *Hong Kong's manufacturing industries.* Hong Kong: Industry Department.

———. 1991c. *Property review: 1991.* Hong Kong: Government Printer.

———. 1992a. *Hong Kong's manufacturing industries.* Industry Department.

———. 1992b. *Report on industrial automation study.* Hong Kong: Government Printer.

Hovenkamp, H. 1991. *Enterprise and American law 1836–1937.* Cambridge, Mass.: Harvard University Press.

Hsiao, H-H. M. 1991. *Techno-economic and market research study on Hong Kong's electronics industry 1988–1989.* Hong Kong: Government Printer.

———. 1992. The labor movement in Taiwan: A retrospective and prospective look. In *Taiwan: Beyond the economic miracle,* ed. D. F. Simon and M. Y. M. Kau, 151–67. New York: M. E. Sharpe.

Hughes, H. 1969. From entrepot to manufacturing. In *Foreign investment and industrialisation in Singapore,* ed. H. Hughes and P. S. You, 1–45. Canberra: Australian National University Press.

Huntington, S. 1993. The clash of civilisations? *Foreign Affairs* 72(3):22–49.

Ingham, G. 1984. *Capitalism divided?* London: MacMillan.

International Monetary Fund. 1988. *Direction of Trade Statistics.* Washington, D. C.: IMF.

———. 1993a. *Direction of trade statistics.* Washington, D.C.: IMF.

———. 1993b. *World economic outlook.* Washington, D.C.: IMF.

———. 1994. *World economic outlook.* Washington, D.C.

Jao, Y. C. 1988. Monetary system and banking structure. In *The economic system of Hong Kong,* ed. H. C. Y. Ho and L. C. Lau. Hong Kong: Asian Research Service.

Japan. 1990. *White Paper on international trade.* Tokyo: MITI (Ministry of International Trade and Industry).

Jessop, R. 1990. *State theory.* Oxford: Polity.

JETRO (Japanese External Trade Organization). 1990. *Japanese Business Facts and Figures.* Tokyo: JETRO.

Johnson, C. 1982. *MITI and the Japanese miracle*. Palo Alto: Stanford University Press.

———. 1987. Political institutions and economic performance: The government-business relationship in Japan, South Korea and Taiwan. In *The political economy of the new Asian industrialization*, ed. F. Deyo, 136–64. Ithaca: Cornell University Press.

Joint Associations Working Group. 1989. *Report on Hong Kong's labour shortage*. Hong Kong. Mimeographed.

Kamath, S. J. 1990. Foreign direct investment in a centrally planned developing economy: The Chinese case. *Economic Development and Cultural Change* 39:107–30.

Kamil, Y., M. Pangestu, and C. Fredericks. 1991. A Malaysian perspective. In *Growth triangle: The Johor-Singapore-Riau experience*, ed. T. Y. Lee, 37–74. Singapore: Institute of Southeast Asian Studies.

Kanamori, H. 1993. Economic cooperation in Northeast Asia. In *Regional economic cooperation in Northeast Asia*, ed. W. B. Kim, B. O. Campbell, M. Valencia, and L. J. Cho, 288–91. Honolulu: Northeast Asia Economic Forum.

Kao, Yueh–shi. 1992. The effects of human resource movements and direct foreign investment on employment in the ROC. *Industry of Free China* 78(5):43–62.

Kim, S. J. 1993. *Korean direct investment in China*. Paper presented at workshop, Emerging Patterns of East Asian Investment in China, 17–18 May, Shanghai, China.

Kim, S. O. 1989. Better labor conditions creep into NICs. *Electronics Korea* (December): 38.

Kim, W. B. 1993a. *China and the Asian NIEs: Emerging symbiotic relations*. Paper prepared for the Conference on China and the Asian NIEs: The Emerging Pattern of Investment, 17–18 May, Shanghai, China.

———. 1993b. Industrial restructuring and regional adjustment in Asian NIES. *Environment and Planning A* 25:27–46.

King, A. Y. C. and P. Man. 1979. Small factory in economic development: The case of Hong Kong. In *Hong Kong: Economic, social and political studies in development*, ed. T. B. Lin, R. P. L. Lee, and Udo-Ernst Simonis, 31–63. New York: M.E. Sharpe.

Koike, Kazuo, and Takenori Inoki. 1990. *Skill formation in Japan and Southeast Asia*. Tokyo: University of Tokyo Press.

Kojima, K., 1973. A macroeconomic approach to foreign investment. *Hitotsubashi Journal of Economics* 14:1–21.

———. *Direct foreign investment: A Japanese model of multinational business operations*. New York: Praeger.

Kojima, K. and T. Nakauchi. 1988. Economic conditions in East and Southeast Asia and development perspective. In *Challenge of Asian developing countries*, ed. S. Ichimura, 102–32. Tokyo: Asian Productivity Organisation.

Korea. 1976. *Survey report on establishment labor conditions*. Seoul: Ministry of Labor.

———. 1981. *Survey report on establishment labor conditions*. Seoul: Ministry of Labor.

———. 1986. *Survey report on establishment labor conditons*. Seoul: Ministry of Labor.

———. 1991. *Survey report on establishment labor conditons*. Seoul: Ministry of Labor.

———. 1992. *Korea business directory*. Seoul: Chamber of Commerce and Industry.

———. 1993. *Special survey on industry rationalization*. Seoul: Ministry of Commerce and Trade.

Korea Footwear Industry Association. 1992. *Report on footwear industry*. Seoul: Korean Footwear Industry Association.

———. 1993. *Report on footwear industry*. Seoul: Korean Footwear Industry Association.

Krause, L. B. 1988. Hong Kong and Singapore: Twins or kissing cousins? *Economic Development and Cultural Change* 36:S46–S66.

———. 1989. Government as entrepreneur. In *Management of success: The moulding of modern Singapore*, ed. K. S. Sandhu and P. Wheatley, 436–51. Singapore: Institute of Southeast Asian Studies.

Krugman, P., and R. Lawrence. 1993. Trade, jobs, and wages. Working Paper 4,478. National Bureau of Economic Research, Cambridge, Mass.

Kuo, S.W.K. 1983. *Taiwan: Economy in Transition*. Boulder: Westview.

———. 1993. *The Taiwan economy in the 1990s*. Paper presented at conference, Taiwan in the Asia Pacific in the 1990s, 12 April, Australian National University, Canberra.

Kurt Salmon Associates, Inc. 1992. *Technoeconomic and market research study of Hong Kong's textiles and clothing industries: 1991–1992*. Hong Kong: Government Printer.

Landsberg, M. 1979. Export-led industrialization in the Third World. *Review of Radical Political Economics* 11:50–63.

Lau, J., ed. 1986. *Models of Development*. San Francisco: Institute of Contemporary Studies.

Lau, L. J. 1990. The economy of Taiwan 1981–1988: A time of passages. In *Models of development*, ed. L. J. Lau, 183–215. San Francisco: ICS.

Lee, C. H. 1990. Direct foreign investment, structural adjustment, and international division of labor: A dynamic macroeconomic theory of direct foreign investment. *Hitotsubashi Journal of Economics* 31:61–72.

Lee, J. 1993. Intensification of subcontracting and changes of location and labor composition in the apparel industry in Seoul. *Journal of Geography* 21:35–51.

Lee, Josephs. 1991. Capital and labor mobility in Taiwan. In *Taiwan: From developing to mature economy,* ed. Gustav Ranis, 305–55. Boulder: Westview.

Lee, Keun. 1993. Structural change in the Korean economy and Korean investment in China and ASEAN. Paper presented at international workshop, Emerging Patterns of Foreign Investment in East Asia, 17–18 May, Shanghai, China.

Lee, M. W. 1992. *Making theory.* Seoul: Knowledge Enterprise Press.

Lee, S. A. 1973. *Industrialisation in Singapore.* New York: Longman.

Leipziger, D., and P. A. Petri. 1993. Korean industrial policy: Legacies of the past and directions for the future. Discussion Paper 197, World Bank, Washington, D.C.

Lethbridge, D., and S. H. Ng. 1984. The business environment and employment. In *The business environment in Hong Kong:* 2d ed., ed. D. Lethbridge, 71–138. Hong Kong: Oxford University Press.

Leung, C. K. 1993. Personal contacts, subcontracting linkages, and development in the Hong Kong Zhujiang Delta region. *Annals, Association of American Geographers* 83:272–302.

Levin, D., and S. Chiu. 1993. Dependent capitalism, colonial state, and marginal unions: The case of Hong Kong. In *Organized labor in the Asia Pacific region,* ed. S. Frankel, 187–222. Ithaca: Cornell University, ILR Press.

Levy, B. 1990. Transaction costs, the size of firms, and industrial policy. *Journal of Development Economics* 34:151–78.

Liang, K. S., and C. H. Liang. 1988a. Development policy formation and future policy priorities in the Republic of China. *Economic Development and Cultural Change* 36:S67–S101.

———. 1988b. Taiwan's new international role in the light of changes in comparative advantage, trade patterns, and the balance of payments. Paper presented at Conference on Economic Development Experiences of Taiwan and its Role in an Emerging Asia Pacific Area, 8–10 June, Institute of Economics, Academia Sinica, Taipei.

———. 1988c. Trade strategy and industrial policy in Taiwan. In *America's new competitors,* ed. T. Bradshaw, 47–79. Cambridge: Ballinger.

Liemt, Gijsbert van. 1992. Economic globalization: Labor options and buiness strategies in high labour cost countries. *International Labour Review* 131:453–69.

Lim, J. D. 1992. Industrial restructuring and changes in regional labor market: Pusan's footwear industry. *Korean Journal of Labor Economics* 15:265–301.

———. 1993a. New industrial policy and old industrial structure: Pusan economy under open system. *Proceedings of Summer Seminar,* 265–69. Pusan: Korea International Economic Association.

———. 1993b. Urban growth and industrial restructuring: The case of Pusan. *Environment and Planning A* 25:95–109.

———. 1994. Restructuring of footwear industry and industrial adjustment of Pusan Economy. *Environment and Planning A* 26:499–664.

Lim, L. 1978. Women workers in multinational corporations: The case of the electronics industry in Malaysia and Singapore. Occasional paper 9, Women's Studies Program, University of Michigan.

Linbert, P. H. 1969. United States investment. In *Foreign investment and industrialisation in Singapore,* ed. H. Hughes and P. S. You, 154–76. Canberra: Australian National University Press.

Liu, P., Ying-Chuan Liu, and Hui-Lin Wu. 1993. The manufacturing enterprise and management in Taiwan. Discussion Paper 9.304, Institute of Economics, Academic Sinica, Taipei.

Liu, Paul K. C. 1992. Science, technology, and human capital formation. In *Taiwan: From developing to mature economy,* ed. Gustav Ranis. Boulder: Westview.

Longxi, Z. 1992. Western theory and Chinese reality. *Critical Inquiry* 19:105–30.

Lui, T. L., and S. Chiu. 1992. *Merchants, small employers, and a non-interventionist state: Hong Kong as a case of unorganized late industrialization.* Paper presented at workshop, Models of Integration, Models of Development: Issues in the Urban and Regional Transformation of the Pacific Basin, 15–18 June, Institute of Advanced Studies, University of Malaya.

———. 1993. Industrial restructuring and labour market adjustment under positive noninterventionism: The case of Hong Kong. *Environment and Planning A* 25:63–79.

———. 1994. A tale of two industries: The restructuring of Hong Kong's garment-making and electronics industries. *Environment and Planning A* 26:53–70.

Mandel, E. 1978. *Late capitalism.* London: Verso.

Markusen, A. 1994. *The interaction between regional and industrial policies: Evidence from four countries—Korea, Brazil, Japan, and the United States.* Washington, D.C.: World Bank.

Markusen, A. R., and S. O. Park. 1993. The state as industrial locator and district builder: The case of Changwon, South Korea. *Economic Geography* 69:157–81.

Massey, D. 1984. *Spatial divisions of labour.* London: Macmillan.

Mayer, C. 1990. Financial systems, corporate finance, and economic development. In *Asymmetric information, corporate finance, and investment,* ed. R. G. Hubbard, 307–32. Chicago: University of Chicago Press.

Mirza, H. 1986. *Multinationals and the growth of the Singapore economy.* London: Croom Helm.

Miyoshi, M. 1993. A borderless world? From colonialism to transnationalism and the decline of the nation-state. *Critical Inquiry* 19:726–51.

Mody, A. 1990. Institutions and dynamic comparative advantage: The electronics industry in South Korea and Taiwan. *Cambridge Journal of Economics* 14:291–314.

Mody, A., and D. Wheeler. 1990. *Automation and world competition.* New York: St. Martin's.

Moon, C. I. 1988. The demise of a developmentalist state? Neoconservative reforms and political consequences in Korea. *Journal of Developing Societies* 6:67–84.

Murray, R. 1989. Fordism and post-Fordism. In *Newtimes,* ed. S. Hall and M. Jacques, 38–53. London: Lawrence and Wishart.

Ng, S. H., F. T. Chan, and K. K. Wong. 1989. *A report on labour supply studies.* Hong Kong: Hong Kong Economic Research Centre.

North, D. 1990. *Institutions, institutional change, and economic performance.* Cambridge: Cambridge University Press.

Obstfeld, M. 1992. Risk-taking, global diversification, and growth. Working Paper 4,093, National Bureau of Economic Research, Cambridge, Mass.

Ogawa, N., G. Jones, and J. Williamson. 1993. *Human resources in development along the Asia-Pacific Rim.* Singapore: Oxford University Press.

Ogle, G. E. 1990. *South Korea: Dissent within the economic miracle.* London: Zed.

Ohno, K., and H. Imaoka. 1987. The experience of dual industrial growth: Korea and Taiwan. *The Developing Economies* 27:310–24.

Onis, Z. 1991. The logic of the developmental state. *Comparative Politics* 24:109–27.

Pang, E. F., and L. Lim. 1982. Foreign labour and economic development in Singapore. *International Migration Review* 16:548–76.

Pangestu, M. 1991. An Indonesian perspective. In *Growth triangle: The Johor-Singapore-Riau experience,* ed. T. Y. Lee, 75–115. Singapore: Institute of Southeast Asian Studies and Institute of Policy Studies.

Park, J. H., T. Lee, and J. Hoh. 1991. *A report on Korean footwear industry.* Pusan: Dong Nam Bank.

Park, S. I. 1990. Industrial relations policy in Korea: Its features and problems. In *Korean economic development,* ed. J. K. Kwon, 393–407. New York: Greenwood.

Park, S. O. 1985. Industrial location policies in major metropolitan areas of Korea (in Korean with English summary). *Journal of Korean Planners Association* 20:202–20.

———. 1987. Recent development and linkages of high technology industries in the Seoul metropolitan area. *Korean Journal of Regional Science* 3:21–36.

———. 1991. Government management of industrial change in the Republic of Korea. In *The state and the spatial management of industrial change*, ed. D. Rich and G. Linge, 74–87. London: Routledge.

———. 1993a. Industrial restructuring and the spatial division of labor: The case of the Seoul metropolitan region, the Republic of Korea. *Environment and Planning A* 25:81–93.

———. 1993b. Structural changes in manufacturing and directions of structural adjustments of industries in the Capital Region (in Korean with English summary). *Journal of Geography* 21:1–16.

———. 1994. Industrial restructuring in the Seoul metropolitan region: Major triggers and consequences. *Environment and Planning A* 26:527–41.

Peck, J. 1992. Labor and agglomeration: Control and flexibility in labor markets. *Economic Geography* 68:325–47.

People's Republic of China. 1985–1992. *China Statistical Yearbook*. Beijing: State Statistical Bureau.

Plosser, C. I. 1989. Understanding real business cycles. *Journal of Economic Perspectives* 3:51–77.

Pusan Chamber of Commerce. Various years. *Pusan Business Directory*. Pusan, Korea: Chamber of Commerce.

Reiger, H. C., and W. Veit. 1990. State intervention, state involvement, and market forces: Singapore and South Korea. In *The newly industrialising economies of Asia*, ed. M. Kulessa, 155–79. Berlin: Springer Verlag.

Rich, D. C., and G. J. R. Linge. 1991. The state and industrial change. In *The state and the spatial management of industrial change*, ed. D. C. Rich and G. J. R. Linge, 1–21. London: Routledge.

Riedel, J. 1991. Intra-Asian trade and foreign direct investment. *Asian Development Review* 9:111–46.

Rodan, G. 1989. *The political economy of Singapore's industrialization: National, state, and international capital*. London: Macmillan.

Rose-Ackerman, S. 1991. Risk taking and ruin: Bankruptcy and investment choice. *Journal of Legal Studies* 20:277–310.

Said, E. 1993. *Culture and imperialism*. London: Vintage.

SaKong, I. 1993. *Korea in the world economy*. Washington, D.C.: Institute for International Economics.

Salih, K., M. L. Young, and R. Rasiah. 1988. The changing face of the electronics industry in the periphery: The case of Malaysia. *International Journal of Urban and Regional Research* 12:375–403.

San, Gee. 1991. The status and evaluation of the electronic industry in Taiwan. Technical Paper 29, OECD Development Centre, Paris.

Sayer, A., and R. Walker. 1992. *The new social economy: Reworking the division of labor*. Cambridge, Mass.: Blackwell.

Schelling, T. C. 1960. *The strategy of conflict*. Cambridge: Harvard University Press.

Schiffer, J. 1991. State policy and economic growth: A note on the Hong Kong model. *International Journal of Urban and Regional Research* 15:180–96.

Schive, C. 1988. *Foreign investment and technology transfer in Taiwan: Past experience and future potentials*. Paper presented at Conference on Economic Development Experiences of Taiwan, 8–10 June, Institute of Economics, Academia Sinica, Taipei.

Scott, A. J. 1987. The semiconductor industry in Southeast Asia: Organization, location, and the international division of labor. *Regional Studies* 21:143–60.

Scott, M. 1989. *A new view of economic growth*. Oxford: Clarendon.

Sekiguchi, S., and M. Noda. 1992. An overview of East Asia. Paper presented at Workshop on Prospects of Economic Relations in East Asia, 28–29 Nov., Ushiba Memorial Foundation, Odawara, Japan.

Shieh, G. S. 1990. *Manufacturing "bosses" subcontracting network under dependent capitalism in Taiwan*, Ph.D. diss., University of California, Berkeley.

Shieh, S. C. 1989. Financial liberalization and internationalization in ROC: Current status and policy directions. *Industry of Free China*, 72(6):9–18.

Shiller, R. J. 1992. *The report of the Twentieth Century Fund Task Force on market speculation and corporate governance*. New York: Twentieth Century Fund.

Shleifer, A., and R. Vishny. 1993. Corruption. Working Paper 4,372, National Bureau of Economic Research, Cambridge, Mass.

Shubik, M. 1982. *Game theory and the social sciences: Concepts and solutions*. Cambridge: MIT Press.

SIAA (Singapore Industrial Automation Association). 1990. *National automation survey 1989/1990*. Singapore: SIAA.

Singapore. 1981. *Census of population 1980*, release 4, *Economic characteristics*. Singapore: Department of Statistics.

———. 1983. *1982 land and building use*. Singapore: Ministry of National Development.

———. 1986a. *Action plan for the property sector*. Singapore: Ministry of Finance.

———. 1986b. *Economic survey of Singapore, 1986*. Singapore: Ministry of Trade and Industry.

———. 1990. *Survey of business expectations of industrial establishments*. Singapore: Economic Development Board.

———. 1991a. *Economic survey of Singapore, 1991*. Singapore: Ministry of Trade and Industry.

———. 1991b. *The strategic economic plan: Towards a developed nation*. Singapore: Ministry of Trade and Industry.

————. 1992. *Report on the success of industrial production, 1991.* Singapore: Economic Development Board.

————. 1994. *Economic survey of Singapore, 1993.* Singapore: SNP Publishers.

Sit, V. F. S. 1989. Industrial outprocessing: Hong Kong's new relationship with the Pearl River Delta. *Asian Profile* 17:1–14.

Sit, V. F. S., and S. L. Wong. 1989. *Small and medium industries in an export-oriented economy: The case of Hong Kong.* Hong Kong: Centre of Asian Studies, University of Hong Kong.

Sit, V. F. S., S. L. Wong, and T. S. Kiang. 1979. *Small scale industry in a laissez-faire economy.* Hong Kong: Centre of Asian Studies, University of Hong Kong.

Skeldon, R. 1986. Hong Kong and its hinterland: A case of international rural-to-urban migration? *Asian Geographer* 5:1–24.

So, A. 1986. The economic success of Hong Kong: Insights from a world system perspective. *Sociological Perspective* 29:241–58.

————. 1993. Political determinants of direct investment in mainland China. Paper presented at international workshop, Emerging Patterns of Foreign Investment in East Asia, 17–18 May, Shangai, China.

Song, B.-N. 1990. *The rise of the Korean economy.* New York: Oxford University Press.

Stein, A. 1990. *Why nations cooperate: Circumstances and choice in international relations.* Ithaca: Cornell University Press.

Stiglitz, J. 1990. Symposium on bubbles. *Journal of Economic Perspectives* 6:13–18.

Storper, M. 1992. The limits to globalization: technology districts and international trade. *Economic Geography* 68:60–93.

Storper, M., and Allen J. Scott. 1990. Work organization and local labor markets in an era of flexible production. *International Labour Review* 129: 573–91.

Straits Times. 1987. *Republic among major users of industrial robots.*

————. 1988a. *Automation makes for better use of labour,* 10 September.

————. 1988b. *Automation pays off for three firms,* 5 November.

————. 1988c. *Govt gives automation $60m boost-incentives to help firms reduce dependence on foreign labour,* 23 November.

————. 1989a. *Boon or bane,* 6 February.

————. 1989b. *Overreliance on foreign workers is bad in the long run,* 6 February.

————. 1991a. *S'pore lacks skill to run overseas investments: Dr Hu,* 19 June.

————. 1991b. *BG Lee spells out EDB's new priorities,* 2 August .

————. 1991. *Foreign investments by Singapore firms trebled,* 13 December.

Strong, J., and J. Meyer. 1990. Sustaining investment, discretionary investment, and valuation: A residual funds study of the paper industry. In *Asymmet-*

ric information, corporate finance, and investment, ed. R. G. Hubbard, 127–48. Chicago: University of Chicago Press.

Suh, J. I. 1993. *Restructuring of Pusan footwear industry.* Seoul: Korea Institute of Economics and Technology.

Summers, R., and A. Heston. 1988. A new set of international comparisons of real product and price levels: estimates for 130 countries, 1950–1985. *Review of Income and Wealth* Series 34:1–25.

———. 1991. The Penn world table (Mark 5): An expanded set of international comparisons, 1950–1988. *Quarterly Journal of Economics* 106:327–68.

Taiwan. 1988. *Report on the 1986 Taiwan Industrial and Commercial Census* (in Chinese). Taipei: DGBAS (Directorate General of Budget, Accounting, and Statistics).

———. 1989. *Monthly statistics of exports and imports.* Taipei: MOEA (Ministry of Economic Affairs).

———. 1990. *Statistics on overseas Chinese and foreign investment.* Taipei: MOEA.

———. 1991a. *Statistical yearbook of the Republic of China.* Taipei: MOEA.

———. 1991b. *Statistics on overseas Chinese and foreign investment.* Taipei: MOEA.

———. 1992a. *Preliminary report on the 1991 Taiwan Industrial and Commercial Census* (in Chinese). Taipei: DGBAS.

———. 1992b. *The 1991 White Papers in the small and medium-sized enterprises in Taiwan* (in Chinese). Taipei: MOEA.

———. 1992c. *Taiwan statistical data book.* Taipei: DGBAS.

———. 1993a. *Monthly statistics of exports and imports.* Taipei: MOEA.

———. 1993b. *The 1992 yearbook of earnings and productivity statistics in Taiwan* (in Chinese). Taipei: DGBAS.

———. 1993c. *Report on the 1992 Enterprises Survey on Labor Employment* (in Chinese). Taipei: DGBAS.

———. 1993d. *Report on the 1992 Survey of Management Performance of the manufacturing industry in Taiwan.* Taipei: MOEA.

———. 1993e. *Statistical yearbook of the Republic of China.* Taipei: MOEA.

Tang, M., and M. Thant. 1993. *New Developments in regional economic cooperation: Growth triangles.* EDRC (Economic Development Research Center) staff paper, Asian Development Bank, Manila.

Tesar, L., and I. Werner. 1992. *Home bias and the globalization of securities markets.* Working Paper 4,218, National Bureau of Economic Research, Cambridge, Mass.

Tham, L. 1992. Packing up, going north. Department of Sociology, National University of Singapore, Singapore.

Thurow, L. 1992. *Head to head.* New York: William Morrow.

Tribe, L. 1989. The curvature of constitutional space: What lawyers can learn from modern physics. *Harvard Law Review* 103:1–39.

Tsai, Hong-chin, and Ching-lung Tsay. 1991. *Social problems of foreign workers in Taiwan* (in Chinese). Commission on Research, Development, and Evaluation, Technical paper, Executive Yuan, Taipei.

Tsay, Ching-lung. 1993. Industrial restructuring and international competition in Taiwan. *Environment and Planning A* 25:111–20.

Turnbull, C. M. 1972. *The Straits Settlements, 1826–1867*. London: Athlone Press.

Turner, H. A., P. Fosh, and N. S. Hong. 1991. *Between two societies: Hong Kong labour in transition*. Hong Kong: Centre of Asian Studies, University of Hong Kong.

Tyson, L. 1992. *Who's bashing whom?* New York: Basic Books.

UN (United Nations). 1991. *Economic and social survey of Asia and the Pacific 1990*. New York: United Nations.

UNCTC (United Nations Centre on Transnational Corporations). 1987. *Transnational corporations and the electronics industries of ASEAN economies*. New York: United Nations.

———. 1990. *Regional economic integration and transnational corporations in the 1990s: Europe 1992, North America, and developing countries*. New York: United Nations.

Wade, R. 1985. East Asian financial systems as a challenge to economics. *California Management Review* 27:106–27.

———. 1990a. *Governing the market: Economic theory and the role of government in East Asian industrialization*. Princeton: Princeton University Press.

———. 1990b. Industrial policy in East Asia: Does it lead or follow the market? In *Manufacturing miracles, Paths of industrialization in Latin America and East Asia*, ed. G. Gereffi and D. L. Wyman, 231–66. Princeton: Princeton University Press.

———. 1993. Managing trade: Taiwan and South Korea as challenges to economies and political science. *Comparative Politics* 25:145–67.

Ward, M. 1991. Fashioning the future: Fashion, clothing, and the manufacturing of post-Fordist culture. *Cultural Studies* 5:61–76.

Watanabe, T. 1990. Bringing China out of its shell: The Asian NIEs. *JETRO China Newsletter* 87:2–5.

———. 1991. Nichi-Bei-NIEs sankyoku no sekaizou (The tripolar world of Japan-United States-NIEs). Chapter 2 in *Ajia keizai kenkyu* (The study of Asian economy), ed. S. Sekihuchi and O. Akihiko. Tokyo: Chuokeizai.

Webber, M. J. 1987. Rates of profit and interregional flows of capital. *Annals, Association of American Geographers* 77:63–75.

———. 1991. Garnaut: The implications of Northeast Asia for Australian industry. *Australian Journal of International Affairs* 44:39–44.

————. 1994. Enter the dragon: Lessons for Australia from Northeast Asia? *Environment and Planning A* 26:71–94.

Webber, M. J., G. L. Clark, J. McKay, and G. Missen. 1991. *Industrial restructuring: Definition*. Working Paper 91–3. Melbourne: Monash-Melbourne Joint Project on Comparative Australian-Asian Development.

Whiting, A. S. 1992. China and Japan: Politics versus economics. *Annals, AAPSS* 519:39–51.

Wilairat, K. 1975. Singapore's foreign policy. Field report 10, Institute of Southeast Asian Studies, Singapore.

Williams, J. F. 1992. Environmentalism in Taiwan. In *Taiwan: Beyond the economic miracle*, ed. D. F. Simon and M. Y. M. Kau, 187–210. New York: M.E. Sharpe.

Willson, A. L., ed. 1982. *German romantic criticism*. New York: Continuum.

Winckler, E. A. 1988. Elite political struggle, 1945–1985. In *Contending approaches to the political economy of Taiwan*, ed. E. A. Winckler and S. Greenhalgh, 151–71. New York: M.E. Sharpe.

Wong, J. 1988. Integration of China into the Asia-Pacific region. *World Economy* 11:327–54.

Wong, S. L. 1986. Modernization and Chinese culture in Hong Kong. *China Quarterly* 106:306–25.

————. 1988. *Emigrant entrepreneur*. Hong Kong: Oxford University Press.

————. 1990. Chinese entrepreneurs and business trust. *University of Hong Kong Gazette Supplement* 37:25–34.

Wong, T. Y. C. 1991. A comparative study of the industrial policy of Hong Kong and Singapore in the 1980s. In *Industrial and trade development in Hong Kong*, ed. E. K. Y. Chen, M. K. Nyaw, and T. Y .C. Wong, 256–93. Hong Kong: Centre of Asian Studies, University of Hong Kong.

Woo, J. E. 1991. *Race to the swift: State and finance in Korean industrialisation*. New York: Columbia University Press.

World Bank. 1984. *Korea's development in a global context*. Washington, D.C.: World Bank.

————. 1991. *World development report: The challenge of development*. New York: Oxford University Press.

————. 1993a. *The East Asian miracle*. New York: Oxford University Press.

————. 1993b. *World tables 1992*. Baltimore: Johns Hopkins University Press.

Wu, J. 1988. Entrepreneurship. In *The economic system of Hong Kong*, ed. C. Y. Ho and L. C. Lau, 155–68. Hong Kong: Asian Research Service.

Wu, R.-I. 1988. The distinctive features of Taiwan's development, in *In search of an East Asian development model*, ed. P. B. Berger, H.-h. M. Hsiao, 179–96. New Brunswick, N.J.: Transaction.

Wu, H.-L., and K.-J. Lan. 1991. Labor shortage in Taiwan. Paper presented at workshop, Labor Flows to Taiwan, 6–8 June, Institute of Economics, Academia Sinica, Taipei.

Yen, T. 1991. Taiwan investment in mainland China and its impact on Taiwan's industries. *Issues and Studies* 27:10-42.

Yoffie, D. B., ed. 1993. *Beyond free trade: firms, governments, and global competition.* Boston: Harvard Business School Press.

Young, A. 1992. A tale of two cities: Factor accumulation and technical change in Hong Kong and Singapore. In *NBER Macroeconomics annual 1992,* ed. O. J. Blanchard and S. Fischer, 13–63. Cambridge: MIT Press.

———. 1993. Lessons from the East Asian NICs: A contrarian view. Working paper 4,482. National Bureau of Economic Research, Cambridge, Mass.

———. 1994. The tyranny of numbers: Confronting the statistical realities of the East Asian growth experience. Working paper 4,680, National Bureau of Economic Research, Cambridge, Mass.

Yoon, Y. K. 1990. The political economy of transition: Japanese foreign direct investments in the 1980s. *World Politics* 43:1–27.

Youngson, A. J. 1982. *Hong Kong: Economic growth and policy.* Hong Kong: Oxford University Press.

Yu, Tzong-shian. 1992. The two sides of the Taiwan Straits: economic interdependence and cooperation. Occasional Paper 9203, Chung-hua Institution for Economic Research, Taipei.

Zheng, D. L. 1987. *Modern Hong Kong economy* (in Chinese). Beijing: China's Financial, Political, and Economic Publisher.

Additional References

Liu, Philip. 1993a. Investing in the neighborhood. *Free China Review* 43:28–35.

Liu, Philip. 1993b. Is manufacturing on the ropes? *Free China Review* 43:52–57.

Shen, Jia-You. 1993. The composition and changes of Taiwan's petty bourgeoise, 1976–1987. *In Discovery of the middle classes in East Asia,* ed. H. H. M. Hsiao, 177–200. Institute of Ethnology, Academia Sinica, Taipei.

Contributors

Stephen Chiu (Ph.D., Princeton) currently teaches sociology at the Chinese University of Hong Kong. He has published several papers on the labor movement and industrial relations in Hong Kong and contributed to recent issues of *Environment and Planning A* (with Tai-lok Lui) and the *International Journal of Human Resource Management*. His other research interests include urban social movements, industrial restructuring, and employment practices in Hong Kong's cotton-spinning industry.

Gordon L. Clark (Ph.D., McMaster University) is the Halford Mackinder Professor of Geography at the University of Oxford. His research is principally on the patterns and regulation of industrial restructuring in Western economies including reference to income and pension security policies. Recent books include *Pensions and Corporate Restructuring in American Industry* and *Unions and Communities Under Siege: American Communities and the Crisis of Organized Labor.*

K. C. Ho (Ph.D., University of Chicago) is a senior lecturer in the Department of Sociology at the National University of Singapore and associate editor of the *Southeast Asian Journal of Social Science*. His research interests include urbanization, information technologies, development, and change. Recent published works, on industrial restructuring are published in *Environment and Planning A*. Dr. Ho is working with Tai-lok Lui and Stephen Chiu on a book comparing Singapore's and Hong Kong's development experiences and is also editing a book with Eddie Kuo entitled *Videotex Development in the Asia Pacific.*

Won Bae Kim (Ph.D., University of Wisconsin) is a fellow in the Program on Population of the East-West Center, Honolulu. The editor of *Regional Economic Cooperation in Northeast Asia,* the proceedings of the 1992 Vladivostok Conference, Dr. Kim's research interests include regional economic development and Asian urban growth. He has published many papers on Northeast Asia, including "The Korean Peninsula and the Future of Northeast Asia" (forthcoming in *Prospects for Economic Interactions Among Countries in East Asia,* edited by Sueo Sekiguchi and Makito Noda).

Jung Duk Lim (Ph.D., University of South Carolina) is professor of economics and director of the Labor Research Institute at Pusan National University, Korea. His research interests include regional economic development, industrial economics, and organization and labor economics. His most recent publications are on regional labor markets (mostly in Korean) and industrial restructuring (published in *Environment and Planning A*). He is currently writing a book on the performance of labor-intensive industries in Korea.

Tai-lok Lui (Ph.D., Oxford) is a lecturer in sociology at the Chinese University of Hong Kong. His recent research has been on the restructuring of Hong Kong's manufacturing industries, including reference to the links between Hong Kong and China. He is also involved in a project on the formation of the middle class in Asia, sponsored by the Chiang Ching Kuo Foundation. Dr. Lui is currently completing a book manuscript on the social organization of industrial outwork in Hong Kong.

Sam Ock Park (Ph.D., University of Georgia) is professor of geography at Seoul National University, Korea. His research is principally on the patterns of industrial restructuring and the organization of industrial and production spaces in oriental countries. Dr. Park is a regular contributor to international academic journals, including *Economic Geography,* on topics such as technology and industry policy. His recent book in English is *Korea: Geographical Perspective.*

Ching-lung Tsay (Ph.D., Brown University) is research fellow and chief of population and development studies at the Institute of Economics, Academia Sinica, Taipei, Taiwan. His research interests concern labor issues in the process of rapid socioeconomic transformation. He has published widely in international journals on issues related to labor supply and labor mobility and is presently engaged in a major study of illegal migration in the Asian NIEs.

Michael Webber (Ph.D., Australian National University) is professor of geography at the University of Melbourne. The author of numerous papers and books, including *Impact of Uncertainty on Location*, his current research is on changes in the global economy, geography of production, and the performance of local labor markets. Two forthcoming books are *Postwar Capitalism: The Golden Illusion* (with David Rigby) and *Global Restructuring: The Australian Experience* (with Bob Fagan).

Author Index

Subject Index

Library of Congress Cataloging-in-Publication Data

Asian NIESs and the global economy: industrial restructuring and corporate strategy in the 1990s / edited by Gordon L. Clark and Won Bae Kim.
    p. cm.
Contains ten essays based on papers presented at an international conference, held in May 1993 at the East-West Center in Honolulu.
  Includes bibliographical references (p.   ) and index.
  ISBN 0-8018-5105-X (alk. paper)
1. Business planning—East Asia—Case studies—Congresses. 2. Business planning—Asia, Southeastern—Case studies—Congresses. 3. East Asia—Economic policy—Case studies—Congresses. 4. Asia, Southeastern—Economic policy—Case studies—Congresses. 5. Economic history—1990—Congresses. I. Clark, Gordon L.
II. Kim, Won Bae.
  HD30.28.A84 1995
  338.95—dc20   95-21624